Europe's Transformations

Essays in Honour of Loukas Tsoukalis

Edited by

HELEN WALLACE

NIKOS KOUTSIARAS

GEORGE PAGOULATOS

OXFORD
UNIVERSITY PRESS

OXFORD
UNIVERSITY PRESS

Great Clarendon Street, Oxford, OX2 6DP,
United Kingdom

Oxford University Press is a department of the University of Oxford.
It furthers the University's objective of excellence in research, scholarship,
and education by publishing worldwide. Oxford is a registered trade mark of
Oxford University Press in the UK and in certain other countries

© OUP 2021

First Edition published in 2021

Impression: 1

Published in the United States of America by Oxford University Press
198 Madison Avenue, New York, NY 10016, United States of America

British Library Cataloguing in Publication Data
Data available

Library of Congress Control Number: 2021938590

ISBN 978-0-19-289582-0

DOI: 10.1093/oso/9780192895820.001.0001

Printed and bound by
CPI Group (UK) Ltd, Croydon, CR0 4YY

Preface

The stimulus for this volume came from friends and colleagues of Professor Loukas Tsoukalis. All of us had followed the development of his many contributions to the discussion of European public policies. These remain so pertinent to contemporary Europe that as co-editors we agreed that their themes and judgements deserved further exploration. Loukas Tsoukalis deserves plaudits for his many achievements, to be sure. However, this volume is not at all intended as simply or mainly a celebratory *Festschrift*. On the contrary, it is intended as a collection of thoughtful and reflective responses to the analyses and arguments that have shaped Loukas Tsoukalis' career.

Loukas Tsoukalis has played many parts across nearly half a century. The bedrock of his career has been thoughtful and carefully evidenced scholarship. A second strand has been his role as a teacher—in national institutions, in plurinational institutions, in Greece, for many years based in the United Kingdom, and across Europe and in the wider world. His role as a teacher has left strong imprints on his students, many of whom have gone on to European affairs careers, some in the world of academia and others in the field of policy practice. Close contacts, networking, and friendships have proliferated from these connections. Not for Loukas Tsoukalis the ivory towers of academia. He has cared too much about reality to confine himself to the classroom or the printed page. Hence, he has been and still is an active public intellectual, ever keen to engage with the challenges and dilemmas of practice. His insights have been fertilized by his multiple personalities. Yes, he is and has remained Greek—patriotic but not at all parochial or nationalistic. Yes, he is thoroughly European in his outlook—that is to say, at home across the continent, sensitive to the differences in perceptions, cultures, and concerns in different parts of it, and tenacious about the overlapping and collective concerns of Europeans. And, yes, he is an internationalist, concerned with the capability of Europeans to shape global processes and global well-being.

The overarching theme of Europe's transformations chose itself given that this has been a recurrent preoccupation of Loukas Tsoukalis and it aptly fits with the times. Chapter 2 discusses the development of his analyses and commentary on the European political economy, his primary field of expertise. Appropriately the line-up of authors provides reflections from the worlds of both analysis and practice. Part I on democracy and welfare sheds light on the contested social, economic, and political considerations that complicate the European process. Part II on lopsided integration turns our attention to the diversity of situations, aspirations, and interests across the continent which define the scope for—and the limits to—integration, strikingly important in these Brexit and post-Brexit times. In Part III our authors have been invited to reflect on scenarios for change that locate the EU in the wider and more complex context of the global system. The chronology in the appendix lists Loukas Tsoukalis' main publications across the timeline of evolution and critical junctures for the European Union.

A collection of essays as wide ranging as this does not turn itself straightforwardly into a coherent manuscript. A great debt is owed to Matina Meintani for her work in anchoring the process and for many technical contributions. Her work has been aided by the capable editing hand of Michael Eleftheriou. Dominic Byatt and his colleagues at Oxford University Press have added this volume to their several publications authored by Loukas Tsoukalis; they have encouraged and guided us along the editorial path with skill and empathy. Our appreciation goes to all the authors who have contributed to this volume. It has been a pleasure to work with a team who have been so positive and enthusiastic about the value of the exercise.

HW, NK, GP

July 2021

Contents

III. WHAT KIND OF POWER IN WHAT KIND OF GLOBAL SYSTEM?

List of Contributors

Matthew Bevington is Public Policy and Foreign Affairs Analyst at 'The UK in a Changing Europe', King's College London.

Anthony Gardner is a former US Ambassador to the European Union.

Nikos Koutsiaras is Associate Professor at the National and Kapodistrian University of Athens (Department of Political Science and Public Administration).

Brigid Laffan is Director of the Robert Schuman Centre for Advanced Studies, European University Institute (EUI), Florence.

Enrico Letta is Secretary of the Democratic Party and former Prime Minister of Italy; President of the Institut Jacques Delors; and former Dean of the Paris School of International Affairs, Sciences Po.

Anand Menon is Director of 'The UK in a Changing Europe' and Professor of European Politics and Foreign Affairs, King's College London.

Yves Mény is a former President of the European University Institute.

George Pagoulatos is Director General of ELIAMEP, Professor of European Politics and Economy at the Athens University of Economics and Business, and Visiting Professor at the College of Europe, Bruges.

Jean Pisani-Ferry is Tommaso Padoa-Schioppa chair of the European University Institute, Florence, and Senior Fellow at Bruegel and the Peterson Institute for International Economics.

Xavier Prats-Monné is Special Advisor at 'Teach For All' and Senior Advisor for Strategic Initiatives at the Open University of Catalonia (UOC).

Jacques Rupnik is Director of Research at the Centre d'Études et de Recherches Internationales (CERI), Fondation nationale des Sciences politiques, and a Professor at Sciences Po, Paris.

André Sapir is a Professor at Solvay Brussels School of Economics and Management, Université Libre de Bruxelles and a Senior Fellow at Bruegel.

Vivien A. Schmidt is Jean Monnet Professor of European Integration and Professor of International Relations and Political Science at Boston University.

Nathalie Tocci is Director of the Istituto Affari Internazionali and Special Adviser to EU HRVP Josep Borrell.

Herman Van Rompuy is President of the European Council Emeritus and former Prime Minister of Belgium.

Helen Wallace is an Honorary Professor at Sussex European Institute.

Wolfgang Wessels is Director of the Centre for Turkey and European Union Studies (CETEUS), University of Cologne.

Ngaire Woods is Dean of the Blavatnik School of Government and Professor of Global Economic Governance at Oxford University.

1

Setting the Scene

Helen Wallace

Introduction

It is just over 70 years since the Schuman Declaration of 9 May 1950 proclaimed the plan to create the European Coal and Steel Community, the first step towards what is now the European Union (EU). Much has changed across those decades. The European integration process has been transformed as old challenges were faced, some more effectively than others, and as new challenges crowded on to the agenda. Indeed the EU has never had the chance to stand still. There has been one transformation after another—of membership, of policies, and of governance. The history is one of both making experiments and acquiring experience. The experiments have generated extensions of scope and innovations of method. Learning by doing has occurred as experience has accumulated as regards which policies and programmes work better and which less well. The record contains both successes and failures—it is always possible to do better. Nor are the judgements about success and failure subject only to a dry and technical process of evaluation. On the contrary they have also to be derived from the court of public opinion, or rather the courts—plural—since public opinion is of course variegated across countries, regions, sectors, societal cohorts, and political families.

How then should we evaluate our current prospects? First, the challenges that we Europeans face multiply rather than decrease—both internally and externally. Secondly, we need to recognize that the rationales that have underpinned the European process have been buffeted by events across the decades. Thirdly, it turns out that the narratives about the purposes and outcomes of European integration vary across countries, regions, and societal sectors, as well as across time. Fourthly, this is not surprising in that the EU of now 27 consists of countries with diverse needs and aspirations, which leads to questions about whether and how to differentiate the work of the EU. In the past much has been made of the distinctiveness of the EU as anchoring a process of deep integration rather than shallow collaboration. This rests on the assumption that reciprocity can be diffuse and cumulative—cross-sectoral and cross-temporal. But is this assumption too demanding, or too unrealistic for current circumstances?

The authors in this volume take their prompts from the work of Loukas Tsoukalis, who has been a continually inquisitive and thoughtful analyst of the

Helen Wallace, *Setting the Scene* In: *Europe's Transformations: Essays in Honour of Loukas Tsoukalis*. Edited by: Helen Wallace, Nikos Koutsiaras, and George Pagoulatos, Oxford University Press. © OUP 2021.
DOI: 10.1093/oso/9780192895820.003.0001

way that the European integration process has evolved. His major works are listed in the Chronology and thoughtfully analysed by Nikos Koutsiaras in Chapter 2. Our authors share as a theme the search for a better understanding of Europe's transformations and, in particular, the character of the European political economy, notwithstanding deep structural economic changes. They come at this from many different angles and with many different focuses. We have encouraged them all to engage in a process of reflection based on their diverse professional experiences and areas of expertise. This resulting volume is a contribution to the debate about the transformations of European integration.

A Crowd of Challenges

It is self-evident that Europeans face no shortage of challenges. The historical record may have dealt with some, but within the territories of the EU and of its near neighbours in Europe, to the east and to the south, there is a proliferation of challenges at all levels of concern from the macro to the micro, from the overarching to the local, and across the political, economic, societal, and security dimensions. Similarly, the world is a troubled place within which Europeans are vulnerable and have limited tools to promote their shared concerns. The post-Second World War international system of institutions is creaking badly across domains from the broad multilateral to the functionally focused. The belief in the value of institutionalized collaboration and transnational rules that was such an important part of the second half of the twentieth century has been eroded, leaving islands of order in seas of contestation and without the political hegemony of notably the USA to provide a guiding hand. The Covid-19 pandemic has arrived on a scene that was already troubled. Its implications remain hard to foretell, although there is no shortage of speculations.

So how do Europeans address these challenges? How should they address them? For which of them is the European framework the appropriate one to choose? Or for which of them does the European framework seem to offer viable responses? Which of them resonate with public opinion inside the member states? What should be the process through which it is to be determined when and where and how European responses should be crafted? It is all too easy to produce a list of critical questions, but it is much harder to answer them. Our authors offer a range of preferences and priorities that reflect their own experiences, expertise, and judgements.

Early Rationales for Integration

Once upon a time it seemed relatively straightforward to identify the main rationales that underpinned the creation and development of the European

Community (EC) which we now know as the EU. The initial pair were: first, the stabilization of [western] Europe after the Second World War, and especially the anchoring of a peaceful and democratic [West] Germany; and, secondly, economic recovery after the dislocation of the 1930s followed by the ravages of war. A third rationale soon came into the mix, namely the safeguarding of western Europe vis-à-vis the Soviet sphere in eastern Europe—in tandem with NATO. With the passage of time a fourth emerged, the promotion in its European neighbourhood of democratization and socio-economic transformation—initially in the southern Mediterranean countries and then those in central and eastern Europe, as their autocratic regimes withered. The discussion that follows focuses on the main and framing rationales for European integration as distinct from the many other reasons for which the EU has become a very convenient and pro-ductive platform for collaboration.

Here then were four powerful rationales for the European integration project as one which developed *deep* integration rather than *shallow* collaboration as the vehicle for constructive and democratic development across the continent. These were cogent rationales which by and large were resonant for the citizens of the founder member states. Even the communist parties in France and Italy eventually bought into the project. The questions that follow are about: how convincing the record of achievement has been in addressing these core purposes and in carrying public opinion along; how well these rationales serve the EU of 27 member states in the 2020s; and whether nowadays they need to be revisited or reframed or replaced.

Across the decades Europe became a largely stable and peaceful continent—except not quite so in the western Balkans. Yes, the western European economy prospered—or at least it did so for a few decades until things became a bit more complicated. Yes, the ending of the Cold War set aside the Soviet imperium, although alas it was not followed by the transformation of Russia into a liberal democracy and parts of the former Soviet Union remain outside the integration tent. Thankfully, Greece, Portugal, and Spain have become well-functioning democratic members of the family of European countries, although there is a mixed picture across central and eastern Europe. So here is a positive record and a genuinely important one—but it is one where the clearest of achievements relate to the resolution of historical problems as much as to contemporary challenges.

Stabilization after the Second World War

The stabilization of western Europe is nowadays largely taken for granted and lacks the power to continue to mobilize public enthusiasm across the countries of the continent. Moreover, its resonance was concentrated in the six founder members of the EC and not so keenly echoed in later members of the EC club, whose experiences and memories of the Second World War have been different and less focused on Franco-German reconciliation. Alas this big achievement has never quite caught the political imagination in the UK. Is this stabilization rationale now to be taken as a given? Well, yes, but, no, not quite. There is a less loudly articulated purpose of continuing relevance: namely, the anchoring of Germany as a good and not overly hegemonic partner given its preponderant weight in the EU family. Here is an issue that presents itself as an understandable but defensive concern.

Economic Collaboration

A key economic purpose remains at the core of the collective European enterprise, with a partially achieved agenda proceeding from the original customs union through towards Economic and Monetary Union. On some criteria this purpose has been remarkably successful. The western European economy prospered for *les trente glorieuses* (1945–75) on the back of the Marshall Plan, the Bretton Woods institutions, and the European Community, providing an encouraging context for the development of the western European welfare states. The mechanisms of deep economic integration, backed by an embedded legal jurisdiction, have indeed tied the member states' economies tightly together, maybe not irreversibly but so tightly that to unpack the involvement is both complex and costly—as the British are finding out. Indeed the commitment of the EU27 to this model of deep integration partly accounts for the hard line that they took in the EU/UK negotiations over future partnership, which Matthew Bevington and Anand Menon discuss in Chapter 11. The rationale for this economic and monetary agenda has evolved over time, although without generating agreement on a single predominant policy paradigm. Integration has had to contend with wide disparities and varied characteristics among the member states of what became a club of 28. Moreover, the EU process has itself, at least according to some commentators, notably Loukas Tsoukalis (2003), generated losers as well as winners within and among member states, both geographically and socially, as Brigid Laffan discusses in Chapter 9. In Chapter 10 George Pagoulatos stresses the relevance of these tensions and strains within the Eurozone. Collective EU remedies may be desirable, but they have tended not to rally public support. The consolidation of the single European market has been a big achievement but not really a popular one. In addition, the global character of economic transactions nowadays, as well as the rise of economic powers in Asia, means that reliance on European instruments is insufficient and less persuasive, although the case for an effective EU caucus has so much to commend it.

East–West Division

Western European integration was one of the key factors in limiting Soviet expansion and in anchoring the western part of the divided Germany. The ending of the Cold War, now already 30 years ago, led to the break-up of the Soviet empire, the unification of Germany, and the folding of 11 central and eastern European countries into the EU (and also into NATO). Here was a large geopolitical achievement for which the EU provided many tools and an insurance policy. At first sight this seems to be a job done, despite some unfinished business in the western Balkans and parts of the former Soviet Union. The Iron Curtain has become a forgotten phenomenon for many citizens across the continent, even apparently in parts of central and eastern Europe. Thus perversely it lacks resonance as a shared achievement or rallying call. Moreover, the EU is much more heterogeneous since it absorbed the central and eastern European countries into the EU. As Jacques Rupnik argues in Chapter 6, there are persistent tensions between the interests and priorities of these countries and those of the old western European members. Thus far they have been passengers rather than pioneers in the development of the EU. There is unfinished work to be done to develop the framing and substance of the EU's core purposes in ways that reflect more explicitly the concerns and circumstances of central and eastern Europe. In addition, there remains an agenda of tricky engagement with the eastern neighbourhood.

Democratization

The record of the EU as an anchor of democratization is a bit hazy. On the one hand, joining the EC/EU was made subject to demanding conditionality for the candidates, both initially those from southern Europe and later those from central and eastern Europe. On the other hand, political developments that challenge democratic practice have occurred inside some EU countries, notably recently and most explicitly in Hungary and Poland, leaving the EU institutions and other EU member states confused and ambivalent about how to respond. Politicians in and around the EU have sought to make much of the EU as a space for the active projection of democracy, human rights, and the rule of law—so much so that there has been a growth of academic literature extolling the role of *normative* Europe. But there is something of a tension between the rhetoric and the practice and not least against the backcloth of increasingly vocal Eurosceptic critiques and political movements. The range of views is wide on both the character of this set of issues and ways of reacting to them. Vivien Schmidt suggests in Chapter 5 that improving governance might be one remedy at least in the context of monetary union. Xavier Prats Monné stresses in Chapter 4 that a greater investment in social

Europe would help to connect citizens more explicitly to the European collective process. Yves Mény in Chapter 7 calls for a rethink of how we define the fundamentals of democracy. Anthony Gardner in Chapter 16 reminds us that these are issues not only for Europeans but also more broadly for 'the West', and is optimistic about the continuing scope for Europeans and Americans to work together in promoting shared values. Interestingly, Ursula von der Leyen, as president of the European Commission since 2019, has chosen to appoint one of the vice-presidents, Margaritis Schinas, to a portfolio on 'Promoting our European Way of Life', while Dubravka Šuica, another vice-president, has the portfolio for 'Democracy and Demography'. How well these ambitions will stand up to political engagement remains to be seen.

Renewing the Rationales for Integration

Here then is a history of big ambitions and solid achievements. The resonance of some, however, has been of diminishing intensity across the years, and varying intensity across the membership of eventually 28 but now 27 member states. Hence these core rationales have been periodically accompanied by efforts to develop successor core purposes. These have been of three kinds: first, suggested new or revised macro rationales; secondly, an emphasis on the interest-based or transactional rewards from EU collaboration; and thirdly, the celebration of *Europe* as such as a successful enterprise that should be repeatedly reinforced. To note: in this volume we have avoided the term 'crisis' as a label for the current context, even despite the shockwaves generated by the Covid-19 pandemic. However, the rise of public scepticism about the merits of European integration (discussed in several chapters) is a clear cause for concern. The contributors to this volume offer a range of responses to the quest for renewal of the integration project and especially as regards sustainable growth and economic governance (both policies and institutions) in the European political economy and especially in the Eurozone. In what follows we take a parsimonious approach and resist the temptation to overload the EU agenda with a plethora of purposes of varying cogency and resonance.

As regards potential core macro rationales, four stand out from the chapters that follow: the climate emergency; the challenges of the digital age; a reinvigorated economy; and a stronger role in global affairs. So what is new or different here? All four are palpably relevant to today and to successor generations, holding out the search for future benefits. All four are ones for which there are distinct European aspects. All four depend on engagement with the wider world, which has become much less 'Western' over recent years. And all require a multifunctional or cross-disciplinary set of tools and actions. How well do these priorities chime with the analyses in this volume? The focus on the climate emergency is a widely shared priority and strongly advocated, in particular by Enrico Letta (Chapter 15) and Herman Van Rompuy (Chapter 17). There is evidence that this resonates with public opinion and especially young people. Letta is the only one of our authors to stress the importance of addressing the agenda of the digital age and the salience of pursuing 'technological humanism'. André Sapir (Chapter 3), however, echoes this in his emphasis on the crucial role of technological prowess in shaping the capacity of the European economy to thrive in today's increasingly digital world. Of course, the case for a core purpose of economic vigour remains at the centre of the EU process. However, there is not a universally shared consensus on how to achieve that or about which tools and actions would be needed. On the one hand, there are differences of view about the distribution of powers and responsibilities within the EU and among its member states. On the other hand, the context of a messy global landscape does not make the agenda for the EU straightforward. Chapters 3, 10 and 13 all address these issues from different angles. The search for effective European autonomy in a tough global context is the key priority for Nathalie Tocci in Chapter 14, a concern that she shares with Van Rompuy, Sapir, and Jean Pisani-Ferry in Chapter 13. This is not a new core purpose, but a new factor that stands out in these chapters is the insistence that economic and geopolitical considerations are mutually interdependent in a world characterized by asymmetries of attributes and power. Anthony Gardner (Chapter 16) shares the insistence that the EU should step up to the mark as an international actor—in tandem with the USA.

Overarching rationales such as these may be cogent in the light of current evidence. Whether or not, and if so how far, they resonate with public opinion is another question. Whether or not they chime with the concerns of all the member states of the EU is also another question. The need to tackle the climate change emergency stands out as particularly compelling, though not straightforward for public opinion or for all member states or all age groups or all socio-economic actors. The pressure of adaptation to the digital age is probably among the most important challenges for European public policy but it is something of a technocratic topic which might not capture the public imagination and, on the contrary, might attract hostility for its potential impacts on the labour market.

One awkward potential core purpose is raised by Letta: namely, the challenge of migration, given the pressures of both economic migration (especially from Africa) and refugees from failed or failing states. It is a troublesome purpose, however, not only given the striking inconsistences of approach across the EU, which make it hard to imagine a sustainable and shared EU approach, but also because it is an issue that invites defensive rhetoric and responses. It is a subject that also much complicates the development of credible polices towards eastern and southern neighbours.

It is instructive in this context to see the incoming agenda of Ursula von der Leyen as president of the European Commission. Her six priorities were identified as: a Green Deal; an economy working for all; fitness for the digital age; the European way of life; a stronger Europe in the world; and improved democracy. There is an overlap with those of our authors but not an exact correspondence. Another potential core purpose is both missing from this Commission list and neglected by our authors: namely, the issue area dealing with internal security under the rubric of justice and home affairs. This is an issue area that escapes the capacity of individual countries but on which it is hard to agree about collective European goods.

A different approach to the identification of core rationales for integration is to stress the cost–benefit analysis of European integration as offering tangible and positive substantive outcomes from the processes of collaboration. This has from the outset been a theme and it continues to play into the development of the EU and its various programmes and policies. For some commentators it provides the key to gaining 'output legitimacy' for the EU in the eyes of its citizens—and it is certain that an EU which fails to demonstrate some evidence of benefits delivered is bound to escape popularity. Part of what lies behind this is the view that goes back to functionalist and neofunctionalist analysts: that loyalty would be built in sectors or localities by tangible rewards from integration which improved their welfare. The record contains both contributions by way of collective goods and measures to deliver on substantive, largely economic, interests. Part of the trick of the European integration process has been to develop both ideational and trans-actional components.

However, critics of the EU question this record and the Eurosceptic movements across the continent tend increasingly to the argument that policies fit for the circumstances of individual countries are much to be preferred. So the argument goes, one size does not fit all. Jacques Rupnik in Chapter 6 argues that this is a factor which continues to limit the appropriateness of EU policies for the countries of central and eastern Europe. As George Pagoulatos shows in Chapter 10, the financial 'crisis' of the period from 2008 has not made it easier to defend the record of EU policy achievement given the tensions and controversies that have dogged it. Indeed the term 'crisis' has become a repeated and often simplistically used label in the debate. After all, it has repeatedly been the case across the years that member governments have been quick to claim the credit for successes and to blame the European process for the failings, as Loukas Tsoukalis (2006) has forcefully argued and as Nikos Koutsiaras reminds us in Chapter 2. A further complication is that many of the economic challenges facing Europeans are shaped and framed by wider global factors over which Europeans have decreasing leverage, given the rise of Asian economies, the idiosyncrasies of recent US behaviour, and the increasing asymmetries in the global landscape. Pisani-Ferry (Chapter 13) argues thoughtfully that the structures and patterns of the global economy have changed in systemic ways that require a different approach from the EU to pull together the economic and the geopolitical factors so as to project a more powerful influence in a world full of troublesome asymmetries. Ngaire Woods (Chapter 12) provides a trenchant critique of the deficiencies in what was supposed to be a cooperative and rules-based global landscape.

The third kind of rationale for European integration is the promotion of the endeavour for its own sake: that is, the celebration of 'Europe' as such. This rests on the belief that the binding of European states into a kind of confederal system is intrinsically virtuous as an insurance policy against potentially dangerous and introverted nationalism and as a logical response to the limits on the capacities and capabilities of individual countries. This purpose was part of the foundational compact. It has been a strand in the debate each time treaty reform emerges as the next advocated step and it is one which generally pleads for a greater investment in the collective EU institutions, and for some a move from confederation to federation.

Most recently a plan has emerged to establish a Conference on the Future of Europe. Over a couple of years this would draw on deliberations across the range from citizens' assemblies to the EU institutions. Its remit is to identify reforms to the policies and institutions of the EU that would equip it better to tackle its medium- to long-term challenges. The proposed conference has been delayed by the Covid-19 pandemic, and hence it is too soon to tell whether this plan will gain momentum and gather support. Our authors are not of one mind on this subject. The plan carries echoes of the Convention on the Future of Europe held in 2001/2003. Its constitutional proposal was lost to the negative referenda in 2005 in the Netherlands and France, and was replaced by what became the Treaty of Lisbon. Underlying this kind of initiative is a conviction that a more robust EU with more robust democratic foundations would both attract more citizen engagement and deliver more valuable outcomes. How well this trajectory fits with our times is a different question. Thus, for example, Schmidt (Chapter 5) emphasizes the potential for the European Parliament to exercise greater influence on the development of the Eurozone. Prats Monné (Chapter 4) insists on the value of a more elaborate social Europe. In contrast, Mény (Chapter 7) suggests that we need to reconsider the traditional features of democratic practice, not least in the light of so many Eurosceptic tendencies across the EU.

Differing Narratives

Politicians craft narratives about what they do and why they do it. Some of these are fleeting and ephemeral, while others become embedded in political discourse. Some are intentionally partisan, while others seek to frame a broader consensus. What seems evident from the discussion so far is that there is not a single preponderant narrative of European integration that is shared across all of the member states and recounted by politicians across political families to their citizens. Perhaps there was in the early foundational years when the memories of the Second World War were still fresh and raw. However, we should be wary of exaggerating the alignment of narratives told to domestic audiences even in the early years. Thus, for example, there is a splendidly heroic narrative about Franco-German reconciliation which every now and then looks a little tarnished when conflicts of approach and interest are revealed. What does seem very important is that the narratives matter. The stories that member state politicians tell their publics make a difference to public perceptions and public attitudes. The ways in which domestic politicians attribute praise or blame to the policies of the EU make a difference to whether these provide welcome opportunities or irritating constraints. How far politicians from this or that member state seek to claim the credit for a particular European initiative is also relevant in giving the impression that this or that member state is more or less influential in the process.

It seems to be the case that in recent years the variations in the narratives about EU integration have become more and not less diverse. On the one hand, this reflects differences in the political situation across and within EU member states. On the other hand, this also generates pressures for differing assessments of the values of European integration, depending on who you are and where you are. A German populist narrative on the recklessly irresponsible cicadas of the South was the reverse side of the Greek stereotype on the callousness of the austerity-imposing Germans who were incapable of solidarity. The pro-European narrative about the winners from economic integration sits uneasily alongside the resentful narrative of the losing regions and social groups. Or—to recognize a contrasting story about relative influence—politicians in some member states have succeeded in crafting narratives that imply that governments from 'their' country have exercised disproportionate influence over agreed outcomes, while others have characterized themselves as regime-takers rather than regime-makers.

Interestingly, the statistics on explicit voting within the EU Council of Ministers show that the French government is hardly ever recorded as dissenting from emerging agreements whereas in recent years the UK government became the star-performing no-sayer. Both of these records have made it more tempting and plausible for the French to claim an achievement of successful influencing while the British have a cultivated self-image of pushing against the flow. Neither narrative is entirely well founded since voting records tell only a tiny part of the story. Part of the sad story of the UK's failed membership is that its history was one of heavy influence on core purposes—especially the single market, eastern enlargement, and the embryonic common foreign and security policy—but these successes were hidden secrets as far as the British public was concerned. For more on the road to Brexit see the commentary by Matthew Bevington and Anand Menon in Chapter 11. We should also note that the reverse approach of French governments to present themselves in the leading group of EU governments has not been enough to prevent the emergence of a substantial Eurosceptic political movement in the *Rassemblement National* (previously *Front National*).

Our discussion above about core rationales suggests that, although there may have been a shared narrative across the membership of the European Community as was, this has been overtaken by the emergence of dispersed and differentiated narratives by country, by political family, by socio-economic sector or position, by locality . . . We should be careful here not to concentrate the explanation for this as a feature of EU politics. Similar trends can be seen within countries and not only in Europe. Given that there is declining trust in politicians, it is hardly surprising that there should be limited trust in the EU system. Given that the [western] European pattern of left/right and catch-all parties has been eroded, we should not be surprised at the rise of parties and movements with quite different poles of attraction for the electorate. As the lyric goes, 'The times they are a-changin'.'

One further complication has been the difficulty of framing the narratives as regards the reform agenda of the EU. In the UK discussions about Brexit it became virtually impossible to make the case for EU reform without stirring up the more radical criticisms of the Eurosceptics and determined 'leavers'. This polarization of narratives—keen pro-Europeans defending the EU record versus vehement Eurosceptics—gets in the way of constructive discussions about how to repurpose the EU so as to address current and future core challenges.

Diverse Needs and Aspirations

The EU has grown from six to 27(8) members embracing a variety of features—political, economic, societal, and geographic—as well as historical baggage. The variety has become more, not less pronounced in recent years, partly but not only as a result of serial enlargement, and it holds for many of the earlier members of the EU family as well as for the more recent arrivals. The debate about differentiated integration goes back a long time. Its earliest articulation was—ironically—around the time of the accession of the UK to the then EC in the early 1970s, when doubts were expressed as to whether the UK would as a member really buy in to the core purposes and policies of the EC. It took a long time—40 years or so—for these doubts to come to a head in the form of Brexit. Differentiation in the form of exceptionalism for the UK—budget rebate, not in the euro, and outside Schengen—served to cultivate the UK an outsider. There is a distinction to be drawn here between differentiation as constructive flexibility and differentiation as a form of exclusion from the mainstream (even if self-imposed). On the other hand, the search for uniformity of rules and practice may also be counterproductive. Rupnik's (Chapter 6) warnings about the consequences of the EU being quite so insistent on exporting its western template to the new members from central and eastern Europe need to be taken seriously in this context.

Diversity of situation shows up in several contexts. The split between the Eurozone and the other member states is an evident example. The richer/poorer spectrum is a related example which does not entirely correlate with countries given the rising inequalities within them. A range of factors bear on mixed responses (current and future) to the climate emergency. Attitudes to migration are another case in point, with the Schengen system having become even more fragile during the Covid-19 pandemic. Differences in influencing ability are also pertinent, since there are asymmetries of power among the member states. This is one of the factors affecting political developments in Hungary and Poland. Differences in preferences, priorities, and even values are part of the European patchwork. We must make a distinction here between, on the one hand, those differences that can nonetheless be bargained into a shared policy or rule and, on the other hand, those differences that are more resistant. In assessing the prospects for future transformations a judgement has to be reached on cases where one size does—or can be made to—fit all as opposed to those differences that are structural and obstinate. The shorter the core agenda of the EU, the better the chances of keeping it focused on issues where the needs and preferences are shared. The more wide ranging the agenda, the greater the likelihood of coming up against stubborn national differences.

One Path Ahead or Several?

So there are some tough choices ahead for the practitioners in the EU, both those concerned with national policies and politics and those whose primary concern is with the collective EU enterprise. The choices are especially tough given that the global landscape is so troubled and its instruments for collaboration so constrained. Moreover, the Covid-19 pandemic adds to the uncertainties, not least as to whether the hurriedly crafted EU responses and budgetary propositions will become permanently embedded. None of our authors has a quick fix answer to the dilemmas. Rather from their various perspectives they share their insights into the character of the several challenges and indicate where the search for remedies should be focused. In this unique exercise of collective governance over ever-deepening complexity, which is the European integration, flagging the issues, being aware of the trade-offs, and explaining the options might be almost as important as attempting to sketch the solutions.

References

Tsoukalis, Loukas (2003/2005). *What Kind of Europe?* Oxford and New York: Oxford University Press.

Tsoukalis, Loukas (2006). 'The JCMS Lecture: Managing Diversity and Change in the European Union.' *Journal of Common Market Studies* 44(1): 1–15.

2

Tsoukalis and the Political Economy
of European Integration

Nikos Koutsiaras

A Reverse Chronological Order

This chapter is a review study of Loukas Tsoukalis' published work on the political economy of European integration.[1] A reverse chronological order (with minor twists) is followed, its benchmarks being provided by Tsoukalis' books; his journal articles and chapters in edited volumes are also reviewed, albeit selectively.

Readers might reasonably ask what makes such an approach preferable. Would it not be more suitable to construct a thematically organized review of Tsoukalis' contribution to the academic research on the economics and politics of European integration? His research interests would thus be straightforward to locate; and the significance—and added value—of his work could accordingly be assessed. Yet, a thematically organized discussion would risk insufficient attention being paid to the 'holistic' perspective on European integration with which Tsoukalis has been widely credited. Or, would it not be simpler—indeed, more conventional—to arrange the material along a path stretching from the earlier to the latest phase of Tsoukalis' academic and public presence? Would this not make the evolution in both his research interests and intellectual and ideological leanings easier to trace and contextualize?

The reverse chronological order deployed in this chapter retains all the advantages of the conventional—chronological—approach, while presenting some further advantages. One may, reasonably, be better acquainted with Tsoukalis' more recent work, simply because one is young (and at an early stage in one's research on European matters), or because one's long memory may be fading as time goes by. Furthermore, as cognitive psychologists and behavioural economists have shown, an availability bias is often present in mental processes. Thus, when we evaluate an issue or a choice, or a person and their work for that matter, we often rely on information which is easier to recall; judgements and expectations are, therefore, formed with reference, primarily, to more recent information. In this

[1] I am grateful to my co-editors for their constructive comments on an earlier draft.

Nikos Koutsiaras, *Tsoukalis and the Political Economy of European Integration* In: *Europe's Transformations: Essays in Honour of Loukas Tsoukalis.* Edited by: Helen Wallace, Nikos Koutsiaras, and George Pagoulatos, Oxford University Press.

sense, a reverse chronological order conforms to the availability bias inherent in cognitive processes.

Readers may thus find it easier to follow a narrative of Tsoukalis' academic and public presence which starts with things—books and articles, ideas and proposals—that come to mind first and which also deal with recent developments in Europe and the world. More importantly, though, the latest work of Tsoukalis—or, indeed, almost any academic—embodies the knowledge, experience, and wisdom accumulated over his many years engaging with and studying the European project; and, perhaps implicitly, it reflects the intellectual and ideological transformations he has gone through as a consequence. Hence, not only are Tsoukalis' recent contributions easier to recall, they are also more representative of his broader convictions, including his beliefs and aspirations regarding his role as an academic who has engaged with practice, too.

In fact, Tsoukalis' published work and academic and public presence can be divided into two phases, the latest and the earlier one. In his most recent work, he has mainly sought to shed light on the big challenges facing the process of European integration, following the establishment of the Economic and Monetary Union (EMU), the advent of hyper-globalization and, subsequently, the emergence of the Great Recession and the euro area crisis. In Tsoukalis' view, such challenges are quite often reinforced by policy inertia attributed to hard political constraints inherent in the European system of market integration and policy coordination. Thus, in the latest phase of his published work and presence, Tsoukalis has sought to enrich the political dimension in his approach to the political economy of European integration; largely as a consequence of this, he has endeavoured both to broaden the scope of his analysis and to enhance its practical relevance—to the benefit of academic research, European political discourse, and informed public opinion.

In the earlier phase of his research into European integration, Tsoukalis focused more on the economic aspect, paying more attention to sectoral issues and certain policy areas—primarily monetary cooperation. Yet the political element was never in short supply; nor was the bigger picture overlooked in his earlier writings. As a matter of fact, Tsoukalis developed very early on a quite distinctive approach to studying the political economy of European integration; as a consequence, he set the relevant bar high.[2]

---

[2] If I may add a more personal note at this point—a subjective justification, if you wish, for deploying a reverse chronological order in this review of Tsoukalis' published work: this author's academic and intellectual collaboration and, principally, friendship with Loukas Tsoukalis have gathered strength and grown in substance during the latest phase of Tsoukalis' research and contributions to the study of European political economy. The beginnings of this rich relationship date back 30 years, which is to say to when Loukas Tsoukalis initiated this author into the political economy of European integration. The many intervening years have been full of fruitful arguments and, mostly, joy. And it is the latest part of this period that comes up first in this reviewer's mind and heart.

The Latest Phase: Defending the European Project

In the wake of the Great Recession and the euro area crisis—which inevitably became an EU crisis—Tsoukalis published a book entitled *In Defence of Europe*, whose central question was whether the process of European integration was still sustainable (Tsoukalis 2016). As implied by the work's title, Tsoukalis' purpose was neither solely academic nor principally analytical. Rather, being mainly normative in outlook, the book was—notwithstanding its academic audience— targeted at European policy makers, institutional agents, and informed citizens.

Tsoukalis had little hesitation arguing that the way European political authorities handled the euro area crisis was poorly thought out economically, and that its political implications were also poisonous. There is enough evidence to support his argument. Response to the crisis was delayed (and insufficient), while, in particular, a timely—and probably efficacious—restructuring of Greek government debt was averted, largely to the benefit of (primarily French and German) banks holding Greek bonds. Furthermore, austerity was imposed across the euro area, regardless of its macroeconomic and social impact, and much to the detriment of much-needed macroeconomic rebalancing and economic and social cohesion in the European Union (EU). The insistence on structural reforms being promptly implemented was often ideologically motivated: their economic benefits were doubtful and the distributional consequences ignored. Unsurprisingly, divisions between the euro area countries deepened, which would be reinforced—and reconfigured—following the migration and refugee crisis and spill over into the rest of the EU membership. What was more, the popular legitimacy of the EU was seriously undermined.

Be that as it may, Tsoukalis has little patience with the prophets of doom and gloom, which is to say those who systematically belittle the resilience of the European project. Indeed, a costly break-up of the monetary union was avoided largely as a result of institutional reforms, mainly the establishment of the European Stability Mechanism and (the still incomplete) banking union. No doubt, such institutional reforms, as well as the ECB's monetary policies, could hardly have been contemplated prior to the crisis. They were the 'unthinkables', as Tsoukalis remarks emphatically in a paper published while the crisis in the euro area was still unfolding; alas, they have also been extremely painful politically (Tsoukalis 2012).

Tsoukalis (2016) is worried about the long-term sustainability of the European institutional system of economic integration and political cooperation. He doubts whether an Economic and Monetary Union can walk for long on just one—its monetary—leg. Furthermore, in Tsoukalis' view, governance arrangements in the euro area can hardly be deemed suitable. Imposing institutional homogeneity, often indirectly, across national political economies is hardly advisable; it ignores structural economic heterogeneity, pays little regard to (domestic) redistributive consequences, and, in all likelihood, reinforces asymmetry and undermines economic convergence. What is more, such a model of governance seems to be oblivious to national social contracts and domestic democratic institutions. The resurgence of (economic) nationalism and the growth of centrifugal political forces have almost inevitably been driven by (unequally distributed) economic hardship and popular dissatisfaction.

On purely normative grounds, Tsoukalis (2016) advocates a new pact for the EU: in his words, a new historical compromise between EU member states, between the main political families—one may plausibly take a broader view of potential signatories—and between generations. The attainment of such a compromise depends to a large extent on Germany's willingness to underwrite the European project and, for that matter, to embrace a more enlightened conception of its own economic and political interest. Yet, it also hinges on other countries' commitment to reforming their economic and social institutions; that is, by overhauling—rather than deregulating—their regulatory frameworks, thereby allowing for a closer match between policies and social preferences in regard to the average level of welfare and its distribution across society. Domestic economic reform may also enable France to reclaim its co-leadership of the process of European integration. A widely shared commitment to economic reform might have even persuaded the British to assume a more active role in the EU; alas, Tsoukalis' (modest) optimism about the UK's place and role in the European project—one might just call it hope—was subsequently proved false by events.

An ever-closer union—a common European (political) identity—is obviously not within reach in the foreseeable future; nor will the EU be able to punch above its weight in a multipolar world. Thus, a new pact for the EU, as envisaged by Tsoukalis (2016), should principally address challenges facing European integration in the twenty-first century and adapt the EU's institutional architecture and enhance its policy capacity accordingly. Resolving the contradiction of a currency without a state—the fundamental cause of the 'original sin' of EMU[3]—should certainly be the key objective of any new pact. Centralization of competences in some policy areas may be deemed essential, though in other policy areas repatriation of powers may well be desirable—and also advisable; differentiated membership options should certainly also be made available in certain policy domains. Furthermore, a new pact for Europe should provide for the encouragement of

---

[3] A metaphor coined by Barry Eichengreen and Ricardo Hausmann (1999) to describe a country's—mostly in the developing world—failure to use its domestic currency to borrow abroad or even to borrow long-term domestically. The metaphor is here meant to reflect Paul De Grauwe's (2011) hypothesis that sovereign bond markets within a monetary union are more vulnerable to self-fulfilling liquidity crises, which are likely to degenerate into solvency crises, than they are in countries which retain their own currency and central bank, thereby ensuring that cash will always be available to pay out bondholders. A very similar argument is also put forth by proponents of the Modern Monetary Theory (Kelton 2020).

economic activity and increases in social welfare, while also bolstering democratic institutions and strengthening economic and social cohesion across and within EU member states.

But how else, other than by a new treaty, could such a pact be credibly concluded? Tsoukalis' (2016) proposal for a new treaty—more concretely, for a revision of the Treaty of Lisbon—is tied to a crucial, albeit controversial, condition; that, notwithstanding the need for such a new treaty to pass the democratic test, it should no longer have to do so unanimously. In other words, by emphasizing those willing and able to proceed further, the unanimity constraint on treaty revision could be overcome. Tsoukalis admits, nevertheless, that it is highly unlikely his proposal will be widely embraced—that is, other than in academia and by a smallish circle of politicians devoted to the European cause—let alone officially contemplated. However, the issue he raises remains wide open: how else could the European project be rescued from, at best, muddling through the handling of the short-term impact of a crisis, while failing to address its longer-term causes? Which brings us to the issue of the relevance and desirability of the European project itself. Somewhat unfortunately, neither issue would really be put to the test until much later, this time in the midst of a pandemic killing people and wreaking havoc on the European and global economy.

In Defence of Europe is mostly about the economics and politics of muddling through European integration, the euro area crisis being the principal case study. But there have been precedents. Shortly after the onset of the euro area crisis, Tsoukalis argued that a wave of euro-enthusiasm at the beginning of the twenty-first century, which had been overly—and overtly—sustained by academic writings, political discourse, and media hype, had been transformed into euro-distrust in the course of a decade. Illusions have been shattered, he bluntly proclaimed (Tsoukalis 2011). The crash-landing of the European constitution, to use Tsoukalis' metaphor, was at least partly an early manifestation of popular dissatisfaction with European integration. Weak productivity and income growth and miscalculations on the part of European and member-state authorities notwithstanding, the eastern enlargement of the EU was also a causal factor. Tsoukalis did not argue that the eastern enlargement should not have taken place. He only suggested that it was hastily carried out at the expense of the internal cohesion of the EU. The latter's fundamental deficits and functional shortcomings were consequently reinforced.

Thus, not only has intergovernmentalism increased, but institutional niceties (which are costly in time and substance) have also effectively been circumvented, with the bigger countries, in particular, seeking to make decision making better attuned to the real balance of power. However, intergovernmental arrangements do not adequately provide for collective ownership, continuity, surveillance, and implementation control, as Tsoukalis (2011) submitted, thereby rendering European economic governance virtually circumscribed and, therefore, inadequate. Economic interdependence has often been poorly managed—and externalities have been only partly addressed. Markets—financial markets, in particular—have often been insufficiently regulated, and asymmetries barely checked. Furthermore, the global role of the EU has been little more than projection of soft power—a concept that has sometimes been confused with mere rhetoric. EU foreign policy, in particular, has had a long history of grand initiatives, many of which have proved to be embarrassing failures, and hard to attain—sometimes contradictory—goals. Ambitions have rarely been fulfilled, and policy instruments have been in short supply. In fact, foreign policy has remained the stronghold of the nation-state.

Tsoukalis raised early warnings about the unsteady state of the Union; the risk of the EU drifting towards a bad equilibrium should not be discounted, he constantly advised. In 2003 Tsoukalis published a book entitled *What Kind of Europe?*; an updated edition was published in 2005 (Tsoukalis 2003/2005). His principal argument in this book was that there is no morally or politically neutral way to settle the issue of allocating the powers in the EU's multilevel system of governance—the rest amounts to pretentiousness. Hence, the aims of the EU should first be clearly specified, the broad objectives of European economic and social policies defined accordingly, and dilemmas and trade-offs acknowledged and, in principle, resolved. In plain words, the question of how much Europe we need should come second to—and actually be informed by—the question of what kind of Europe we want. Politics comes first: readers should have been left in little doubt as to Tsoukalis' intellectual point of view and social democratic ideological perspective.

Writing in the midst of a period of euro-euphoria, regardless of decelerating economic growth, Tsoukalis (2003/2005) took stock of recent European successes. Indeed, the introduction of the euro and the eastern enlargement of the EU had been sources of optimism for the European project; at least, they were perceived as such. Furthermore, the constitutional treaty had been concluded—and, at that time, there was little speculation that it would be dealt a death blow by domestic democratic politics. Besides, Europeanization—a vague concept at best—was advancing, primarily as a result of growing cross-border transactions and the soft coordination of economic and social policies.

Nonetheless, Tsoukalis (2003/2005) remained cautious. The EU suffered from a political deficit, he argued, which goes deeper than the (widely perceived) democratic deficit of the EU institutions, thereby reducing the effective capacity of the EU and undermining its legitimacy. And, as he posited in a chapter written later (Tsoukalis 2005), EMU was actually in tune with the strong tradition of elitism and depoliticization in European integration. For some, as Tsoukalis observed, EMU formed part of the 'golden straitjacket'—which metaphor, coined by the US journalist Thomas Friedman, is meant to indicate that democracy in advanced capitalist societies has been transformed into a competition among managers (of a Schumpeterian variety) aiming at (economic) efficiency. The delegation of policy powers to unelected experts—the stateless ECB in this case—has also been a major transformative factor. For Tsoukalis (2005), such a transformation may not last long, at least in the EU; as he wisely warned, EMU was a high-risk strategy.

The EU's political deficit, the main theme of *What Kind of Europe?*, allows for the entrenchment of intellectual fallacies and the engendering of policy failures. An intellectual fallacy at the heart of orthodox economics was reflected in weak financial regulation and market forces being left to allocate funds and price risks inefficiently—indeed irresponsibly, from a social point of view. The decentralization of financial rules and institutions, coupled with a lack of effective coordination at the EU level, was partly motivated by false expectations regarding the role unbridled financialization would play in bolstering economic growth; for that matter, it also led to the capture of the regulatory agencies and to collective inertia.

In general, the EU's political deficit meant that there was little, if any, genuine political debate in respect to the dilemmas and trade-offs facing the European system; namely, efficiency vs. equity, growth vs. stability, scale economies in the provision of (broadly defined) public goods vs. heterogeneity of preferences.

Thus, perhaps unsurprisingly, the EU failed to acknowledge—and, most importantly, address—the redistributive consequences of globalization. As a matter of fact, the two processes of European integration and globalization have largely been complementary, both being premised on the welfare gains brought about by market openness and economic interdependence. The EU, in particular, has made little attempt to manage—rather than merely accommodate—the process of globalization. Hence, in Tsoukalis' (2003/2005) view, European integration has been a kind of regional globalization, only much more advanced.

Globalization has surely increased economic welfare in Europe and the world at large. Within the advanced economies, however, its benefits have been distributed unequally, with losses largely concentrated among the most vulnerable members of the labour force: the unemployed and less-skilled, low-wage earners. Economic research on the effects of trade globalization on US wage inequality has been accumulating since the early 1990s (Freeman et al. 1995; Burtless 1995). Yet, the issue received little attention in European economic scholarship at that time. That may partly be attributed to a great deal of research ascribing increased US wage inequality to skill-biased technological change (Johnson 1997). It may also be explained by the fact that unemployment, rather than wage inequality, was the main European economic problem at that time, with mainstream economic theory ascribing it principally to labour market rigidities (OECD 1994; Siebert 1997). Furthermore, a relatively sanguine view of the effects of globalization on European labour markets had gradually become the EU official view (Commission EC 2005: 155–79; Economic Policy Committee 2005).

Thus, Tsoukalis (2003/2005) was among the few European political economists to draw timely attention to the issue of those emerging as losers from (European and) global economic integration. He warned that, besides being undesirable per se, neglecting this issue in EU policy making could also be politically unwise. The popular legitimacy of the European project would likely be eroded and Euroscepticism fuelled, too. And that might also be reinforced by national governments seeking recourse (often unjustifiably but still irresistibly) to the politics of blaming the EU institutions for domestic economic ills and policy shortcomings. In fact, Tsoukalis' concerns would soon prove to be well founded. The constitutional treaty was rejected in referenda in France and the Netherlands; the spectre of the 'Polish plumber', symbolizing many people's fears of economic dislocation stemming from the enlarged single European market, haunted the French referendum campaign on the constitutional treaty.

Hence, managing diversity and change, while mitigating feelings of insecurity among many Europeans, was the imminent challenge facing the EU. That was the theme of Tsoukalis' 2006 Journal of Common Market Studies Annual Lecture (Tsoukalis 2006a). As he argued, there has to be clarity and realism about what the EU can practically deliver. However, the EU had often failed that test. The Lisbon strategy was a case in point: regardless of its great ambitions and intense (soft) coordination processes, the Lisbon strategy had little impact on the domestic politics of economic and welfare-state reform. As a result, it provided little for revitalizing the EU economy and increasing the relevance and resilience of the European social model. A lack of effective means and, most importantly, an absence of sufficient (financial) incentives had undermined the implementation of the Lisbon strategy. Still, national governments could add yet another item to their repertoire of scapegoating-the-EU.

On the other hand, though, the establishment of the European Globalization Adjustment Fund in 2006 was, in Tsoukalis' view, the kind of EU action that makes good economic sense while also being politically prudent. Tsoukalis was one of the leading proponents of the Globalization Adjustment Fund—and played a direct role in its creation while wearing the hat of adviser to the then president of the European Commission. In making the case for such a fund, he argued that the EU needed a stronger caring dimension, thereby addressing the economic pain induced by trade globalization and industrial restructuring while also fostering European solidarity, in particular by making the Union more visible in those parts of the EU that had not benefited from the structural and cohesion funds. Besides, having exclusive competence over external trade policy, the EU should undertake part of the fiscal responsibility for dealing with the dislocation effects of trade globalization (Tsoukalis 2006b). The European Globalization Adjustment Fund has changed considerably since its introduction—it has become broader in scope and, effectively, lesser in size. Still, its political visibility has indeed been evidenced, although its economic effectiveness has probably left much to be desired (Claeys and Sapir 2018). A (highly) qualified success, as Tsoukalis would presumably concede.

The Earlier Phase: Upgrading the Political Economist's Approach to European Regional Integration

Perhaps the most important, academically influential and, indeed, pioneering of Tsoukalis' published works has been *The New European Economy*. The book was originally published in 1991, with a revised edition following in 1993 (Tsoukalis 1991/1993) and a radically revised third edition in 1997 (Tsoukalis 1997); it has also been translated into several languages. Holding fast to traditional political economy, Tsoukalis placed the economic questions within their political context, the latter being institutionally diverse and spread across (economic) policy areas. In order to provide a synthetic view of the many different and individually analysed aspects of European regional integration, and to put the latter in per-spective, he trod a fine methodological line between theory (be it economic theory, new political economy, grand regional integration theories, or institutionalist accounts of European integration) and plain empiricism. Methodological eclecti-cism has actually been the key element in Tsoukalis' distinctive approach to the political economy of European integration. This approach is probably the main reason why *The New European Economy* has found a place on the reading lists of nearly every academic European studies course, irrespective of national origin. It also helped that the book was accessible to people from a variety of disciplinary backgrounds—and to practitioners as well as academics.

Tsoukalis' main argument was that, following the continuous widening and deepening of regional integration, especially in its post-1985 phase, a European economic system was effectively formed which was qualitatively different from the group of highly interdependent economies studied in the regional integration literature until then. Cross-border transactions were growing rapidly as a result of market integration and liberalization coupled with diminished governmental intervention. Market regulation, in particular, was only partly redressed at the European level, while industrial policy was now little more than a relic of the past. National governments' authority over social insurance and redistribution had remained virtually intact. However, as a result of increased capital mobility—with labour mobility staying low—national redistributive policies had been fur-ther constrained, despite the growing risk of increased economic inequality.

Granted, regional policy had become more ambitious and transfers to the less advanced regions and member states had increased substantially; however, accel-erating productive investment and achieving convergence dynamics hinges more on national policies and institutions providing for the efficient allocation of both domestic resources and Community regional transfers. Tsoukalis argued that the relaunching of the European integration process had become associated with a liberal transformation of the European economic and political landscape, which is to say a reallocation of real economic power between the state and the market in favour of the latter. In his view, that raised concerns about social justice and would eventually incite questions as regards the legitimacy of European integration.

In *The New European Economy Revisited*, Tsoukalis (1997) took into account developments that had taken place in the meantime on the European economic system's widening and deepening front, further reinforcing the relevance of his approach. Having long been engaged in research on European monetary integration (more on that later), he was in an almost unique position to draw lessons from the crisis facing the European Monetary System (EMS)/Exchange Rate Mechanism (ERM) in the early 1990s. Indeed, in the face of compelling evidence that asymmetry was inherent in a (virtually) fixed exchange-rate system comprising divergent national growth models—as recent literature has postulated (Baccaro and Pontusson 2016)—and anchored on the monetary and macroeconomic preferences of a (relatively) big surplus economy, Tsoukalis had his doubts: how could EMU, being modelled on German institutional norms and morals, alleviate asymmetry in national macroeconomic adjustment and encourage cross-country convergence?

Tsoukalis was not fascinated by the new classical macroeconomics; nor was he convinced by the so-called endogenous optimum-currency-area (OCA) theory, for that matter.[4] Drawing on the insights of traditional OCA theory, he warned of the risk of economic diversities being amplified and political divisions heightened, thereby causing the risk of redenomination (as the risk of the EMU breaking up would later become known) to rise. Besides, deficiencies in the institutional architecture of EMU, especially in relation to financial regulation and supervision as well as fiscal policy, frustrated incentives for national governments to reform labour markets, economic regulation and public finances. Macroeconomic imbalances were thus likely to worsen, making adjustment, in deficit countries for the most part, too costly to administer. Tsoukalis would, alas, be proven right: a sudden cessation of capital inflows into such countries would later bring EMU almost to its knees. Furthermore, his speculation that Germany

---

[4] New classical macroeconomics was, to a large extent, clarified in the celebrated Lucas critique (1976): namely, the proposition that the effects of a change in economic policy cannot be predicted solely on the basis of historically observed relationships. Besides, policy changes induce adjustments in the behaviour of economic agents. Keynesian (large-scale) macroeconometric models are thus structurally flawed; or, more precisely, they lack genuinely structural content and have little predictive power as a consequence—they are hardly relevant for policy making. Instead, macroeconomic modelling should explicitly account for individuals' (optimizing) behaviour—enter microfoundations—thereby allowing for the incorporation of policy changes in agents' decision making. Furthermore, rational expectations, as opposed to the adaptive expectations employed by monetarists, ensure that economic agents can hardly be surprised by policy change; in essence, agents act in a forward-looking manner. Thus, demand management is largely ineffective, even in the short run. Economic growth and stabilization should, therefore, rely on supply-side policies exclusively.

The endogenous character of the relationship between various OCA criteria, primarily trade integration and business cycle synchronization, is a direct application of the Lucas critique, the implication being that a country is more likely to satisfy the criteria for joining a currency union *ex post* rather than prior to its joining (Frankel and Rose 1998).

might develop into the dominant, and largely self-referential, EMU partner would also come true.

Nevertheless, Tsoukalis did not advocate an unconditional transfer of policy powers and responsibilities to the EU institutions; in other words, he embraced the principle of subsidiarity in making his case for an efficient and equitable European economic system. A common EU social policy—let alone an EU welfare state—was neither feasible nor desirable, he argued. Yet, that in no way implied that national welfare states would wither away and social contracts be dismantled. Besides, rescuing the welfare state and reforming socially outdated institutions— and optimizing policy trade-offs, for that matter—was crucial for legitimizing European integration. Thus, from its very first edition *The New European Economy* offered intellectual justification for coordinating the economic and social policies of EU member states. However, Tsoukalis' recommendations for the institutional reform of the European economic system went far beyond what European politicians would be willing to consider.

The New European Economy, in all its three editions, may be said to epitomize Tsoukalis' long-time research into European regional integration. Remarkably, his main research interests had lain alongside some of the most contentious economic issues pertaining to the politics of regional integration, with money at the forefront of his research endeavours. Thus, in 1989 (the year the Committee for the Study of Economic and Monetary Union headed by the then president of the European Commission, Jacques Delors, published its *Report on Economic and Monetary Union in the European Community*), a chapter about the EMS authored by Tsoukalis appeared in a volume on the political economy of European integration edited by two Italian economists, one of whom, Pier Carlo Padoan, was later to become Italy's minister of finance (Tsoukalis 1989). Though the chapter was written shortly after the EMS celebrated its ninth birthday in March 1988, Tsoukalis' tone was not exactly celebratory.

As a matter of fact, after its first nine years, both macroeconomic analysis and the political-economy balance sheet of the EMS were still some way from producing incontrovertible evidence of the economic effectiveness and political sustainability of the EMS, including the feasibility of various options for reforming the prevailing monetary arrangements. Thus, the nominal and real exchange-rate variability among participating currencies was reduced; and national rates of inflation converged downwards. Yet, as Tsoukalis observed, there was little sign of convergence in fiscal (and economic) policies, although contractionary monetary policies had evidently been pursued in nearly all EMS countries; thus, monetary instruments had principally been relied upon to reduce inflation rates and differentials and achieve exchange-rate stability. Furthermore, favourable developments in nominal variables had not been matched with improvements in real economic variables; rates of intra-EMS trade expansion, investment, and (real) economic growth had all slowed down during the period, especially towards its end. Keynesian and supply-side explanations had surely been on offer; yet, problems of measurement and identification bedevilled econometric analysis, as they always do. Tsoukalis did not explicitly take sides; implicitly, however, he recognized that a deflationary bias was likely to be deep-rooted in the EMS.

Furthermore, the EMS had developed into an asymmetrical system with the D-Mark as its anchor currency. Hence, by pegging to the D-Mark—and thereby coming into line with the Bundesbank—foreign-exchange interventions, capital controls, and currency realignments could be deployed by the other EMS countries, singly or in some combination, in order to stay anchored. National choices differed, reflecting *inter alia* divergent preferences as regards financial liberalization and monetary independence. Yet, the commitment of central banks to the existing parities was often tested by way of speculation in foreign-exchange markets. Asymmetry was therefore evident in the intra-marginal interventions which had increasingly been relied upon, even though they placed a disproportionally large part of the burden of keeping the EMS afloat on the shoulders of the countries with the weaker currencies. In addition, the existing credit facilities had only been used sporadically. Although currency realignments had mostly been carried out smoothly, the revaluation of the D-Mark had occasionally caused political confrontations.

Whether it was currency realignments, institutional development and the day-to-day management of the EMS, or macroeconomic coordination in general, collective choices were formed through intergovernmental procedures. Inevitably, as Tsoukalis (1989) pointed out, some had more influence than others. And he took pains to construct the political-economy balance sheet, focusing on the regional and international position, the domestic political economy, and the macroeconomic policy preferences—and legacies—of the EMS member states. He argued that the EMS had laid the foundations for the development of a truly regional currency, but that gains—or losses—in competitiveness had not been distributed equally in the process. Current-account imbalances grew rapidly and pressures for internal adjustment diverged, notwithstanding the existing margins of exchange-rate fluctuations—and monetary policy manoeuvres. Owing to its leading role, Germany was spared the painful complexities of the Mundell–Fleming trilemma: free flow of capital, monetary autonomy, and a fixed exchange rate. On the other hand, the countries with weaker currencies—and legacies of imprudent macroeconomic management—gained (anti-inflation) credibility, or so it was maintained. Yet, one may wonder whether that was a fair trade-off as regards the distribution of benefits and costs, let alone an economically meaningful one.

In discussing the options for consolidating and reforming the EMS, Tsoukalis (1989) raised several issues ranging from the long-debated participation of sterling in the ERM to the use of the European Currency Unit (ECU) in private and official transactions and, not least, Europe's dependence on the dollar. Tsoukalis was undoubtedly in favour of relaunching the process of European monetary integration and, indeed, of creating a European monetary identity. To this end, he acknowledged the hegemonic role that West Germany could play, provided the latter adopted a more far-sighted approach to its own and European interests—in effect, by authorizing the setting up of mechanisms designed to counter asymmetry in the European Monetary System. As it happened, the process of monetary integration accelerated rapidly, but not in the exact manner—including institutional changes—that Tsoukalis had proposed. After all, besides being the accelerator, the reunification of Germany amounted to a momentous transformation of the European political economy.

The establishment of the EMS, in December 1978, was probably the most important development in international exchange-rate arrangements since the demise of the Bretton Wood institutions and, in particular, the abandonment of fixed exchange rates in 1973. There were other regional exchange-rate arrangements too, but these paled in significance; currency pegs and 'dirty' or 'managed' forms of floating, albeit unregulated, were also deployed. In 1985, Tsoukalis edited a volume of research papers on international money authored by some of the leading experts in the field. In his own paper, Tsoukalis took stock of broader developments in international monetary arrangements and made the case for reform (Tsoukalis 1985).

Tsoukalis noted that floating exchange rates coupled with independent monetary policies aimed at controlling the money supply, the privatized provision of large amounts of international liquidity, and the marginalization of the International Monetary Fund (IMF) could hardly be thought of as the best of all possible worlds. Adjustments to the balance of payments via floating was neither an inexpensive nor an effective policy. Exchange-rate volatility and frequent 'overshooting' was a high price to pay, while the low (short-run) responsiveness of demand for imports and exports to price movements and labour market rigidities reduced the effectiveness of the exchange rate. Furthermore, national money supply targets had all but lost their relevance in a world of increased capital mobility and constant shifts in currency portfolios. Last but not least, risks to financial stability caused by irresponsible bank lending practices had made their presence amply clear; the international debt crisis of the early 1980s was surely a case in point—and Tsoukalis was prescient in his remarks.

A comprehensive international monetary reform could hardly be contemplated; nor was it advisable under the circumstances. Even an international exchange-rate arrangement, coupled with a coordination of national monetary (and fiscal) policies, amounted to a radical step forward—or backwards?—given that preferences on the two sides of the Atlantic diverged substantially. Tsoukalis (1985) argued, rightly, that the joint management of exchange rates would necessitate a much bigger shift in American attitudes than anything required from the EMS countries, or Japan for that matter. In addition, exchange-rate volatility implied little cost for the US economy, the dollar being the international reserve currency, and the independence of US monetary policy was largely preserved. No doubt, controversies went deeper as regards the supply and control of international liquidity, the regulation of the international activities of commercial banks, and official lending of last resort, including the role of the IMF.

Could a gradual reform of international monetary arrangements be envisaged? Would major countries be willing to accept constraints on their national autonomy and restore a form of collective management that was more in keeping with the degree of financial interdependence that had already been reached? And how relevant was the experience of the European Community (EC) in that respect? A favourable perception of the EMS was widespread at that time. And yet the EMS could hardly be thought of as a realistic benchmark for international policy coordination and the joint management of exchange rates. The economics and politics of the EMS were largely, though not solely, endogenous to the process of European regional integration, and so too were its broader implications for monetary cooperation. Thus, problems of international liquidity, exchange-rate management and policy coordination—or the lack thereof—would henceforth remain relevant, often painfully so.

In a 1983 publication (a contribution to a much-cited volume on policy making in the EC), Tsoukalis argued that setting up an exchange-rate regime in the EC, by way of the EMS, had been both advisable and realistic (Tsoukalis 1983). The similarity of national economic structures and social and political institutions, a high degree of regional economic interdependence, and common policies and institutions (the Common Agricultural Policy being a good case in point) had diminished the attraction of the exchange rate as a policy instrument, and reinforced the case for some degree of exchange-rate stability. In addition, a higher degree of flexibility than in the Bretton Woods system—which also reflected the fact that the ambitions of the early 1970s in regard to monetary integration had finally been cast aside—rendered the EMS acceptable. Undoubtedly, political motivations had been decisive, be they a desire to counter British attempts to dilute the Community into a free trade area, or the strong integrationist attitudes of certain member states (Italy being a case in point). Perhaps what mattered most was the perception of the EMS as an instrument for strengthening western European cooperation at a time when relations with the USA were rather cold—as well as a defence mechanism against the US monetary and exchange-rate policy of 'benign' or 'aggressive neglect'.

Tsoukalis' 1977 book on *The Politics and Economics of European Monetary Integration*—in essence, a shortened version of his doctoral thesis for Oxford University—was an inquiry into the (short) history of EMU and the controversies surrounding the strategies advised and/or attempted to achieve it (Tsoukalis 1977). His analysis went far beyond the technical and mechanistic arguments raised by macroeconomists and monetary analysts, regardless of persuasion.

Besides, independent of functional justifications—whether it was the unity of the common agricultural market, or policy coordination to manage economic interdependence—the joint management of exchange rates and monetary cooperation in general had not been appreciated equally by the EC member states. Doubtless, economic interdependence was asymmetrical and so, too, were the pressures on the balance of payments, the adjustments needed, and incentives for policy coordination. What was more, following the demise of the Bretton Woods institutions, asymmetries had grown bigger, dealing a further blow to functionalist expectations. In fact, money was neither neutral (as monetarists suggested) nor a technical issue (as functionalist theorists of European integration implicitly assumed). The management of money was highly political; and attempting to separate money from politics was no less so. Yet, Tsoukalis predicted that the process of European monetary integration would gradually gather strength, mostly as a result of growing regional economic interdependence and, largely pursuant to that, converging national preferences. That book was the *hors d'oeuvre de la haute cuisine* that developed later: the bigger picture, the political dimension of complex monetary arrangements, the emphasis on asymmetries.

Tsoukalis' research on the politics of money and the political economy of international and European monetary cooperation has indeed been wide and deep—as well as exemplary. His engagement in this field of political economy—probably the thorniest one of all[5]—has also been protracted. Nonetheless, that proved no impediment to his other research endeavours, be they the second enlargement of the EC (Tsoukalis 1981) or sectoral restructuring and EC industrial policies (Tsoukalis and Strauss 1987; Tsoukalis and da Silva Ferreira 1980), to name but two (on Tsoukalis and EC industrial policy, see Chapter 3 in this volume). However, there is no space available for a detailed discussion—and this chapter is already on the long side.

An Appraisal

Loukas Tsoukalis belongs to that early cohort of scholars of European integration whose workhorse models of analysis had largely been informed by the so-called grand theories of regional integration and, so far as economics was concerned, neoclassical microeconomics and trade theory as well as Keynesian macroeconomics. Yet, he was evidently sceptical of both the then prevailing neoclassical

---

[5] Bond fund manager Felix Martin points out sarcastically that 'in no other field than money is there a greater risk of being dismissed as a complete crank when you claim to have discovered the meaning of it. I am sure many of you will know Paul Samuelson, the great Nobel Prizewinning American economist. He used to say, "Not one man in 10,000 understands the monetary question, and you meet him every day"' (Martin 2013: 96).

synthesis—mostly developed by John Hicks and Franco Modigliani and popularized by Paul Samuelson—as well as functionalist approaches to European regional integration produced in the main by political scientists. Tsoukalis was thus little inspired by John Maynard Keynes' ideal stereotype of economists as 'humble, competent people, on a level with dentists' (Keynes 1933: 373);[6] nor did he envisage European regional integration as being an almost linear process of market making and (common) institution building, whereby technocratic politics would hold the key to problem solving.

Tsoukalis was one of the first to talk of the European economic system as something much more than a set of interdependent national systems. He was also one of the first to highlight the problem of the losers of globalization, which was later to become a key political issue. He began warning about the asymmetries and imbalances of monetary union from the EMS era, as well as about the inherent instability of financial markets. What is more, he never confined his research—either in substance or in scope—to the limits of conventional economic analysis. Instead, Tsoukalis has sought to make sense of the political perplexities and dynamics inherent in European economic integration, political and institutional inertia notwithstanding; and he has always looked at the bigger picture.

At the methodological level, Tsoukalis has constantly been critical of mainstream economic theory—and, in particular, of the microfoundations-cum-rational-expectations approach which has near-dominated academic macroeconomics since the late 1970s, or thereabouts. And he has regularly set himself free from the rigours of formal methodology, having adopted an approach akin to 'disciplined empiricism'. Furthermore, during his latest phase of research and writing, he has often embraced a normative rather than strictly analytical perspective, thereby articulating policy suggestions—and feeding ideas into the European political discourse. There can be no doubt that he has consistently supported the European project, while remaining critical of the official orthodoxy.

One could suggest—contrary to Tsoukalis' own epistemological stance, obviously—that neither relative theoretical indifference nor methodological eclecticism account for the widespread appreciation of his work and its outstanding influence on the European political-economy scholarship. One may nonetheless admit that, often, such an epistemological stance can soften science's hard constraints on mental processes, thereby allowing for greater intuition and more careful observation. Tsoukalis has certainly excelled in both. And, what is more, he has been remarkable in his synthesis, imaginative in his metaphors, and awesome in his prose.

---

[6] Tsoukalis would also draw little inspiration from Gregory Mankiw's (2006) suggestion that economists need to be more like engineers—that is, problem solvers—rather than being pure scientists; and he would not relish Esther Duflo's (2017) idea that economists should be like plumbers, and engage with the details of policy making.

Tsoukalis has been influenced by Keynes' other ideal stereotype for economists—which he advanced before the aforementioned one:

> [T]he master-economist must possess a rare combination of gifts. He must reach a high standard in several different directions and must combine talents not often found together. He must be mathematician, historian, statesman, philosopher— in some degree...He must contemplate the particular in terms of the general, and touch abstract and concrete in the same flight of thought. He must study the present in the light of the past for the purposes of the future. No part of man's nature or his institutions must lie entirely outside his regard.
>
> (Keynes 1924: 322)

Subscribing to that professional code, and following the line of inquiry thus prescribed, Tsoukalis has unequivocally (and repeatedly) made the case for European integration, while taking into account objective constraints and subjective sensibilities. He is a European idealist and a realist at one and the same time.

References

Baccaro, Lucio, Jonas Pontusson (2016). 'Rethinking Comparative Political Economy: The Growth Model Perspective.' *Politics and Society* 44(2): 175–207.

Burtless, Gary (1995). 'International Trade and the Rise in Earnings Inequality.' *Journal of Economic Literature* 33(2): 800–16.

Claeys, Grégory and André Sapir (2018). 'The European Globalisation Adjustment Fund: Easing the Pain from Trade?' Policy Contribution, Issue No. 5, March, Bruegel.

Commission EC (2005). *The EU Economy Review: Rising International Economic Integration Opportunities and Challenges*. Brussels.

De Grauwe, Paul (2011). 'The Governance of a Fragile Eurozone.' Working Document, No. 346, Centre for European Policy Studies (CEPS).

Duflo, Esther (2017). 'The Economist as Plumber.' Working Paper, No. 23313, National Bureau of Economic Research (NBER).

Economic Policy Committee (2005). *Responding to the Challenges of Globalisation*. ECFIN/EPC (2005) REP/54448 final.

Eichengreen, Barry and Ricardo Hausmann (1999). 'Exchange Rates and Financial Fragility.' Working Paper, No. 7418, National Bureau of Economic Research (NBER).

Frankel, Jeffrey A. and Andrew K. Rose (1998). 'The Endogeneity of the Optimum Currency Area Criteria.' *Economic Journal* 108 (July): 1009–25.

Freeman, Richard B., J. David Richardson, and Adrian Wood (1995). 'Symposium: Income Inequality and Trade.' *Journal of Economic Perspectives* 9(3): 15–80.

Johnson, George E. (1997). 'Changes in Earnings Inequality: The Role of Demand Shifts.' *Journal of Economic Perspectives* 11(2): 41–54.

Kelton, Stephanie (2020). *The Deficit Myth: Modern Monetary Theory and How to Build a Better Economy.* London: John Murray.

Keynes, John Maynard (1924). 'Alfred Marshall, 1842–1924.' *Economic Journal* 34 (September): 311–72.

Keynes, John Maynard (1933). 'Economic Possibilities for Our Grandchildren (1930).' In *Essays in Persuasion.* London: Macmillan and Co., Limited: 358–73.

Lucas, Robert E. Jr. (1976). 'Econometric Policy Evaluation: A Critique.' In Karl Brunner and Alan H. Meltzer (eds.), *The Phillips Curve and Labor Markets.* Carnegie-Rochester Conference Series on Public Policy. Amsterdam: North-Holland: 19–46.

Mankiw, N. Gregory (2006). 'The Macroeconomist as Scientist and Engineer.' *Journal of Economic Perspectives* 20(4): 29–46.

Martin, Felix (2013). 'Session 4: The Meaning of Money.' In Robert Skidelsky and Edward Skidelsky (eds.), *Are Markets Moral?* London: The Centre for Global Studies: 96–109.

OECD (1994). *The OECD Jobs Study: Facts, Analysis, Strategies.* Paris: Organization for Economic Cooperation and Development.

Siebert, Horst (1997). 'Labor Market Rigidities: At the Root of Unemployment in Europe.' *Journal of Economic Perspectives* 11(3): 37–54.

Tsoukalis, Loukas (1977). *The Politics and Economics of European Monetary Integration.* London: George Allen & Unwin Ltd.

Tsoukalis, Loukas (1981). *The European Community and its Mediterranean Enlargement.* London: George Allen & Unwin.

Tsoukalis, Loukas (1983). 'Money and the Process of Integration.' In Helen Wallace, William Wallace, and Carole Webb (eds.), *Policy-Making in the European Community.* Chichester: John Wiley & Sons Ltd: 115–41.

Tsoukalis, Loukas (1985). 'The New International Monetary "System" and Prospects for Reform.' In Loukas Tsoukalis (ed.), *The Political Economy of International Money: In Search of a New Order.* London: Sage Publications for The Royal Institute of International Affairs: 283–304.

Tsoukalis, Loukas (1989). 'The Political Economy of the European Monetary System.' In Paolo Guerrieri and Pier Carlo Padoan (eds.), *The Political Economy of European Integration: States, Markets and Institutions.* London: Harvester Wheatsheaf: 58–84.

Tsoukalis, Loukas (1991/1993). *The New European Economy: The Politics and Economics of Integration.* Oxford: Oxford University Press.

Tsoukalis, Loukas (1997). *The New European Economy Revisited.* Oxford: Oxford University Press.

Tsoukalis, Loukas (2003/2005). *What Kind of Europe?* Oxford and New York: Oxford University Press.

Tsoukalis, Loukas (2005). 'The Long-Term View.' In Loukas Tsoukalis (ed.), *Governance and Legitimacy in EMU.* Florence: European University Institute— Robert Schuman Centre for Advanced Studies: 111–17.

Tsoukalis, Loukas (2006a). 'The JCMS Lecture: Managing Diversity and Change in the European Union.' *Journal of Common Market Studies* 44(1): 1–15.

Tsoukalis, Loukas (2006b). 'Why We Need a Globalisation Adjustment Fund.' In *The Hampton Court Agenda: A Social Model for Europe.* London: Policy Network: 81–7.

Tsoukalis, Loukas (2011). 'The JCMS Annual Review Lecture: The Shattering of Illusions—And What Next?' In Nathaniel Copsey and Tim Haughton (eds.), The JCMS Annual Review of the European Union in 2010. *Journal of Common Market Studies* 49: 19–44.

Tsoukalis, Loukas (2012). 'Markets, Institutions and Legitimacy.' *Journal of Democracy* 23(4): 47–53.

Tsoukalis, Loukas (2016). *In Defence of Europe: Can the European Project Be Saved?* Oxford: Oxford University Press.

Tsoukalis, Loukas and António da Silva Ferreira (1980). 'Management of Industrial Surplus Capacity in the European Community.' *International Organization* 34(3): 355–76.

Tsoukalis, Loukas and Robert Strauss (1987). 'Community Policies on Steel 1974–1982: A Case of Collective Management.' In Yves Mény and Vincent Wright (eds.), *The Politics of Steel: Western Europe and the Steel Industry in the Crisis Years (1974–1984).* Berlin: Walter de Gruyter: 186–221.

PART I
DEMOCRACY AND WELFARE

3

Growth and Competitiveness

An Elusive European Quest?

André Sapir

Introduction

After two generally prosperous decades, the European Economic Community (EEC) suffered a serious setback in the late 1970s and early 1980s, with sluggish growth and weak competitiveness, especially in high-tech sectors, compared to the United States (USA) and Japan.[1] The consolidation of the single European market in 1992 was a major boost to growth and competitiveness in Europe. Yet, today, the European Union (EU), as it has been called since 2009, is facing economic troubles again. Growth has been subdued for a while, and the EU is suffering once again from weak competitiveness in high-tech sectors compared to the USA and to China, which is rapidly displacing Japan as the main Asian powerhouse.

Meanwhile the geopolitical situation has changed dramatically. Until the fall of the Berlin Wall in 1989, the world was divided between East and West, and all three main economic powers—the EU, Japan and the USA—were in the same political camp. Their rivalry was therefore mainly economic. Today, there are political dividing lines between the three main economic powers. The USA has dubbed China a 'strategic rival' and the EU has called it a 'systemic rival'. Moreover, although the transatlantic alliance between the EU and the USA endures, it is clearly weaker than it was during the Cold War. The EU's competitiveness problem vis-à-vis China and the USA in some key technologies is therefore not just economic but also geopolitical. Yet, despite its name, the EU remains largely an economic entity, though it has started to think and even to act geopolitically. The obvious question is whether Europe will be able to repeat its achievement of nearly 30 years ago and come up with a new design that will boost its growth and competitiveness once again in this new era, or whether this quest will prove elusory.

This chapter is inspired by Loukas Tsoukalis' writings, which I have always found insightful. Reading them is like travelling through the history of European

[1] I am grateful to Michael Leigh and to this volume's editors for their thoughtful comments.

André Sapir, *Growth and Competitiveness: An Elusive European Quest?* In: *Europe's Transformations: Essays in Honour of Loukas Tsoukalis.* Edited by: Helen Wallace, Nikos Koutsiaras, and George Pagoulatos, Oxford University Press. © OUP 2021. DOI: 10.1093/oso/9780192895820.003.0003

integration. But it is a voyage into the future, not the past. Starting with his maiden book, *The Politics and Economics of European Monetary Integration* (Tsoukalis 1977), which was based on his doctoral dissertation at Oxford University, Tsoukalis has used his sharp intellect to analyse Europe's problem of the day and to offer solutions that would often be implemented a few years (or decades!) later. His success in identifying and analysing Europe's main challenges owes much to a method combining politics and economics in roughly equal measure, which he has (fortunately) retained in all his writings.

In the early 1980s, Tsoukalis wrote an insightful piece, entitled 'Looking into the Crystal Ball', which sought to understand and to offer remedies for Europe's growth and competitiveness problem at the time.[2] It will be the starting point of my contribution, which is organized as follows. The next section examines the economic situation in Europe at the beginning of the 1980s and how the Single Market Programme (SMP) was conceived to remedy the growth and competitiveness problems of the day. The subsequent section fast forwards to the current economic situation in the EU, comparing it to the situation 40 years ago and trying to understand what has changed, what has remained the same, and why. In the spirit of Tsoukalis' writings, the comparison looks not only at the economic but also at the political conditions prevailing then and now. The final section offers some concluding remarks.

Europe's Growth and Competitiveness Problem in the 1980s

In the early 1980s, the mood was pretty sombre in Europe, with the terms 'Eurosclerosis' and 'Europessimism' summing up the situation. After two decades of rapid economic integration and equally rapid economic growth, the European Community (EC) was facing difficulties.

Tsoukalis (1982) shared this worry about the economic situation in Europe, writing (p. 239) that:

> The available economic forecasts for the EC countries are very gloomy indeed. They talk about continuing stagnation of economic activity and investment, further growth in unemployment and a new deterioration in the international competitiveness of those economies.

He recognized that the slowdown of economic growth was not unique to Europe, but he worried that the EC countries were faring worse than other

---

[2] The paper was published as an article in the *Journal of Common Market Studies* (Tsoukalis 1982) and as a chapter in his edited volume on *The European Community: Past, Present and Future* (Tsoukalis 1983).

industrialized countries such as Japan and the USA. He partly ascribed this situation to lower labour market flexibility and lower rates of profitability in private industry in Europe.

He was equally worried about the consequences of Europe's poor economic conditions for the process of integration, stating (p. 239) that:

> If those forecasts prove to be correct, then it seems inevitable that protectionist pressures will mount...If national protectionist measures become widespread, they will make nonsense of both the common market and the common commercial policy, and therefore of much that the Community actually represents.

He considered that 'the survival of the common market' (p. 239) depended on the EC's ability to introduce two new policies.

The first new policy, given the growing disparities in economic structure and income between EC countries (in light of the forthcoming enlargement to include Spain and Portugal), was to complement the common market with 'a sizeable redistribution of resources and a differentiation of measures jointly agreed in the pursuit of common objectives' (p. 240).

The second new policy concerned industrial policy. Tsoukalis (1982) was rightly worried that it would be difficult, but necessary, for the European Commission to control state aid granted by EC countries to help their national industries. But he wanted the Community to go beyond negative integration and simply taming certain national industrial policies. Rather, he also wanted the EC to take positive joint action and implement a form of Community industrial policy, especially in high-tech sectors where the EC was lagging behind Japan and the USA. As he wrote (p. 240):

> Some broad agreement on the intra-EC division of labour and the promotion of transnational ventures may be the only way to create a common market in high technology sectors, which presently does not exist because of national industrial and public procurement policies.

He was under no illusion, however, about the political feasibility of deepening European integration in these two areas, stating (p. 241) that:

> Although there may be greater emphasis on the redistribution of resources at the EC level, the amounts actually transferred are likely to remain small and inadequate. Moreover, in view of the complexity of industrial policy measures, the big differences in terms of ideology, general approach and specific instruments available in each country as well as the political sensitivity of the issues involved, progress towards some form of a common industrial policy may prove to be extremely slow.

Tsoukalis (1982) can be credited for having correctly emphasized two import-ant economic realities prevailing in the early 1980s. First, Europe's economic performance was relatively poor compared to that of Japan and the USA. Secondly, the EC lacked a common market in high-tech sectors as a result of national industrial and procurement policies. In his reasoning, however, the causal link between these two observations ran only from the first to the second. It was because of the poor economic performance of EC countries, especially in terms of unemployment, that these countries adopted the national protectionist measures which in turn jeopardized the common market. What is lacking in the analysis is that there was also a causal link running in the opposite direction: the fragmen-tation of the common market was probably one of the reasons for the poor relative performance of the EC countries compared to Japan and the USA.

The notion that Europe's inadequate performance in terms of growth and competitiveness owed much to national policies that fragmented and rigidified the common market, and that removing national barriers would therefore not only help create a common market in high-tech and other sectors but would also promote growth and competitiveness, was the central thesis of an influential paper by Geroski and Jacquemin (1985), published shortly after Tsoukalis (1982).

Like Tsoukalis (1982), Geroski and Jacquemin (1985) start their analysis from a fairly gloomy picture of the economic situation in Europe, characterized by sluggish growth and poor competitiveness, especially in high-tech sectors, com-pared to Japan and the USA (see Table 3.1). And like him, they came to the conclusion that Europe needs a European industrial policy instead of national industrial policies, and that its aim must be 'to enhance market flexibility, reduce barriers to mobility, and stimulate adaptability within large corporate bureaucra-cies' (p. 202).

There are, however, two main differences between Tsoukalis (1982) and Geroski and Jacquemin (1985). The first concerns the reason why a single European industrial policy was needed. For the former, it was to ensure the survival of the common market, which would otherwise become irrelevant due to national pro-tectionist measures; for the latter, it was to ensure that the common market delivered its potential benefit in terms of growth and competitiveness.

Table 3.1 Share of firms in sales of high-tech products, c.1980

Product	EC based	Japanese	US based	Total
Semi-conductors	9	27	64	100
Computers	9	9	82	100
Software	10	1	89	100
Data services	29	9	62	100
Digital telecom products	35	29	36	100

Source: Geroski and Jacquemin (1985).

The second difference concerns the content of the European industrial policy. In Tsoukalis (1982), it would take the form of government intervention to correct market failures, a form of 'European state aid', possibly through the coordination of national state aids. By contrast, the European industrial policy proposed by Geroski and Jacquemin (1985) would be more market based, reflecting their view that 'industrial policy should be designed not to specify and enforce particular outcomes but to alter market processes by attacking the rigidities which impede both the force of market selection external to the firm, and the pressures for change from within the firm' (p. 170). The policy would comprise four components:

- A vigorous anti-trust and merger policy aimed at reducing entry barriers erected by dominant firms.
- An attack on financial barriers to entry, which favour dominant firms at the expense of new and smaller firms.
- The harmonization of national industrial policies and the reduction of state aid to reduce government-created barriers between EC countries.
- Policies to promote cooperative ventures in sectors such as high-tech.

These measures would, according to their authors, help reduce the fragmentation of the European market and move the EC towards a more 'genuine common market'. In each EC country, the large firms or national champions would then be exposed to greater competition and their market power would be correspondingly reduced, thus promoting Schumpeterian growth.

The ideas discussed in papers such as Tsoukalis (1982) and Geroski and Jacquemin (1985) were influential in shaping the intellectual climate that led to the White Paper on the Completion of the Internal Market put forward by Jacques Delors and Lord Cockfield, respectively president and vice-president of the European Commission, in June 1985. The purpose of the Single Market Programme (SMP) was both to preserve the achievements of European economic integration and to relaunch European economic growth by deepening the internal or single market,[3] as the common market was rebranded by the 1986 Single European Act—the first major revision to the 1957 Treaty of Rome—which set the goal of completing the single market by 1992.

In 1986, Lord Cockfield appointed Paolo Cecchini, a senior Commission official, as responsible for the 'Costs of non-Europe' project, tasked to make an economic evaluation of the potential gains of completing the single market. The work of the 'Cecchini Group' was published in several forms, including a popular version (Cecchini et al. 1988) and a more analytical version (Emerson et al. 1989).

---

[3] The two terms are often used interchangeably.

During the period 1979–85, annual GDP growth in Europe averaged 1.9 per cent, well below the situation in Japan (4.2 per cent) and the USA (2.8 per cent).[4] In *The Economics of 1992*, Emerson et al. (1989) argued that the reason why growth was lagging in Europe was partly due to the fact that European countries tended to specialize in sectors with low or average growth in demand, rather than in sectors in which demand was growing rapidly, like those producing electronic products or data-processing machines. The weak performance of European countries in high-tech sectors was in line with their relatively low productivity in these sectors. Table 3.2 shows that in 1985 the level of (labour) productivity in the three largest EC countries was well below the levels of productivity in the USA and in Japan, and that the gap with these two countries was much larger in high-tech sectors than in the rest of the manufacturing sector. Emerson et al. (1989: 25) ascribed this unfavourable situation to the fact that:

> In these high-tech sectors, the critical mass for R&D is considerable and requires the active cooperation if not the integration of European firms if the Community is to match the level and effectiveness of expenditure in this area by American and Japanese multinational companies. Furthermore, economies of scale play a vital role in these industries and call for production units which can without difficulty serve a unified market which is perfectly integrated as regards standards and marketing requirements.

The remedy was the removal of the EC's internal market barriers along the lines proposed by the White Paper and the creation of a unified European market. But Emerson et al. (1989: 22) were clear that 'more than full implementation of the White Paper is required to achieve the full potential benefits of an integrated European market. There must be a strong competition policy' to ensure that not only administrative barriers are eliminated but anti-competitive barriers to entry and exit, as well.

Table 3.2 Labour productivity in manufacturing sectors, 1985 (USA = 100)

Product	France	Germany	UK	Japan
Electrical and electronic products	47	43	28	236
Office and data-processing machines	43	45	37	94
All manufacturing	65	65	42	100

Source: Emerson et al. (1988).

[4] See World Bank statistics.

The SMP was a huge success. It boosted economic growth and changed the mood in Europe, with 'Europe 1992' replacing 'Eurosclerosis' and 'Europessimism'. This success gave a new impetus to European integration, with the decision to create a European Union and an Economic and Monetary Union enshrined in the 1992 Treaty of Maastricht.

'Europe 1992' also changed the status of the European project. It turned a fragmented common market into a unified single market (soon with a single currency) capable of rivalling Japan and the USA economically, at least in the manufacturing sector. Sadly, the SMP was far less successful in creating a unified and competitive market for services.

During the 1980s and 1990s, the rivalry between the EU on the one hand and Japan and the USA on the other was palpable. Every official EU document about the state of the European economy compared it with the situation in Japan and the USA. But the rivalry was mainly economic. Paris was traditionally suspicious from a political and security point of view of the USA and the North Atlantic Treaty Organization (NATO), an alliance whose integrated military command France quit in 1966, only to re-join in 2009. Elsewhere, in other national capitals and in Brussels, the seat of the EU, there was no—or a minimal—political and security dimension to the rivalry with Japan and the USA, though there certainly were serious reservations about US foreign policy at times.

On the contrary, the USA and NATO were viewed as essential to ensure the security of western Europe. Tsoukalis (1982) largely shared this view, although he worried about growing differences of interests between western Europe and the USA concerning Middle East and East–West relations, which he regarded as 'probably more than a temporary hiccup and rather part of a long-term trend' (p. 236). Barring a return to more closely aligned Euro–American relations, which he regarded as unlikely, he advocated European countries deepening their political and security relations with a view to gradually setting up 'an independent West European defence arrangement' (p. 243).

Europe's Growth and Competitiveness Problem Today

Today, 35 years after the launch of the SMP, there is widespread agreement that the 'European Single Market has been a powerful tool for stimulating growth and competitiveness, but [also that] its functioning could be further improved' (de Guindos 2019).

Using various techniques, recent studies by Felbermayr et al. (2018), Mayer et al. (2018), In 't Veld (2019) and Lehtimäki and Sondermann (2020) all find that the single market substantially increased EU GDP growth.

At the same time, the productivity performance of many EU countries has been relatively weak, which has contributed to relatively disappointing growth. Leaving aside the catching-up countries of central and eastern Europe, the EU has a productivity growth problem. Between 2001 and 2007, hourly productivity grew at an annual average rate of 2.1 per cent in the USA, but barely 1 per cent in the equally mature euro area (EA). The gap between the EA and the USA was much less between 2008 and 2017, but that is only because productivity growth slowed down on both sides of the Atlantic: to 1 per cent in the USA and to 0.8 per cent in the EA.[5]

The reason for the EU's weak productivity performance is well known. Using annual country-sector data for the period 2000–14 across the EU countries, Anderton et al. (2019) find that: (1) business churning appears to be positively related to higher total factor productivity at the sector level, facilitating as it does the entry of new competitive firms and the exit of less productive ones; and (2) competition-enhancing regulation is associated with a higher rate of firm churning. The implication is that further reducing barriers in European product markets, and especially in services markets which remain highly fragmented along national lines, could help to improve productivity growth.

These findings echo those of the Sapir Report (Sapir et al. 2004), which lamented that, despite its formidable achievements since the launch of the SMP in 1985, the EU's growth performance continued to be relatively mediocre.

The central argument of the Sapir Report was that Europe's unsatisfactory growth was a symptom of its failure to transform into an innovation-based economy. The EU had lagged behind Japan and the USA in the information and communication technology (ICT) revolution in the 1970s and 1980s, and was now lagging behind the USA in the burgeoning digital revolution. The Sapir Report considered the European economic system to be largely built around the assimilation of existing technologies, mass production generating economies of scale, and an industrial structure dominated by large firms with stable markets and long-term employment patterns. It concluded that the system was not well adapted to a world characterized by economic globalization and strong global competition.

Like Geroski and Jacquemin (1985) and Emerson et al. (1989), Sapir et al. (2004) argued that the single market must be accompanied by policies which provided for more opportunities for new entrants, greater mobility for employees within and across firms, more retraining, greater reliance on market financing, and higher investment in both R&D and higher education—that is, policies aimed at making the single market more dynamic and the European economy more competitive, dynamic, and innovative.

---

[5] Two of the EU's mature economies, Sweden and the UK, had very fast productivity growth (even faster than the USA) between 2001 and 2007, but it fell dramatically between 2008 and 2017, with growth rates even lower than the EA average.

Europe's problem does not seem to be a lack of successful large companies. According to the most recent *Financial Times* ranking of the world's 500 largest companies by market capitalization at market exchange rates, dating from September 2015, the EU was home to 22 per cent of these global champions and to 19 per cent of their combined market capitalization (see Table 3.3). This was closely in line with the EU's share of global GDP at market exchange rates, which stood at 22 per cent in 2015 according to IMF statistics.

A similar finding can be observed in Table 3.4, which is based on the ranking of the world's 2,500 largest R&D spenders, as compiled by the European Commission. In 2018, EU-based companies accounted for 22 per cent of the top 2,500 companies and 25 per cent of their combined R&D spending. Companies based in the EU accounted for an even larger share of the top 100 companies and their combined R&D spending at 29 and 27 per cent, respectively. However, EU-based companies were less prominent among the top 20, where they accounted for only 20 per cent of the firms and 18 per cent of the money they spent.

Table 3.3 The world's 500 largest listed companies by market capitalization, 2015

Headquarter country	Number of firms (% of total)	Market capitalization (% of total)
USA	42	48
EU	22	19
Japan	7	6
China	7	9
ROW	22	18
World	100	100
$ trillions		32.4

Source: Financial Times (2015).

Table 3.4 The world's top 2,500, 100, and 20 companies in terms of R&D, 2018

Country	Number of firms (% of total)			R&D expenditures (% of total)		
	Top 2,500	Top 100	Top 20	Top 2,500	Top 100	Top 20
USA	31	36	50	38	45	52
EU	22	29	20	25	27	18
Japan	13	15	10	13	12	7
China	20	9	5	12	8	6
ROW	14	11	15	12	8	17
World	100	100	100	100	100	100
€ billions				823	411	201

Source: Own computations based on Hernández et al. (2020).

So, what is Europe's problem? As Table 3.5 indicates, Europe is still very weak in information and communications technology (ICT). In 2018, EU-based firms accounted for barely 14 and 12 per cent of global expenditures on ICT products and services, respectively. This is far behind the global leader, the USA, with market shares of 42 and 68 per cent, respectively; it is also less than China, which has market shares of 15 and 14 per cent, respectively (see Table 3.5, second panel). The third panel of Table 3.5 indicates that only 13 and 7 per cent of R&D expenditures by EU-based companies are in sectors producing ICT products and ICT services, respectively. This is far behind US-based companies, with shares of 26 and 27 per cent respectively; and also far behind China-based companies, with shares of 29 and 18 per cent respectively.

Table 3.5 The country and sectoral distribution of R&D by the world's top 2,500 R&D companies, 2018 (€bn for the top panel and % for the other two panels)

Country	ICT products	ICT services	Health industries	Auto and other transport	Other industries	All industries
USA	80	85	83	24	40	312
EU	27	15	45	65	56	208
Japan	22	5	13	34	35	109
China	28	17	5	11	35	96
ROW	33	3	24	6	31	97
World	190	125	170	140	140	823
Country	ICT products	ICT services	Health industries	Auto and other transport	Other industries	All industries
USA	42	68	49	17	29	38
EU	14	12	26	46	40	25
Japan	12	4	8	24	25	13
China	15	14	3	8	25	12
ROW	17	2	14	4	22	12
World	100	100	100	100	100	100
Country	ICT products	ICT services	Health industries	Auto and other transport	Other industries	All industries
USA	26	27	27	8	13	100
EU	13	7	22	31	27	100
Japan	20	5	12	31	32	100
China	29	18	5	11	36	100
ROW	34	3	25	6	32	100
World	23	15	21	17	17	100

Source: Own computations based on Hernández et al. (2020).

As in the 1980s, EU-based companies continue to have a strong position in more traditional sectors instead, like automobiles and other industries, where demand growth is lower than in the ICT sectors. In these more traditional sectors, which together absorb nearly 60 per cent of the total R&D expenditures of EU-based companies, EU firms account for more than 40 per cent of global R&D expenditures. This is more than double their average share in three high-tech sectors (ICT products, ICT services, and health industries) which together account for nearly 60 per cent of the global 2,500 R&D expenditures.

The strong position of EU-based firms in medium-tech sectors like automobiles, and their weak position in high-tech ICT sectors, is further illustrated by Table 3.6, which lists the global top 20 companies in terms of R&D expenditures. There are only four EU-based companies among the top 20 and none in the high-tech ICT or health sectors.

Table 3.6 also alludes to two worrisome trends in the European situation. The first is that, although it does possess some global champions, including R&D champions, Europe lacks relatively young champions. This is clearly shown by the data in Table 3.7, borrowed from Véron (2008), which indicate that only 8 per cent of the European companies belonging to the FT Global 500 (in 2007) were born after 1950, and that these European companies only account for between

Table 3.6 The world's top 20 companies in R&D spending, 2018

Rank	Company	Country	Sector	R&D (€bn)
1	Alphabet	USA	ICT services	18.3
2	Samsung Electronics	S. Korea	ICT products	14.8
3	Microsoft	USA	ICT services	14.7
4	Volkswagen	Germany	Automobiles and parts	13.6
5	Huawei	China	ICT products	12.7
6	Apple	USA	ICT products	12.4
7	Intel	USA	ICT products	11.8
8	Roche	Switzerland	Pharma and biotech	9.8
9	Johnson & Johnson	USA	Pharma and biotech	9.4
10	Daimler	Germany	Automobiles and parts	9.0
11	Facebook	USA	ICT services	9.0
12	Merck US	USA	Pharma and biotech	8.5
13	Toyota Motor	Japan	Automobiles and parts	8.3
14	Novartis	Switzerland	Pharma and biotech	8.0
15	Ford Motor	USA	Automobiles and parts	7.2
16	BMW	Germany	Automobiles and parts	6.9
17	Pfizer	USA	Pharma and biotech	6.8
18	General Motors	USA	Automobiles and parts	6.8
19	Honda Motor	Japan	Automobiles and parts	6.6
20	Robert Bosch	Germany	Automobiles and parts	6.2

Source: Hernández et al. (2020).

Table 3.7 Age structure by country/region (top panel) and country/regional structure by age (bottom panel) of FT Global 500 companies, 2007 (% of companies)

Year of birth	Europe	USA	Japan	ROW	World
Up to 1900	71	42	49	25	47
1901–1950	21	29	36	30	28
1951–1975	6	15	9	26	14
1976–2000	2	14	5	19	11
Total	100	100	100	100	100
1951–1975	13	38	6	43	100
1976–2000	6	46	4	44	100

Note: Europe includes the EU countries plus Norway and Switzerland.
Source: Véron (2008).

6 per cent (for those born in 1951–75) and 13 per cent (for those born in 1976–2000) of all the FT Global 500 companies born after 1950. The corresponding figures for the US champions are 29 per cent, and between 38 and 46 per cent. As argued in Philippon and Véron (2008), the near absence of new champions from Europe should be a source of concern for European policy makers, because it reflects the weight of long-established corporate entities in Europe and may hamper innovation.

The second worrisome trend is that EU champions are nearly all based in large EU countries. All four EU-based companies listed in Table 3.6 are German, and 15 of the top 20 EU companies in R&D are based in Germany or in France.[6] This suggest that nationality still matters a great deal in Europe, probably because large firms are still viewed as national champions (and helped) by their national governments. In turn, this implies that nearly 30 years after 1992, national considerations (both economic and political) still weigh heavily on the working of the single market.

Concluding Remarks

In the 1980s, Europe's growth and competitiveness problem was mainly economic and the response at the EU level was economic, too: the completion of the single market.

Today, Europe's sustained lacklustre growth and mediocre competitiveness are still primarily an economic problem. Without an improvement in its economic

---

[6] Including Airbus, which is incorporated in the Netherlands, but operates mainly in France and Germany.

performance, it will be impossible for Europe to maintain its living standards—for the retired, too, whose share in the population is fast increasing.

But Europe's difficulties in growing and competing also have an increasingly geopolitical dimension, especially as far as data and data-processing systems are concerned, where the EU's dependency on the USA and China is increasingly worrying. Europe has a distinct socio-economic model compared with both the USA and China, which its governments and peoples generally want to preserve. Doing so does not mean the EU should turn protectionist towards either the USA or China. That would be counterproductive. But it does mean that the EU needs to make itself more autonomous vis-à-vis its two main economic partners and rivals by strengthening its own economic and technological capabilities. This requires that the EU becomes more innovative and economically vibrant. It cannot simply be a large single market, though a large integrated single market is an absolute condition if it wants to be a global economic and geopolitical player alongside the USA, China, and others.

Despite being an economic and geopolitical necessity, a growth and competitiveness agenda will not be easy to implement, due to domestic political opposition from two groups of citizens who have become extremely disgruntled with the current growth model.

One group's objections centre on the fruits of growth having become very unevenly distributed and on the fact that traditional policies that seek to increase growth will simply exacerbate distributional problems and income inequalities still further. Although citizens in this group may reap some benefits from the growth-enhancing policies in question, they are ready to block them because they judge the benefits to them, if any, to be too small both in absolute terms and compared to the benefits accruing to a small minority.

The other group objects that increasing growth will add to CO_2 emissions and render the goal of zero emissions by 2050, to which EU governments are in principle committed, impossible to achieve.

Together, these two groups (which sometime partly overlap and sometime disagree profoundly) form a significant proportion of the EU electorate, at least in the more mature and wealthy countries.

The EU must therefore come up with a new growth agenda that combines growth, social cohesion, and the fight against climate change (Demertzis et al. 2019). Combining growth and the fight against climate change (i.e. achieving green growth) is possible, but requires a two-pronged industrial strategy involving both supply- and demand-side policies. On the supply side of the equation the key is innovation, which requires the right regulatory framework and sufficient public investment to unleash private-sector R&D targeted at affordable low-emission technologies. On the demand side the key is a change in behaviour, which once again requires the right regulatory framework and public procurement policies. These three policy levers—an effective regulatory framework, public funding for

R&D, and public procurement—should be designed at the EU level and imple-mented in a coordinated fashion by the EU and the national governments.

In seeking to create the right environment for green innovation, of which ICT innovation is an important component, the EU ought to seek inspiration not from China, which has an economic and political system too different from our own (though this does not mean we should not measure our performance against China's), but from the USA.

Three US federal institutions—the Defense Advanced Research Projects Agency (DARPA), National Institutes of Health (NIH), and the National Science Foundation (NSF)—have played, and continue to play, a crucial role in pushing forward the frontier of knowledge, and enabling private-sector R&D, in key domains. These three institutions, which in 2020 have a combined budget of $53 billion ($42bn for NIH, $8bn for NSF, and $3bn for DARPA), often work separately but sometimes together (and with others), as they did on the Brain Research through Advancing Innovative Neuro-technologies (BRAIN) initiative. BRAIN 'is part of an ambitious, public–private collaborative effort aimed at developing new experimental tools that will revolutionize our understanding of the brain'.[7] The EU budget, through the 2014–20 Horizon 2020 programme, already devotes sizeable amounts of public money to fund innovative initiatives (roughly €13 billion in 2020), but the amounts are still probably too small, and their effectiveness needs to be improved. Hopefully, the forthcoming 2021–7 Horizon Europe will improve the situation in both dimensions.

This kind of industrial policy, which involves creating appropriate framework conditions through a combination of regulatory policy, public R&D money, and public procurement, holds more promise for the goal of green growth than alternative types of industrial policy that would seek to relax EU competition policy and/or to use the EU budget to subsidize the production of certain firms deemed crucial from a technological viewpoint.

Fostering green growth through regulatory measures like carbon taxes will inevitably have distributional consequences, and unfortunately these will often be adverse. Low- and middle-income households are likely to be hit twice by increased energy prices: once via the increase in their heating and transport costs, especially if they live outside the main cities, and again because their jobs may be in carbon-intensive activities and therefore at risk of disappearing in the event of a significant carbon tax. But these distributional effects can be softened. Although it would be EU-mandated, the proposed carbon tax would be implemented primar-ily at the national level, and its proceeds should be redistributed to reduce the burden on low-income households. Moreover, public funding of innovation will

---

[7] See https://www.braininitiative.org/.

accelerate the emergence of new technologies, which will not only create new activities but also lower the cost of clean energy.

Cohesion policy should not be conceived simply as a way to alleviate the pains associated with growth, whether green or not (i.e. to 'clean up the mess'). Better social policies, including formal education and life-long learning, are also essential to better equip citizens with the means to participate more fully in the knowledge and innovation society, which is developing rapidly in Europe and elsewhere. However, green innovation will not happen rapidly enough both to preserve growth and to protect the planet, unless our societies make a greater effort to educate their citizens not only about the dangers of climate change but also about the possibilities that science offers.

Will the EU be able to rise to the new challenge it is facing? Will it be able to transform the single market to produce greater and more sustainable economic prosperity while also playing a greater geopolitical role at a time when the risk of its being squeezed between China and the USA is increasing?

These are difficult questions to answer; we can only repeat what Loukas Tsoukalis wrote four decades ago, at the end of his 1982 essay: 'Our main conclusion is that the equilibrium which the process of European integration seems to have reached in recent years is likely to prove a very unstable one' (Tsoukalis 1982: 243).

References

Anderton, Robert, Benedetta Di Lupidio, and Barbara Jarmulska (2019). 'Product Market Regulation, Business Churning and Productivity: Evidence from the European Union Countries.' ECB Working Papers, No. 2332. Frankfurt: European Central Bank.

Cecchini, Paolo, Michael Catinat, and Alexis Jacquemin (1998). *The European Challenge, 1992: The Benefits of a Single Market*. Aldershot: Wildwood House.

de Guindos, Luis (2019). 'Growth and Competitiveness in the Euro Area.' Panel contribution by the vice-president of the European Central Bank at the European House-Ambrosetti Forum, Cernobbio, 7 September. https://www.ecb.europa.eu/press/key/date/2019/html/ecb.sp190907~81df41228e.en.html.

Demertzis, Maria, André Sapir, and Guntram Wolff (2019). 'Promoting Sustainable and Inclusive Growth and Convergence in the European Union.' Bruegel Policy Contributions, No. 07–2019. Brussels: Bruegel.

Emerson, Michael, Michel Aujean, Michel Catinat, Philippe Goybet, and Alexis Jacquemin (1989). *The Economics of 1992: The EC Commission's Assessment of the Economic Effects of Completing the Internal Market*. Oxford: Oxford University Press.

European Commission (1985). *Completing the Internal Market—White Paper from the Commission to the European Council*, COM (85) 310 final, June. Brussels.

Felbermayr, Gabriel, Jasmin Katrin Groschl, and Inga Heiland (2018). 'Undoing Europe in a New Quantitative Trade Model.' Ifo Working Papers, No. 250–2018. Munich: Ifo Institute.

Financial Times (2015). 'FT 500 2015.' https://www.ft.com/ft500.

Geroski, Paul and Alexis Jacquemin (1985). 'Industrial Change, Barriers to Mobility, and European Industrial Policy.' *Economic Policy* 1(1): 169–205.

Hernández, Hector, Nicola Grassano, Alexander Tübke, Sara Amoroso, Zoltan Csefalvay, and Petros Gkotsis (2020). *The 2019 EU Industrial R&D Investment Scoreboard*. Luxembourg: Publications Office of the European Union.

In 't Veld, Jan (2019). 'Quantifying the Economic Effects of the Single Market in a Structural Macromodel.' European Economy Discussion Papers, No. 94. Brussels: European Commission.

Lehtimäki, Jonne and David Sondermann (2020). 'Baldwin vs. Cecchini Revisited: The Growth Impact of the European Single Market.' ECB Working Papers, No. 2392. Frankfurt: European Central Bank.

Mayer, Thierry, Vincent Vicard, and Soledad Zignago (2018). 'The Cost of Non-Europe, Revisited.' CEPII Working Papers, No. 2018–06. Paris: CEPII.

Philippon, Thomas and Nicolas Véron (1988). 'Financing Europe's Fast Movers.' Bruegel Policy Brief, No. 01–2008. Brussels: Bruegel.

Sapir, André, Philippe Aghion, Giuseppe Bertola, Martin Hellwig, Jean Pisani-Ferry, Dariusz Rosati, Jose Viñals, Helen Wallace, Marco Buti, Mario Nava, and Peter M. Smith (2004). *An Agenda for Growing Europe: The Sapir Report*. Oxford: Oxford University Press.

Tsoukalis, Loukas (1977). *The Politics and Economics of European Monetary Integration*. London: Allen & Unwin.

Tsoukalis, Loukas (1982). 'Looking into the Crystal Ball.' *Journal of Common Market Studies* 21(2): 229–44.

Tsoukalis, Loukas (ed.) (1983). *The European Community: Past, Present and Future*. Oxford: Blackwell.

Véron, Nicolas (2008). 'The Demographics of Global Corporate Champions.' Bruegel Working Paper, No. 03–2008. Brussels: Bruegel.

4

Education and the European Social Contract

Xavier Prats-Monné

A Grand Illusion

When I first met Loukas Tsoukalis, the Berlin Wall seemed as everlasting as the Great Wall of China, and China was still 20 years away from WTO membership. He was already a charismatic young professor at the College of Europe, I was his student and then teaching assistant, and we both saw the European project with the admiration of people who had experienced life under a dictatorship.

At that time Loukas had just published his second book, *The European Community and Its Mediterranean Enlargement*. Reading it again now, after so many years, I recognize Loukas' rare ability to combine rational argument, political conviction, and clarity of expression.

What his book could not foresee at the time were Europe's transformations, driven not just by half a dozen enlargements but also by technology, globalization, and demographic change. And what I definitely could not foresee—not even three months before writing this—is that I would one day be downloading Loukas' book from the *National Emergency Library* of the Internet Archive: a collection of books that support emergency remote teaching, research, and intellectual stimulation while the world's universities, schools, and libraries are closed due to the Covid-19 pandemic.

No scholarly article could make the case for strong multilateral institutions and global governance more eloquently than the coronavirus pandemic of 2019. And nothing like Covid-19 could have exposed so bluntly the Achilles' heel of the European project: while the EU has acquired powers—relating to trade, competition, macroeconomic stability—that can transform people's lives, the issues that interest European citizens most are still those where the EU has the least direct competence: health, employment, social protection, education.

Healthcare is the most obvious example of the gap between people's concerns and EU powers: public health is an exclusively national competence, and with the exception of self-selected success stories, member states refuse to engage in even the most basic transparency and information sharing about their national systems and policies.

Xavier Prats-Monné, *Education and the European Social Contract* In: *Europe's Transformations: Essays in Honour of Loukas Tsoukalis.* Edited by: Helen Wallace, Nikos Koutsiaras, and George Pagoulatos, Oxford University Press. © OUP 2021. DOI: 10.1093/oso/9780192895820.003.0004

Even in the case of health emergencies—where the importance of cooperation within the single market should be obvious, even without the Covid-19 pandemic—the one and only EU legal instrument is a Decision from October 2013 on serious cross-border threats to health. That Decision, adopted in the aftermath of the H1N1 flu outbreak a good decade after the first SARS coronavirus outbreak, established 'the rules for epidemiological surveillance, surveillance of serious cross-border threats to health, early warning of and response to such threats, including with regard to planning preparation and reaction linked to these activities, in order to coordinate and complement national policies'.[1]

Those 'rules' failed the reality check of the Covid-19 pandemic: predictably, an administrative decision agreed between health ministries in 2013 was not enough to ensure the transparent flow of information between member states, the coordination of restrictions on mobility and trade, let alone the timely distribution of protective equipment to fight the worst pandemic since the Spanish flu of 1918.

With this kind of inaction and solidarity gap, it is difficult to convince the average European citizen of the merits of a European social contract, or of the fact the EU fulfils its core aim 'to provide economic and social solidarity' (Fontaine 2018: 6), or that 'a European sphere of public policy is emerging as part of an embryonic European public sphere' (Mény 1996: 13).

The social contract is a very European concept: an inheritance of Stoic philosophy and Roman Canon Law, it was rediscovered in the age of Enlightenment and has been the main doctrine of political legitimacy for the last three centuries. There are many views of what a European social contract might entail, but the essence of the concept is simple: legitimacy rests on consent—and ever since the financial crisis of 2007, EU institutions have been at pains to explain why citizens should adhere to a project that ostensibly does so little for the issues they care most about.

Ask EU citizens from Riga to Athens what they expect from (any) public authority, and you know the answer you're likely to get: educate the young and keep adults in work; raise the poor out of poverty; preserve the social services, pensions, and health systems of our ageing societies.

Surveys over the years have consistently shown that Europeans are strongly attached to their welfare regime; more importantly still, as Tony Judt put it 25 years ago in his extraordinarily prescient *A Grand Illusion: Essay on Europe*, they sense that protection from the forces of globalization or natural disasters will come from national institutions rather than from European or multilateral organizations (Judt 1996).

Since its inception, the European project has rested on the reductionist assumption that economic integration necessarily creates social and political affinities.

[1] https://eur-lex.europa.eu/legal-content/EN/TXT/?uri=OJ:L:2013:293:TOC.

Time has shown that, while production and finance can become globally integrated and European economies can become more interdependent than at any other time in history, other aspects of human existence do not necessarily follow suit, or at least not at a comparable speed.

Social Europe at 50

If welfare and 'social Europe' are not the EU's strongest suit, it is not for lack of words: for half a century, European institutions have been remarkably productive on the declamatory aspects of the social dimension of the EU. Particularly since the Maastricht Treaty of 1992, there has been a consistent plea for: a 'social Europe' or 'European social model' that combines economic growth, high living standards, and universal social protection. This emphasis on welfare and inclusion is what sets the European Union apart from other less ambitious multilateral organizations and regional economic integration projects, and what supposedly binds Europeans together in contrast to the 'American way of life' or the objectivism of Ayn Rand (1966: vii).

Yet solidarity and a shared sense of identity are difficult to translate into practice. Social Europe has never been a homogeneous set of objectives or instruments. Some elements were born in 1957 with the original EC treaty and evolved through qualified majority voting: the four freedoms, the European Single Act, health and safety, and financial instruments such as the European Social Fund. Other policies acquired a treaty basis in the 1990s, but with the so-called 'Lisbon strategy' and the prospect of the enlargements to come in the following decade, the tentative attempts to strengthen EU social competences through a regulatory approach were abandoned in favour of the soft law of the 'Open Method of Coordination (OMC)'.

If by 'social Europe' or 'European social model' we broadly mean social protection and welfare regimes, the consensus in the academic literature is that there is no single European social model, but rather a number of variations around three broad regimes: Scandinavian, Anglo-Saxon, and Continental. These welfare regimes are complex systems which reflect the radically different ways in which European countries have organized themselves throughout the twentieth century in terms of the structure and volume of benefits, eligibility criteria, subsidiarity in delivery, family policies, etc.[2] More importantly, each of these welfare regimes has its own advantages and shortcomings, and responds differently to the combined impact of globalization, technology, and demographic change.

---

[2] Some authors add a fourth, Mediterranean, variant of the Continental regime. For a discussion on regimes, see for example Esping-Andersen (2002).

The cumulative result of this diversity in social realties and policy developments is a panoply of legal, financial, and policy instruments that are not entirely coherent, but certainly not negligible either. Over 50 years, the EU has developed a wide range of instruments: the European Social Fund from the early days, to promote inclusion and skills upgrading; the Globalization Adjustment Fund from 2006, to support workers made redundant as a result of trade liberalization; legislation to enforce a level playing field in the single market and to prevent gender and other forms of discrimination. Social Europe has also proven its worth less tangibly by supporting mutual learning, promoting the wider involvement of stakeholders, lending impetus to the modernization of social protection systems, increasing awareness of the multidimensional nature of poverty and social exclusion, forging a shared approach to common challenges, and bringing emerging common issues to the fore.

For many years, these instruments did not have to pass a real stress test. With the fall of the Berlin Wall, the 'end of history', and the financial euphoria of the early years of the century, the EU—the Commission in particular—presented itself as a manager of globalization and engine of economic growth—and got away with it.

Then, in 2007, the instruments of social Europe, painstakingly built and tweaked over 50 years and through half a dozen enlargements, were suddenly challenged by an unprecedented financial and economic crisis which quickly turned into a social one, with immigration flows not seen in Europe since the post-war years. With the realization that stability was not the norm and that globalization produced many losers and considerable discontent, inequality and social exclusion forced their way onto the policy and political agenda across Europe—and social Europe was found wanting. As constraints on the funding of social policies increased sharply, the focus of social Europe shifted dramatically: while it once stressed regulation rather than outcomes, now, given the lack of consensus and political will, it focuses on proclamations and process rather than substance.

The latest and clearest example is the European Pillar of Social Rights, jointly 'proclaimed' in November 2017 by the European Parliament, the Council, and the European Commission. It was presented as a turning point in the development of the social dimension of European integration, whereby 'the EU stands up for the rights of its citizens in a fast-changing world';[3] but this solemn declaration and its 'twenty principles and rights' have yet to be translated into tangible measures. Seeing the contrast between European proclamations and the reality for refugees in Aegean islands, few people would argue that this is a social Europe fit for purpose.

---

[3] Commission President J.-C. Juncker's speech on the occasion of the proclamation of the European Pillar, 17 November 2020.

As the EU begins to address the social, political, and economic impact of the Covid-19 pandemic, the debate on social Europe and, more generally, on solidarity, remains handicapped by confusion and contradictory views about the role the European Union should play in employment, education and skills development, social protection, and the reduction of inequalities. European institutions as well as national leaders are paying the price for their habit of over-promising and under-delivering on the social dimension of the EU.

The Limits of Social Europe

Social Europe is not just a collection of exhortations and declamatory statements, but it has its limits. National governments have greater political legitimacy and greater breadth and depth than EU institutions. And given that the views of member states differ significantly, the long debate over the Lisbon Treaty showed that there was little scope for consensus on the transfer of further legal and constitutional powers to the EU in the social field.

Germany set the tone. In its judgement on the Lisbon Treaty, the German Constitutional Court drew a clear line in the sand, stating that the competences of the EU in social matters had been reinforced by the Lisbon Treaty (Article 3.3.1 and the new horizontal clause in Article 9 of the Treaty on the Functioning of the European Union); that political initiatives and programmes gave concrete shape to this legal framework; and that this should be enough: in the future, 'the essential decisions in social policy must be made by the German legislative bodies on their own responsibility. In particular, the securing of the individual's livelihood... must remain a primary task of the member states...This corresponds to the legally and factually limited possibilities of the European Union for shaping structures of a social state.'[4]

But it is policies not treaties that can address Europe's transformations: beyond any constitutional limits, three obstacles stand in the way of a stronger social dimension of the EU. The first obstacle stems from the very nature of social policy. Forging a European approach on, say, energy security requires an analysis of complex economic realities and technical issues, a debate about common goals, and a difficult compromise between national interests. Education, social protection, and healthcare require all of that—and must still make room for the expression of strong personal and cultural values, for income redistribution and its vested interests, for ideology and political beliefs. A social contract, national or European, is about politics, policies, and well-being: the inherent subjectivity and

---

[4] https://www.bundesverfassungsgericht.de/SharedDocs/Entscheidungen/EN/2009/06/es20090630_2bve000208en.html.

political nature of all three should not be under-estimated, particularly since populist forces are stoking nationalist sentiments across Western democracies.

The second obstacle is that, while globalization increases the demand for meaningful EU and international cooperation, social transformations are mostly internally driven and follow different national patterns. For example, Europe's healthcare systems are gradually converging into a hybrid model, but they are still distinct regimes that respond to different preferences and produce distinct outcomes: the Bismarck model in Germany and Belgium, the Beveridge tradition in the UK and Spain, and the Semashko legacy of Soviet times still present in Poland and Hungary. For all the importance of globalization, the main challenges facing Europe's welfare regimes are only indirectly related to globalization: maturing welfare provisions, low fertility and ageing, changing family structures, new technologies. And if the response of EU institutions falls short of expectations, it is because nation-states remain the dominant players, even as governments steadily lose control over information flows, technology, migratory patterns, and financial transactions; at the same time, national social protection policies are still often organized around the model of a stable nuclear family, ignoring the impact of immigration, new family types, female unpaid work, and life-long learning needs.

The third obstacle is the European Union's transformation from a small club of privileged nations into a community of 28 member states, and the diversity of situations this entails. From the employment rate of women and older workers to school dropouts and university education attainment, one would struggle to find a relevant social indicator that does not vary radically from country to country. Even without the UK, if today's 27 member states had to start from scratch, they would still be unlikely to reach the level of consensus and policy development reflected in 50 years of *social acquis*. European institutions and policy makers have been reluctant to acknowledge that there is a trade-off between widening and deepening, or to address the implications of enlargement on the EU's institutional setting and decision-making processes. The obvious example here is the composition of the European Commission: before the fall of the Berlin Wall, the issue could be sidestepped because the number of plausible candidates was limited; after it, overlooking the impact of diversity on the European project was a political necessity, since misgivings about enlargement would have been seen as discrimination against central and eastern Europe. Yet it is disingenuous to assume that the social dimension of EU policies can be deepened, no matter how many members join the club, or how diverse they are.

The aftermath of the crisis of 2007 was a reminder of the striking resilience of European integration and welfare regimes. In Loukas Tsoukalis' words, the doomsayers who predicted the demise of the euro and of the European project 'once again...underestimated the reflex of cooperation strengthened over the years' (Tsoukalis 2016: 6).

On the other hand, the last decade has also reminded us that 'the collective capacity for strategic vision left much to be desired and so did European solidarity' (Tsoukalis 2016: 4). It has shown us, too, the radically different starting points and performance of EU economies, as well as the limitations of the EU when it comes to ensuring equality and social protection. In 2014, Greece's unemployment rate still exceeded 25 per cent, whereas in 2007 it was almost identical to Germany's (8.4 per cent versus 8.5 per cent); in that same year, the unemployment rate also rose to almost 25 per cent in Spain, whereas in Germany and Poland it had already fallen below the 2007 level.

The economic and social impact of the Covid-19 pandemic might give the EU a new sense of opportunity after many disappointments, as inequality finds itself at the top of national and EU agendas once again with the spectre of rising public debt, higher socio-economic and health inequalities, lower labour force participation, and increased labour market segmentation and structural unemployment. For all the EU's history of muddling through crises, this is a chance to explore the prospects of stronger action in areas of low EU competence but high relevance for EU member states and citizens alike. The reform of education is perhaps the best example.

Is There a Role for the EU?

While there is a broad agreement that the worst way to meet Europe's challenges, from pandemic threats to climate change, is uncoordinated action by individual member states, there is little consensus on the specifics of a European strategy in relation to solidarity or social policies.

The European social model of the 1990s, synonymous with continental western Europe's welfare states and social protection regimes, appears as an unsatisfactory answer to the challenges for the EU27. But even the widespread critiques of financial capitalism that surrounded the crisis of 2007 failed to produce a common view on national social policies, or a consensus on the social role of the EU.

Budgetary, fiscal, and redistribution issues follow a familiar pattern. In May 2020, the European Commission put forward its plan to ensure that 'the recovery [from the economic impact of the Covid-19 pandemic] is sustainable, even, inclusive and fair for all member states' through a new recovery instrument, 'Next Generation EU', embedded within a revamped long-term EU budget. The initial response from member states follows the traditional cleavage between net beneficiaries and 'frugal' net contributors to the EU budget.

So, one could be forgiven for seeking refuge in the safety of making proclamations on social Europe which are long on good intentions and short on operational content. And yet, the need for a collective European voice and stronger global governance is strong; EU integration tends to blossom in times of growth and go into hibernation during economic downturns: it should do the opposite now.

Each of the challenges facing the EU over the next decade has a strong social dimension: exploiting the job potential of a greener economy; increasing productivity and competing for talent in a knowledge-based society; adapting Europe's employment and social structures to demographic ageing and migration; tackling emerging threats, of which Covid-19 is the first with a truly disruptive impact but not necessarily the last.

EU policies and institutions will not be the main actors in addressing these issues: the core responsibility for education, employment, and social policies or healthcare, for tackling income inequalities and preventive welfare, will continue to rest with the member states, and the diversity of situations between and within countries will require an approach that is, if anything, more differentiated. But there could be scope for a stronger European contribution to national reform policies.

EU institutions could help define the path to sustainable development and the implications of economic change for public policies; they can make the social justice case for economic reform; they can steer policy development and innovation, particularly as concerns the emerging social risks and cross-border threats that are outside the traditional scope of national welfare regimes and require a high degree of social innovation: managing economic migration and integrating multicultural communities, maximizing the job creation effect and the social impact of green investment and environment-friendly policies, and addressing urban/rural cleavages and labour mobility.

In turn, the most effective way to promote these key strategic goals is to strengthen the links and conditionality between EU policy priorities and financial instruments, and to shift the role of EU funds from mere redistribution tools to financial instruments for the achievement of common objectives.

The credibility of the EU rests on its political will to forge and implement a narrative for sustainable development that addresses inequality and social protection. This is difficult but not impossible, and even more necessary in the wake of Covid-19: the EU needs a social contract in which quality of life and distributive aims play a more prominent role in the European project and its global impact.

The Case of Education

Europeans have been discussing education at least since Plato wrote the Socratic dialogues 25 centuries ago. We still have a variety of viewpoints on the reasons for acquiring knowledge and skills and on the best ways to do so—but I think we can all agree that, for most of human history, the purpose of education has been to make men better people (literally 'men', since it is only in modern times that women have been considered worthy of an education).

Modern European civilization was built on belief in the empowerment of the individual through knowledge, and the driving force behind such personal improvement was education. We have now come to realize another very important thing about education: that its benefits go beyond the individual, as new ideas create economic growth and prosperity. Today, education has an even more urgent purpose: more than ever before, it is the upholder of intellectual freedom and democracy.

So, education can and must have a great future in every country, if only because the demand for new knowledge and new skills will increase, and because critical thinking is the prerequisite of a democratic society. But it cannot be education as we know it.

Three global trends seem to be shaping the global education landscape, and all three plead for stronger cooperation between EU member states and institutions. The first is an extraordinary expansion of the demand for higher education. The OECD foresees that there will be 40,000 new university entrants per day in the world by 2030; the number of 25- to 34-year-old graduates in China will rise by 300 per cent by 2030, and by 30 per cent in Europe and the USA (OECD 2015).

The second trend is a renewed interest in the interaction between technology, education, and society, with the advances made in data technology and artificial intelligence and, suddenly, with the emergency remote learning initiatives patched together in response to the Covid-19 lockdown.

The third trend is a growing concern about inequality and social inclusion: societies will increasingly focus on the 'third mission' of the university: putting research and teaching knowledge at the service of environmental, societal, and economic challenges. Regardless of economic context, be it in times of crisis or expansion, across the wide spectrum of EU and OECD countries there is a positive correlation between education levels, employment rates, and healthy life expectancy: the evidence for the causal link between education and social mobility is undisputable.[5] The emerging evidence on the impact of the Covid-19 pandemic is just one example—albeit a striking one—of the correlation between health, social, and educational inequality on the one hand, and mortality rates on the other.

While this correlation is already a compelling argument for focusing on raising education and skills levels, the case for education reform is broader than that. The challenge is not just to improve education, but to change the way we educate, and to give citizens the best opportunity for social mobility in a knowledge and digital society.

---

[5] For a comprehensive discussion on this causality, see Schleicher (2018).

The extraordinary expansion of university education in Europe since the 1960s was driven by demographics, by changes in social attitudes, and by the idea that creating educated people and generating new ideas creates economic growth and prosperity. But as more and more people acquire a university degree, questions arise about cost and value, about alternatives to the university as we know it, and about the attractiveness and reform of vocational and technical education.

Globalization, technology, and demography are changing the global distribution of talent as well as the demand for and delivery of higher education. We know that a knowledge-based economy needs complex skills, but there is little evidence concerning what skills will be needed. Knowledge today stems from complex networks of institutions and people: it challenges policy makers as well as compartmentalized and discipline-based knowledge in favour of more socially accountable ways of addressing problems in their actual context.

So, the structure of disciplines and the authoritative nature of academic knowledge are being called into question. And since few people will hold onto just one job throughout their life, what is employability today? Employers want workers with the right skills—but they do not know how long they will employ them for (Coaldrake and Steadman 2016).

These complex challenges imply the need to break down the barrier between what C. P. Snow called 'the two cultures': science and the humanities, which as a whole represented the intellectual life of the whole of Western society, have split into 'two cultures'. This division is a major handicap in solving the world's problems (Snow 1959: 3). Students in all types of education will need to understand and combine science, the humanities, and the arts because, while science and technology have a major role to play in our societies and economies, so too do the social sciences in coping with diversity and inequality, and the arts and humanities in developing creative products and services to meet new and unimagined demands. One of the few certainties in the future of education at all levels is that it will have to be far more digital, collaborative, and interdisciplinary.

We are also seeing serious challenges to democracy on Europe's doorsteps, to the east and to the south, and increasingly at home. Better, broader education is the best response: democracy is about giving people, especially young people, the tools that enable them to decide for themselves through rational argument, and only education institutions can achieve that.

If education needs to change, can technology help? This has been the subject of heated discussions ever since Thomas Edison predicted, in 1913, that in 10 years schools would no longer need books: the cinematograph he invented would be a far better pedagogical tool.

Ever since, there has been little consensus or evidence on the impact of technology on education. Many are still sceptical: after all, if Socrates, Aristotle or Newton visited a school or university campus today, their only real surprise would be to see so many women learning, teaching, and conducting research. If the basic principles and tools of education have survived the last 20 centuries through the ages, why shouldn't they survive the twenty-first century too?

Yet this time might be different. The tsunami of technology is about to disrupt education, as it has already disrupted other sectors, and the Covid-19 pandemic will accelerate the widespread adoption of online and blended learning. The world's e-learning market is creating completely new services and audiences: off-campus international learners, modular courses rather than complete pro-grammes, broader student age ranges; as schools and universities across the world are forced to close and enforce social distancing, the experience of digital learning will become familiar and grow exponentially as a result. More importantly, the combination of artificial intelligence and big data is bringing aspects of education to the surface that have so far eluded analytical scrutiny, such as personal learning pathways.

At the same time, technology is posing unprecedented challenges in education, and not just with regard to privacy; there is also the risk of determinism. Since technologies forget nothing, learners could be bound by their own past, or denied recognition from an early age of their ability to improve; they could be limited in their choices and freedom to learn by institutions playing with statistics and predictive algorithms.

The transformation of education, driven by a concerted effort to provide evidence-based incentives for better outcomes, is one of the most important tests of whether the EU, its member countries, institutions, and civil society are determined to shape their own future—to find a path to recovery and progress and, just as importantly, to strengthen equity as the defining characteristic of the European project.

Almost every country in the world, not just in Europe, is trying to reform its general and vocational education and university system. Many nations—countries that find themselves economically where most EU member states were several decades ago—believe more than ever in the role of education, and demonstrate their belief in their spending decisions. In emerging economies, individuals as well as public and private institutions are boosting their investment in education and research, leading to a massive expansion in student enrolment and to higher levels of research. Yet in all but four of the 27 EU member states (Ireland, Latvia, Sweden, and the Netherlands) total public expenditure on education as a percent-age of total government expenditure is below the OECD average (OECD 2018).

Money is not everything in education: you can spend the same amount and the outcomes can be radically different; many improvements require only political will or regulatory changes (more flexibility and autonomy for universities, for example). But it is striking to see that Brazil (6.2 per cent), or South Africa (6.2 per cent), devote a far higher proportion of their GDP to education than almost any EU country (EU27 average: 4.6 per cent).

Reform is equally relevant for every EU member state, notwithstanding the many differences in governance and outcomes, with an agenda which includes: raising the number of graduates to meet the demand for technical and high-level skills in our economies, and opening up the benefits of higher education to a wider cross-section of society; enhancing the quality and relevance of teaching, research, and innovative activities; increasing the capacity and quality of vocational and technical education; creating funding and governance conditions in which universities can reach their full potential while remaining accountable to those who fund them.

Since the creation of Humboldt University in 1810, the greatest ambition of any university has been excellence, as judged by its academic peers. This remains as important as ever. But in these uncertain times of change and complex societal challenges, we must aim for Europe's education systems and higher education institutions to have a greater impact on society; why, for example, offer just a degree when what citizens need is a lifetime subscription that grants them access to the knowledge produced by higher education institutions?

We know what higher education institutions in continental EU member states need to be able to play their role in full: more autonomy to define their strategies, fewer administrative constraints, and more funding to achieve impact. And in exchange, they need to provide more transparency and accountability with regard to their outcomes, not just bureaucratic compliance.

This may sound unrealistic in these times of budget constraints and the bureaucratization of academic life, especially for the governance model in southern Europe. Universities today face many challenges: complex and vertically organized by departments and disciplines, they find themselves operating in an increasingly flat and networked ecosystem. They are losing their monopoly on the transmission and certification of knowledge. At the same time, universities are expected to do ever more with less: meet higher expectations with regard to accountability and performance; fulfil more bureaucratic requirements; compete against other claims on limited public funding; and find an elusive balance between research-intensive activities and teaching quality.

What's more, all education institutions are increasingly under pressure from students, who are demanding change and improvement in content and delivery. As more and more people acquire a university degree, questions arise about cost and added value, as well as about alternatives to the university as we know it.

Furthermore, just as science and technology are advancing with giant steps, so is scepticism about science. We know that vaccination is the most effective public health instrument in human history; we know that homeopathy is to medicine what astrology is to astronomy—and yet trust in vaccines has been steadily decreasing in Europe (at least until the Covid-19 pandemic reminded us of the merits of immunity), and homeopathic products are trusted by many as a natural alternative to clinical trials and scientifically sound medicine, particularly in

France, Germany, and Austria where the prevalence of 'complementary/alternative' medicine is highest. A survey found in 2018 that 74 per cent of French citizens consider homeopathic medicine to be effective;[6] several French universities offer degrees in or courses on homeopathy.

Is There a Role for the EU?

The main policy responsibility and funding instruments for addressing the challenges and the modernization of education systems are, and will remain, at the national or regional level. But the magnitude of the task, the global trends, and the reforms they require call for a strong effort from both the EU and member states.

The point is not who has the right to act, but who can help: EU institutions cannot and should not dictate national policies or innovate in the classroom. But EU policies and financial instruments—obviously Horizon Europe and the Erasmus+ programme, but also others such as Connecting Europe—can provide a supportive policy framework and the right financial incentives; they can help build and communicate the case for change, and articulate a guiding vision for the modernization of education; they can play a key role as platform and broker; and they can use accountability and reporting to encourage new practice. The negotiation of the 2021–7 EU multiannual budget, and the recovery plan that is likely to accompany it, provide an opportunity to rise to the challenge and scale up the scope and ambition of these incentives.

EU institutions have taken modest steps in the right direction: the European Council of December 2017 proposed several initiatives, including the creation of transnational alliances and long-term structural and strategic cooperation between higher education institutions (Council of the EU 2017).

Even without considering the Covid-19 pandemic, the rationale for a stronger EU governance system is not as evident in the field of education as it is in healthcare: the health stakeholders, the causal factors of disease, the determinants of health—from tobacco companies to the coronavirus—are clearly transnational. And while local/cultural factors can play a role in health, there is a fair consensus on the specific goals (e.g. eHealth infrastructure or the eradication of HIV/AIDs), diagnosis, and ways to achieve and measure progress. But health and education are closely related in their potential for human development and as sources of inequality; they both have prominent self-standing as well as transversal roles on the Sustainable Development Agenda. More importantly, while the cross-border impact of education policies is arguably lower than that of health policies, with the Sustainable Development Goals and other international legal instruments in place,

---

[6] IPSOS Survey, published in *Le Parisien*, 8 November 2018.

the education community now has all the key elements it would need to define an EU governance.

The EU created a strategic framework for cooperation in education with clear benchmarks a full decade ago.[7] It also has a very comprehensive monitoring and assessment mechanism: for the eighth consecutive year in 2019, the 'EU Education and Training Monitor' brought together a wide range of evidence on the evolution of national education and training systems. The Monitor measures and compares countries' progress towards the strategic framework; provides insights into measures taken to address education-related issues as part of the European Semester process; offers suggestions for policy reforms that can make national education and training systems more responsive to societal and labour market needs; and, last but not least, helps identify where EU funding for education, training, and skills should be targeted through the EU's next long-term budget: the Multiannual Financial Framework (MFF).[8]

So EU institutions have the means and the evidence required to assert their role as a framework for discussion and policy reform among state and non-state actors in education, with a view to defining and achieving goals, targets, norms, assessment and legal instruments, funding, and (new forms of) partnership. This would not require further normative, water-tight definitions of EU governance in education, even less any change in treaty competences regarding education—just as the global community does not need a consensus on the concept of 'global governance', which is still defined and applied in different ways, descriptively and prescriptively, as an objective, an idea, and a process.

What is missing is enforcement capacity and financial incentives for reform, with two criteria in mind. Thus, EU action is justified when it aims to encourage common practices and goals in the absence of a central authority and in response to growing demands on shrinking public resources; and when it includes the entire spectrum of actors, local, national, regional, and transnational.

Time will tell whether political leaders in member states and EU institutions will have the will and the capacity to enforce effective common policies in areas of limited EU competence such as healthcare, education, social protection, or child poverty—it is, after all, essentially a matter of political will. The determining factor should not be legal competence but actual relevance: not who has the right to act, but who brings added value. And what is required is not new proclamations or a reshuffling of old ones, but clarity of purpose—because the

---

[7] Council conclusions of 12 May 2009 on a strategic framework for European cooperation in education and training ('ET 2020'). OJ C119 of 28.5.2009 https://eur-lex.europa.eu/legal-content/EN/TXT/PDF/?uri=CELEX:52009XG0528(01)&from=EN.

[8] EU Education and Training Monitor 2019 and country reports. European Commission, 24 September 2019.

real challenge is not to define the right priorities but to ensure focus, ownership, and implementation.

Overcoming Europe's Pessimism

Saying that education can transform Europe's society is not wishful thinking: it has already happened. Western Europe's economic reconstruction in the post-war period was based not on natural resources but on immaterial wealth: people, their talent, and their attitude to personal development. Although this seems to have faded away in our collective memory, Europe's education systems have made extraordinary progress over the last 50 years.

In 50 years, the proportion of people with at least an upper secondary education in the EU has doubled to above 80 per cent. And the proportion of Europeans with a university degree has risen from under 15 per cent and mostly men, to almost 40 per cent with women constituting a slight majority (Eurostat 2019).

This radical transformation was possible thanks to changing social values, the emancipation of women, and the simple, compelling idea that creating educated people is the path to a better society. It can be done again.

The European idea—the intellectual challenge to which Loukas Tsoukalis has devoted most of his professional life—is a simple one: a society based on rational informed choice, in which pluralism, non-discrimination, tolerance, justice, solidarity, and equality between women and men prevail. These values are the foundation of the European Union. With the end of the Cold War, we thought we could take them for granted. Not any more: they are being challenged on our doorsteps and increasingly at home, here in Europe, by new forms of populism and illiberal authoritarian regimes. And by new versions of the same old nationalisms.

These are uncertain times: inevitably, many European citizens feel apprehensive about the present, pessimistic about the future, and distrustful of public institutions. We see this anxiety every day: in the media, in surveys, and in cultural expression. This pessimism can be explained in part by the lasting impact of the economic crisis, the rise in inequality, and the realization that the world is drifting in ways we do not understand and cannot control. But this sense of anxiety and apprehension about our own future is not inevitable: most countries are more deeply unequal, and most people have weaker social protection, than they are and do in Europe, and yet their civil societies and institutions can sometimes be more confident about their personal and collective future than we are.

Amin Maalouf (2006) once said that the success or failure of the European project will determine whether the human adventure will find the path of progress, and that with our words and actions, as fellow Europeans, we can all make a difference. Ever since I met him at the College of Europe four decades ago, Loukas Tsoukalis has made a difference.

References

Coaldrake, Peter and Lawrence Steadman (2016). *Raising the Stakes: Gambling with the Future of Universities*. Queensland: University of Queensland Press.

Council of the European Union (2017). https://www.consilium.europa.eu/en/press/press-releases/2017/12/14/european-council-conclusions-external-relations/.

Esping-Andersen, Gøsta (2002). 'A New European Social Model for the XXIst Century?' In M-J. Rodrigues (ed.), *The New Knowledge Economy in Europe*. Cheltenham: Edward Elgar.

Eurostat (2019). 'Tertiary Education Statistics.' https://ec.europa.eu/eurostat/statistics-explained/index.php?title=Tertiary_education_statistics&oldid=473425.

Fontaine, Pascal (2018). *Europe in 12 Lessons*. Luxembourg: EU Publications Office.

Judt, Tony (1996). *A Grand Illusion: Essay on Europe*. New York: New York University Press.

Maalouf, Amin (2006). 'URV Honoris causa Address.' Tarragona: Universitat Rovira i Virgili.

Mény, Yves (ed.) (1996). *Adjusting to Europe*. London, New York: Routledge.

OECD (2015). 'How Is the Global Talent Pool Changing (2013, 2030)?' *Education Indicators in Focus*, no. 31. https://www.oecd.org/education/EDIF%2031%20(2015)—ENG—Final.pdf.

OECD (2018). 'Education at a Glance.' https://www.oecd-ilibrary.org/education/education-at-a-glance-2018/indicator-a7-to-what-extent-do-adults-participate-equally-in-education-and-learning_eag-2018-13-en;jsessionid=kFrgJRigT-3cgVMyuT_w6reM.ip-10-240-5-85.

Rand, Ayn (1966). *Capitalism: The Unknown Ideal*. New York: New American Library.

Schleicher, Andreas (2018). *World Class: How to Build a 21st Century School System*. Paris: OECD. https://www.oecd.org/education/world-class-9789264300002-en.htm.

Snow, Charles Percy (1959). *The Two Cultures*. London: Cambridge University Press.

Tsoukalis, Loukas (2016). *In Defence of Europe: Can the European Project Be Saved?* Oxford: Oxford University Press.

5

Europe's (Euro) Crisis of Legitimacy

Vivien A. Schmidt

This chapter is dedicated to Loukas Tsoukalis, a major intellectual force through his thoughtful scholarly work and insightful policy analysis on Europe, and a great friend. Years ago, he wrote a wonderful textbook on European political economy that I used year after year in my courses on European integration, until it was no longer available. Loukas' contributions go beyond his writings and role as a public intellectual, however, to include his organizational skills as founding director of Greece's premier think-tank on Europe, *Eliamep*, with its stimulating conferences in picturesque villages and on dreamy islands.

Introduction

Prior to the Covid-19 pandemic, the Eurozone's 2010 sovereign debt crisis was arguably the European Union's (EU) most challenging moment. But this moment constituted not just a crisis of economics or of politics. It was also a crisis of legitimacy, as citizens lost trust in the EU as a governing authority as a result of its governing activities—in terms of what it did, but also of what it didn't do. The EU chose the wrong course in 2010 in its response to the Eurozone crisis. Rather than taking bold initiatives, EU actors ended up 'governing by rules and ruling by numbers' in the Eurozone, with a focus on austerity and structural reform (Schmidt 2020). By framing the crisis as one of public profligacy (rather than private excess) and by diagnosing the causes as behavioural (member states not following the rules) rather than structural (linked to the euro's design), EU leaders saw little need initially to fix the euro or to moderate the effects of the crisis. Instead, they chose to reinforce the rules enshrined in the treaties, based on convergence criteria for countries' deficits, debt, and inflation rates. And they agreed to provide loan bailouts for countries under market pressure in exchange for rapid fiscal consolidation and 'structural reforms' focused on deregulating labour markets and cutting social welfare costs. As a result, the crisis went on and on, quickly transforming itself from a purely economic crisis into a more general crisis of legitimacy, as rules-driven governance led to deteriorating economics and increasingly toxic politics.

Vivien A. Schmidt, *Europe's (Euro) Crisis of Legitimacy* In: *Europe's Transformations: Essays in Honour of Loukas Tsoukalis*. Edited by: Helen Wallace, Nikos Koutsiaras, and George Pagoulatos, Oxford University Press. © OUP 2021. DOI: 10.1093/oso/9780192895820.003.0005

By 2012, as European leaders and officials came to recognize that things had gone awfully wrong, they began to change Eurozone governance slowly and incrementally, by reinterpreting the rules and recalibrating the numbers. But because EU actors reinterpreted the rules 'by stealth'—that is, without admitting it to citizens or even, often, to one another—legitimacy remained in question. Fundamental flaws persisted, with suboptimal rules hampering economic growth and feeding populism, as citizens punished mainstream parties and anti-system parties prospered. And even though, by 2015, most EU actors had begun to acknowledge their rules reinterpretations, the damage had been done.

Only in 2020 was there a major reversal in policy, as the EU responded to the health pandemic, which was predicted to create an economic shock even greater than the sovereign debt crisis. After a brief moment of *déjà vu* with the Eurozone crisis, it seemed that the EU had learned its lesson. Suspension of the rules and numbers was accompanied by massive national bailouts and EU pledges for an unprecedented European recovery fund based on solidarity. Grants funded through EU-level bonds were to be provided for countries that had suffered the most alongside a smaller percentage of loans, with no conditionality. Legitimacy, so much at risk during the Eurozone crisis—as evidenced by the poor political economic outcomes, the questionable quality of the governance, and the subsequent populist revolt—may very well improve as a result of this new EU-level solidarity. But it will undoubtedly take time, and depends, too, on an adequate follow-through.

This chapter begins by conceptualizing legitimacy. This is followed by a deeper analysis of EU institutional actors' different pathways to legitimacy, and a discussion of how legitimacy applies to the Eurozone crisis. It concludes with a brief discussion of the response to the Covid-19 health pandemic, and the lessons learned from the Eurozone crisis.

Conceptualizing Legitimacy

This chapter uses the lens of democratic legitimacy to analyse the Eurozone crisis. Legitimacy here is understood as involving not only citizens' trust in a public body's governing authority (in the traditional Weberian sense), but also their acceptance of such a body's governing activities. Building on the systems theory terms of EU studies (Scharpf 1999), we can identify three mechanisms for the legitimation of governing activities. Output legitimacy depends on the extent to which policy choices provide for the common good, and is predicated on those policies' effectiveness and performance. Input legitimacy depends in turn on the extent to which policy choices reflect 'the will of the people', which is predicated on citizens' engagement in representative processes and government responsiveness to citizens' concerns and demands (Scharpf 1999: ch. 1; 2012). Throughput legitimacy sits between the input and the output, in the 'black box' of governance (Schmidt 2013; Zürn 2000; Benz and Papadopoulos 2006).[1] It depends on the procedural quality of the policy-making processes, including the efficacy of the policy making, the accountability of those engaged in making the decisions, the transparency of their actions, and their openness and inclusiveness with regard to civil society (e.g. Harlow and Rawlins 2007; Héritier 2003; Coen and Richardson 2009).

All three mechanisms are important for legitimacy, but they are not created equal. Notably, whereas political input and policy output may be seen to involve trade-offs in terms of legitimacy—with good policy performance making up for little citizen participation or vice versa—there is no such positive trade-off for procedural throughput. High-quality governance processes cannot make up for flaws in political input or policy output. Poor-quality throughput—whether it is due to governance being perceived as incompetent, oppressive, biased, or corrupt— can call both input and output into question by appearing to skew the politics or taint the performance (Schmidt 2013; 2020: ch. 2). The danger, therefore, lies in supranational actors assuming that simply following the existing procedural rules can make up for a lack of citizen participation in the decisions, or even for bad results. And this was the problem for the Eurozone.

Using these three mechanisms of legitimation suggests particularly interesting ways of stylizing our understanding of the Eurozone crisis of legitimacy. Put succinctly, it could be said that Europe's (euro) crisis of legitimacy stems from the fact that EU actors initially assumed that all they needed to do was to reinforce the rules (throughput) to guarantee good policy performance (output) and citizen acceptance (input), only to find that performance worsened along with citizens' attitudes. And when they subsequently reinterpreted the rules without admitting it, although (output) performance improved, perceptions of the quality of the (throughput) processes plummeted while the (input) politics continued to worsen.

In what follows, we focus attention mainly on throughput legitimacy, because countless scholars and analysts have already demonstrated that legitimacy in the Eurozone crisis was very much in question in terms of policy output and political input. Many, Loukas Tsoukalis (2016) among them, have written about the Eurozone's worsening macroeconomic performance in the first years of the crisis, as well as about the growing socio-economic problems, including increasing inequality and poverty (e.g. Blyth 2013; Tooze 2018; Mody 2018). Others have delved into the resulting anti-system politics (see Chapter 7 in this volume), with the rise of populist leaders and challenger parties accompanied by the decline of mainstream parties (e.g. Hopkin 2020; Mair 2013; Hutter and Grande 2019). However, relatively few analysts have compared and contrasted EU actors' procedural (throughput) pathways to legitimacy, and how these affected both output

---

[1] Note that Easton (1965) uses the term 'throughput', but limits it to administrative processes.

performance and input politics during the Eurozone crisis. This is why this chapter concentrates on the 'inside' story of the legitimacy crisis: that is, on how to assess the different governance of EU actors—including the Council, the European Central Bank (ECB), the Commission, and the European Parliament (EP)—during the crisis.

For the inside story of the crisis, much of the literature is concerned not with the question of procedural legitimacy, but rather with which actor had the most power in the process. Some authors insist the Council was in charge, either through coercive imposition (traditional intergovernmentalists—e.g. Schimmelfennig 2015) or deliberative persuasion (the 'new' intergovernmentalists—e.g. Bickerton, Hodson, and Puetter 2015). Others contend that the Commission and ECB were in control, either through institutional position (traditional supranationalists—e.g. Ioannou et al. 2015) or ideational innovation (the 'new' supranationalists—e.g. Bauer and Becker 2014). And yet others maintain that the European Parliament was gaining influence via institutional manoeuvres and discursive persuasion (what I call the traditional and 'new' 'parliamentarists'—e.g. Héritier et al. 2016; Hix and Høyland 2013). Although this is a very important part of the story, the focus on who drives Eurozone governance does not provide a complete picture of the crisis, because we lack an adequate account of the interplay among actors, let alone of how they considered their own actions in terms of power but also of legitimacy. Elsewhere, I have argued that irrespective of specific views on the balance of power among EU actors, the most significant point is that the actual powers of all such actors increased over the course of the crisis (Schmidt 2018).

Politicization has also grown (as argued by the 'post-functionalists'), with the rise of Eurosceptic pressures at the bottom creating bottom-up pressures at the EU level, in particular for the Council (Hooghe and Marks 2009). This has been accompanied by politicization 'at the top', with the increasing politicization of the interactions among EU institutional actors. Although evident in many different areas, this was most notable in Eurozone governance during the crisis. In the Council, for example, while some member state leaders contested the Commission's increasing 'flexibility' with regard to the application of the rules in the European Semester, claiming that it was 'politicized', others defended such action as appropriate administrative discretion. The Commission itself also pushed back against member states' rebukes about politicization at the same time that after 2015 it declared itself a 'political' body responsive to European citizens. Meanwhile, the ECB also became increasingly politically sensitive, engaging in more informal dialogue with Council members to gain tacit agreement for its increasingly bold monetary policy initiatives, and in more communication with the 'people' (as well as the markets) regarding its increasingly expansive monetary policy. And finally, the EP also became increasingly contestational politically as it criticized Council and Commission actions in its hearings and reports. The result is a new politicized dynamics of interaction among EU actors (Schmidt 2019). Although politicization has always been present to some extent, it has increased immensely in recent years, albeit due not only to the Eurozone crisis but also to the refugee crisis and Brexit. This fact also calls for a revision of the catchphrases I used in my 2006 book *Democracy in Europe* to describe the impact of the EU on its member states' democracies. In that book, I argued that the national level was increasingly characterized by 'politics *without* policy', as decision making moved up to the supranational level, whereas the EU continued to be 'policy *without* politics', via national interest-based decision making in the Council, technocratic and organized interest-based policy making in the Commission, and public interest-oriented legislation in the EP (Schmidt 2006). Today, things have changed: the national level has increasingly become 'politics *against* policy' or even 'politics *against* polity' (as in the case of Brexit). In contrast, the EU level consists much more of 'policy *with* politics' in contested areas, particularly Eurozone governance.

Recognition of the new politicized dynamics of interaction is necessary for an understanding of how EU institutional actors governed together during the Eurozone crisis, but it is not sufficient. EU actors not only exercised power in increasingly politicized interactions, they also sought to govern with legitimacy, and to legitimize their governance through discourse and action. But they did so differently, given their very different sources of and pathways to legitimacy.

EU Actors' Different Pathways to Legitimacy

There are significant differences among EU actors with regard to their pathways to legitimacy and their problems in achieving it. The differences concern not only how scholars might assess that legitimacy normatively, according to standards of evaluation related to policy effectiveness, political responsiveness, and procedural quality, but also how the actors themselves empirically think about their own legitimacy, and/or how other actors and citizens may perceive it. Among such actors, it is useful to distinguish in particular between the 'political' actors in the Council and the EP, and the 'technical' actors in the European Central Bank and the Commission.

Among political actors, those who operate in both the Council and the EP tend to assume that they retain legitimacy through their (input) representation of the citizens—the member state leaders in the Council indirectly via national elections, the members of the EP directly via European parliamentary elections. In reality, the Council is far from an (input-legitimate) representative forum, while the EP is only minimally representative. Not only do the Council's intergovernmental decisions often go beyond any individual member state's national aggregation of interests, but most member states' parliaments also lack the information and competences to hold their governments to account. At best, the Council may establish a kind of (throughput-legitimate) mutual accountability as a deliberative body in intergovernmental decision making, or with the EP and Commission in co-decision making (Schmidt 2020: ch. 5). Its transparency is minimal, however, given the secrecy of its meetings. At the same time, the EP serves as a weak representative forum due not only to low citizen electoral turnout and awareness, but also because it has no formal remit to hold the Council to account, particularly in Eurozone governance.

As for technical actors such as those who operate in the ECB and the Commission, neither has any significant input legitimacy. The ECB is by charter the most independent of central banks and thus fully outside the 'shadow of politics' characteristic of so many nationally based central banks, which are expected to be subject to a modicum of input-responsiveness (Scharpf 2010). The Commission is an unelected bureaucracy, and as such is accountable to the Council and EP as input-legitimate bodies. Only with the 2014 *Spitzenkandidat* procedure linked to the EP elections (when EP political parties successfully pushed for the leader of the winning majority party to become Commission president) did the Commission presidency gain an element of input-representation (which lapsed with the 2019 EP Commission presidency appointment process in the Council).

For both groups of technical actors, therefore, legitimacy is mainly characterizable in terms of output performance and throughput procedures. For the most part, ECB officials tend to conceive of their legitimacy as gained primarily from the (output) effectiveness of the ECB's policy outcomes in relation to maintaining the stability of the euro. They also claim (throughput) legitimacy through the ECB's formal charter-based accountability to the EP, however weak this may be (given that it need only listen to the EP in its quarterly meetings). There is no line of ECB accountability to the Council, given its explicit independence as laid down deliberately in its charter (although the ECB has lately developed informal 'political' channels of coordination, as noted above). At the same time, for reasons of efficacy, ECB transparency in terms of internal deliberations is limited. That said, in recent years it has increased its communication to the markets to ensure better outcomes, and to the people to improve perceptions of accountability and even political responsiveness. In contrast, the Commission tends to assume its legitimacy derives in the main from both the (output) effectiveness of its policies and the (throughput) efficacy with which it implements such policies and administers the rules; from its double accountability to input-legitimate actors, encompassing both the Council and the EP; and from the transparency, openness, and inclusiveness of its interface with citizens.

Institutional configurations of power and circuits of influence also matter for legitimacy. In the case of technical actors, the ECB has the autonomy to (re) interpret the rules set out in its charter, so long as its officials can build a sense of agreement about what to do not only internally, via its research departments, but also externally, by actively shaping a supportive epistemic community of banking officials and economic experts. Any such agreements can help to persuade members on the ECB's Board of Governors of the economic validity of the reinterpretations—although often the ECB president will also need both to convince powerful Council members of the reinterpretation's appropriateness (not to mention legal validity) and to report on it to the EP in his quarterly encounters. The only significant challenge to the ECB's reinterpretations has come from decisions by the German Constitutional Court, which issued rulings questioning the legality of its monetary policies.

The Commission has much less margin for manoeuvre because the rules it devises and administers have to be agreed by the Council (as well as with the EP in the 'ordinary legislative procedure', formerly called the co-decision process), and it has much less capacity to exercise voice. That said, within the limits of the rules, the Commission does have room for manoeuvre, given its administrative discretion with regard to interpreting the rules.

Compared to technical actors, political actors such as the Council and the EP may be in a better position in principle to change the rules, since as legislators they make the rules. In practice, however, here too there are significant limits to what the EP or Council could do. For the EP, much depends on whether a policy area is part of the ordinary legislative procedure. Where it is not, which was the case with much Eurozone governance (such as decisions taken in the European Semester and by the Troika for programme countries), the EP had little sway. In contrast, the Council has a great deal of power to impose its decisions in all domains, if it can reach a consensus on what to do. The challenge for the Council is that it has been boxed in by diverging preferences—in the Eurozone crisis, between 'creditor' and 'debtor' countries in particular—and caught up in a 'politics of constraint' that is very difficult to reverse (Laffan 2014).

The Legitimacy of EU Institutional Actors in the Eurozone Crisis

To gain a full sense of Europe's euro crisis of legitimacy, it is useful to consider first the (output) effectiveness and performance of EU institutional actors' policies, then citizens' views of their political (input) responsiveness, and finally the (throughput) quality of EU actors' governance. Such assessments lead to Janus-faced characterizations of EU actors' legitimacy, with split images of all such actors (see Schmidt 2020). Was the Council an unaccountable (German) 'dictatorship' or a mutually accountable deliberative body (in the shadow of Germany)? Was the ECB the 'hero' saving the euro or an 'ogre' imposing austerity and railroading countries into programmes? Was the Commission made up of 'ayatollahs of austerity' imposing fiscal consolidation and structural reform or 'ministers of moderation' reinterpreting the rules for better results? And was the European Parliament merely a talking shop or a potentially equal partner?

Eurozone Policy (Output) and Political (Input) Legitimacy

The narrative with regard to the Eurozone's poor output legitimacy runs as follows. During the heat of the Eurozone crisis from 2010 to 2012, EU leaders in the European Council decided on a range of policies that sought above all to contain the conflagration. First, they rejected calls for greater social solidarity in the form of debt restructuring or debt mutualization in favour of loan bailout funds with harsh terms for countries in danger of default, supervised by the 'Troika' (made up of the International Monetary Fund, the European Central Bank, and the EU Commission) and later the 'Institutions' (made up of the three plus the European Stability Mechanism). At the same time, through successive legislative packages and treaty agreements, they reinforced the rules of Eurozone governance by setting specific numerical targets for deficits and debt (through the six-pack, the two-pack, and the Fiscal Compact), with austerity and structural reform mandated for all those falling foul of the rules, and sanctions for those who failed repeatedly to reach the targets (as determined via the excessive deficit and macroeconomic imbalance procedures). Additionally, EU leaders agreed to enhanced oversight over all member states by Brussels officials through the 'European Semester', meaning that the Commission was charged with vetting national governments' yearly budgets even prior to their being reviewed by national parliaments.

These governance policies failed to deal effectively with the problems of the European economy, raising questions about the EU's legitimacy when defined in terms of policy performance. The USA, which had faced what were arguably even greater economic problems earlier on as a result of the financial crisis, nonetheless managed to emerge from its crisis more quickly, and without the double-dip recession experienced by the Eurozone (Mody 2018). Economic growth remained sluggish while deflation remained a threat in a Eurozone characterized by increasing divergence between the export-rich surplus economies of northern Europe and the rest (Blyth 2013; Tooze 2018; Mody 2018). Europe more generally was also facing a 'humanitarian crisis', affected as it was by rising poverty and inequality along with continuing high levels of unemployment, especially in southern Europe and in particular among young people (Council of Europe 2013; European Parliament 2015). Largely to blame for prolonging the economic crisis in the Eurozone were the demands for austerity in the south together with the lack of investment in the north—as even the IMF (2013; 2014) and the OECD (2016) reported. And adding to this were the 'one-size-fits-all' remedies implemented in diverse national political economies with different institutional configurations and potential engines for growth (Scharpf 2012; Mody 2018).

Citizens' disappointment with the EU's poor economic performance also fuelled questions about the EU's political input legitimacy, related to citizens' increasing dissatisfaction with and disaffection from EU and national politics. Eurobarometer surveys, for example, chart the decline in the positive image of the EU, which went from 52 per cent in 2007 to 30 per cent in 2012, while the negative image went up from 15 per cent in 2007 to 29 per cent in 2012—neck and neck with the positive responses (Eurobarometer, December 2012). And although, in 2019, the number of those with a positive image had come back up to 45 per cent, it was still lower than in 2007 (Eurobarometer, Spring 2019). Citizens came to perceive the EU as more and more remote (read technocratic), and national governments as less and less responsive to their concerns—often as a result of EU policies and prescriptions (Hobolt 2015). The dilemma facing national governments—caught between the need to act responsibly by implementing unpopular EU policies and the need to be responsive to citizens' demands (Mair 2013)—translated into more and more volatile national politics. National elections became increasingly unpredictable, as incumbent governments were regularly turned out of office while new parties with anti-euro and anti-EU messages got attention, votes, and more and more seats in parliaments (Hopkin 2020). Much of this has been a function of the growth of Euroscepticism and the mounting strength of the populist extremes, but it also reflects the increasing divisions between winners and losers in the crisis, within member states as well as between them.

Eurozone Procedural (Throughput) Legitimacy

Adding to these policy-based and politics-related challenges to EU legitimacy have been the policy-making processes involved in the Eurozone's governing by restrictive rules and numerical targets. Here, much of the problem with regard to throughput legitimacy has had to do with EU actors' implementation of 'one size' rules that were a poor fit for most member states, and the fact that after an initial two-year period of harsh enforcement they eased the application of the rules without admitting it. Not acknowledging up front that the rules did not work meant that EU actors continued to operate under rules that were suboptimal and constrained the range of possible solutions. Moreover, it left their actions open to being contested at any time as illegitimate due to insufficient accountability or transparency. By the same token, however, not saying what they were doing gave EU actors the space they needed to reinterpret the rules incrementally, so they would work somewhat better, while waiting for a time when they could secure agreement for changing the rules more formally. Even though by 2015, most EU actors had admitted that they were indeed reinterpreting the rules, it did little to change the dynamics of interaction among EU actors, which had become increasingly politicized over whether such reinterpretations were technically justified or normatively legitimate (Schmidt 2016, 2020).

At the inception of the crisis, the Council became dominated by the 'one size fits one' rules of intergovernmental negotiation that gave the most economically powerful member state (i.e., Germany) outsized influence to impose its preferences. German short-term interests were served economically, because it would pay the most in any 'transfer union'; politically, as the conservative party was worried about membership opposition to bailouts, electoral losses, and the rise of the AfD; and legally, through the Constitutional Court's rulings on ECB policy. Subsequently, however, despite continued German predominance, the increasingly politicized dynamics of deliberation and contestation among the member states intermittently led to positive change. Along with innovative instruments of deeper integration, such as banking union, came acceptance of the need for growth by 2012, when German chancellor Angela Merkel acceded to pressure from Italian prime minister Mario Monti, who was supported by French president François Hollande; for flexibility by 2014, when German chancellor Merkel acceded to pressure from Italian prime minister Matteo Renzi, who was also supported by French president Hollande; and for investment in 2015, when new Commission president Jean-Claude Juncker insisted on the creation of a new investment fund for the Eurozone. At the same time, however, the Council continued with the discourse of rules-based austerity (until 2013, when ECB president Mario Draghi himself called for an end to it) and structural reform, while imposing strict conditionality on member states forced into loan bailout programmes.

In consequence, the Council's intergovernmental mode of operation can, on the one hand, be condemned as an unaccountable (German) 'dictatorship' imposing *diktats* (e.g. Fabbrini 2013; Schimmelfennig 2015), in particular in the first couple of years, and on the other hand, be praised as a mutually accountable 'deliberative body' driven in the crisis by the search for consensus (Puetter 2014). But while the question as to whether the Council should be seen as a dictatorship or a deliberative body remains open with regard to the 'normal' countries, it does not with regard to what happened to the 'programme' countries under conditionality (Greece, Ireland, Portugal, and Cyprus) (Schmidt 2020: ch. 5). Here, in the case of Greece at least, the main alternative views are harsh dictatorship by the Eurogroup of Finance Ministers, backed up by member state leaders in the European Council, which forced the Syriza government to accept its terms in the third bailout of Greece (see e.g. Joerges 2014, Varoufakis 2016), or deliberative authoritarianism, where government leaders in programme countries deliberated on the terms that they felt forced to accept.

Similarly, the ECB at the beginning of the crisis continued to follow its own 'one size fits none' rules of monetary policy, in which its inflation-targeting policy produced increasing divergence rather than the expected convergence in member states' economies (Enderlein et al. 2012). At the same time, the ECB's repeated claims that it would not back member state sovereign debt by acting as a 'lender of last resort' through quantitative easing increasingly worried the markets (despite the ECB's bond-buying Securities Market Programme). It wasn't until July 2012 that the ECB moved definitively from its 'one size' rules to 'whatever it takes', in the famous phrase of ECB president Mario Draghi, as he announced the Open Monetary Transactions (OMT) policy of unlimited bond buying for Italy and Spain. This stopped market attacks dead in their tracks, and OMT was therefore never deployed. Only in 2015 did the ECB engage in full-scale quantitative easing. The ECB legitimized its incremental reinterpretation of the rules by claiming to have remained true to its charter, hiding its successive reinterpretations 'in plain view' as it switched from a discourse of 'credibility' to one of 'stability' in the medium term (Schmidt 2016; 2020: ch. 6). But in exchange for 'saving the euro', the ECB pressed EU member states to be stricter with regard to the rules, by tightening their belts and reforming their economies, while it forced countries in trouble into conditionality programmes.

As a result, the ECB can be portrayed both as the 'hero' on grounds of output performance, for repeatedly rescuing the euro, and as the 'ogre' pushing austerity and structural reform. Its ogre-like characteristics were especially pronounced with regard to its role in the Troika, where it pushed hard for strict conditionality in ways that could be deemed unaccountable and non-transparent. But the ECB could also be faulted in terms of efficacy for its slow response to the crisis, taking over five years to move to the scale of quantitative easing other central banks had begun with the financial crisis. Moreover, ECB president Jean-Claude Trichet's letters in 2010 and 2011 to member state leaders whose countries were in trouble (which included Greece, Italy, and Spain), threatening to pull the plug on their banking access unless they undertook harsh austerity and structural reform programmes, was not only unaccountable and non-transparent, it was arguably also input illegitimate, given the ECB's lack of remit in this area.

The EU Commission, much as the other actors, also initially applied its own 'one size fits all' rules of budgetary austerity and structural reform to very different member state economies. But after a couple of years, despite the fact that the EU Commission stuck to a harsh discourse of rigorous enforcement of the 'one size' rules, it began to use its discretionary powers to become ever more flexible in applying the rules and calculating the numbers (Schmidt 2015, 2016, 2020: ch 7). It twice gave France and Italy two-year extensions to meet the deficit criteria (in 2013 and again in 2015); it agreed to recalculate the numbers for Spain's structural deficit on the basis of its unusually high unemployment rate, so that it too could avoid violating the rules (in 2013); and it recommended suspending fines for

Spain and Portugal (in 2016). While this improved output legitimacy in terms of micro-economic and socio-economic outcomes, it cast doubt on procedural throughput legitimacy, given the reduced accountability and transparency. Moreover, between 2010 and 2015, the disconnect between words and deeds ensured that while southern Europeans continued to feel oppressed due to the Commission discourse, even though they had been accommodated, northern Europeans felt deceived, regardless. Only in 2015 did the newly appointed Commission return to greater accountability and transparency when it admitted to easing its application of the rules, but insisted it had the right to do so, since it established 'rules' for its own flexibility (Commission 2015).

EU Commission officials therefore should not only be derided as 'ayatollahs of austerity' in the first years of the crisis, because they were intent on imposing austerity and structural reform. They should equally be admired as 'ministers of moderation' for navigating between the Council and the ECB as they (re)interpreted the rules for better results. Here, too, however, the only way to characterize the Commission in its role in the Troika with regard to the programme countries was as 'ayatollahs of austerity', although here a mitigating factor post 2012 was that it was essentially the messenger for the *diktats* of the Eurogroup of Finance Ministers.

As for the European Parliament (EP), it had almost 'no size at all' when it came to setting policy for the Eurozone, before as well as at the start of the crisis. Over time, however, the EP developed a growing presence if not yet a major influence in Eurozone governance (Schmidt 2015, 2020: ch. 8). That influence can be seen through its increasing involvement in both informal and formal legislative processes, its greater exercise of oversight over the main Eurozone actors, and those actors' concomitant recognition of the EP as the 'go-to' body for legitimacy (Héritier et al. 2016). The hopes and fears of those most concerned about the political legitimacy of the EU as a whole therefore hinge on whether the EP will continue to be dismissed as little more than a 'talking shop' in Eurozone governance, or come in time to exemplify something more like an 'equal partner' in a renewed set of governance processes for the Eurozone based on co-decision (Hix and Høyland 2013).

Thus, what became increasingly clear over the course of the Eurozone crisis is that the challenge for EU institutional actors was how to get beyond the original rules to more workable ones. This was not just a question of overcoming the institutional architecture that made formally changing the rules very difficult so long as there was significant disagreement among the member states about what to do and how to do it. The challenges also involved the political divisions that reinforced the institutional gridlock, given diverging national perceptions of the crisis that exerted political pressures on EU member state leaders. The potential legal constraints that limited what they could do 'constitutionally' (meaning in terms of the treaties) represented additional obstacles. Moreover, the very structure of the euro served to exacerbate the political divisions and legal problems as it continued to produce increasing economic divergence among member states. Equally important, however, was the question of how to build legitimacy for reinterpreting the rules—no easy task given the complexity of governance resulting from the economic structure of the Eurozone, the EU's political institutions, EU and national politics, and EU law.

Conclusion

Europe's (euro) crisis of legitimacy stems from the European Union's 'governing by rules and ruling by numbers' during the sovereign debt crisis, which played havoc with the Eurozone economy while fuelling political discontent. Subsequent reinterpretation of the rules 'by stealth' may have improved performance, but it did nothing to change the suboptimal rules and only further contributed to EU and national politicization. Although a general acknowledgement of increasing flexibility would come as of 2015, along with quantitative easing and investment, the damage had been done. Legitimacy remained in question, understood not only with regard to political responsiveness (input) but also in terms of the quality of the governance procedures (throughput). That said, once economic performance (output) began improving generally as countries in the periphery graduated their austerity programmes and returned to strong GDP growth after 2014–15 (with the exception of Greece, which remained under a programme until 2018), input legitimacy improved overall (as judged by opinion polls), even as the populist extremes continued to gain political strength.

The question for today is whether the EU's general response to the Covid-19 crisis is enough to make up for the previous decade of declining legitimacy. Much depends on whether the EU has fully learned the lessons of the Eurozone crisis. Or even if it has, whether that is enough to quell the sirens of populism.

The response to the pandemic has already been a game-changer in many ways, despite initial hesitations that led to worries that this would be a replay of the Eurozone crisis, in which EU actors' hesitations and discordant views had only made matters worse. In the first weeks of the pandemic, EU institutional actors were very slow to respond, with a deleterious impact on EU-related (throughput) efficacy and accountability as well as (output) performance. The Commission was nowhere; the EP played no role; the president of the ECB claimed it was not within its mandate to deal with spreads between German and Italian bonds (which triggered an increase in the spreads for Italian bonds); and member state leaders in the Council failed to act in concert, even as they quickly introduced national policies without EU-level consultation or coordination.

Moreover, at the national level, member states' economic policies represented a major reversal of Eurozone budgetary orthodoxy, as they provided massive infusions of money to sustain businesses, protect jobs, and support individuals and families in the interests of output legitimacy. At the same time, their simultaneous closing of national borders, without informing neighbouring countries or the EU, seemed like the refugee crisis *redux*, while the export bans on medical protective equipment, ventilators, and pharmaceutical supplies seemed to violate the single market as well as European solidarity. Taken together, all such responses suggested that member states were concerned solely with national-level efficacy, accountability, and effectiveness, to the detriment of their EU-level obligations. It might have seemed that they had forgotten that the virus does not respect borders, and that the very interdependence of the Eurozone economy required some form of joint action.

Very quickly, however, EU institutional actors stepped up to the plate. After its initial misstep, the ECB became the 'hero' of the Covid-19 crisis, as it announced major bond purchasing programmes to do 'whatever it takes' to save the euro again, but this time without the ogre-like demands for austerity and structural reforms of the Eurozone crisis. Its Pandemic Emergency Purchase Programme (PEPP), at an initial €750 billion in March 2020 (increased to €1.35 trillion in June 2020), came much faster than in the case of the Eurozone crisis, when it had waited until 2015 to introduce its major quantitative easing programme.

The Council became even more of a mutually accountable deliberative body, in particular once France and Germany together proposed a major recovery fund of €500 billion to be mainly financed by EU-level bonds, which would provide the member states in greatest need with grants rather than loans. But this came only after discussions of an initial package of funding by the European Stability Mechanism (ESM) through loans, this time led by the Netherlands, which pushed for conditionality on ESM loans—leading to an outcry in Italy in particular, which feared a replay of Council 'dictatorship'. Moreover, these discussions were followed by the continued resistance of the 'frugal four' (the Netherlands plus Austria, Denmark, and Sweden) to any EU-level bonds, and then by their insistence that any such bonds should be loans rather than grants. But in this case, there was to be no German-led dictatorship, because Germany had switched sides. Not even the German Constitutional Court could produce a return to Germany's previous approach to Eurozone governance, despite the court's challenge to ECB independence through its negative judgement on quantitative easing as well as to the Court of Justice of the European Union (CJEU) and the supremacy of EU law, which had judged QE as within the ECB's mandate.[2]

In the end, the Council continued to act as a mutually accountable deliberative body by agreeing to a recovery fund that, in line with the Commission

---

[2] BVerfG, Judgment of the Second Senate of 05 May 2020–2 BvR 859/15 -, paras. 1–237, http://www.bverfg.de/e/rs20200505_2bvr085915en.html.

recommendation of €750 billion, was way above the Franco-German request. But, in contrast to the Commission proposal of two-thirds grants, one-third loans, the Council decided on a mix of €390 billion in grants and €360 billion in loans. This was certainly a historic achievement, though not a 'Hamiltonian moment', since this was a temporary fund focused on the pandemic, rather than the fabled 'Eurobonds' that many had called for during the Eurozone crisis.

As for the Commission, during the pandemic its officials acted from the start as ministers of moderation, with no sign of the ayatollah-like characteristics they had displayed during the Eurozone crisis. Almost immediately after member states' unilateral pledges on spending without regard to deficit or debt limits, the Commission suspended the budgetary criteria of the European Semester to allow for unlimited government spending (legally possible under the Stability and Growth Pact general escape clause). It also cleared the way for member states to rescue failing companies by suspending the state aid rules, at the same time that it put into place the European instrument for temporary Support to mitigate Unemployment Risks in an Emergency (SURE), to help maintain employment, proposed the creation of an EU-level health authority, and closed the EU's external borders to travellers from outside the EU. Its most important initiative, of course, in response to a Council request, was to recommend the massive €750 billion 'Next Generation' recovery fund to be financed by market-based EU bonds and made up of two-thirds grants and one-third loans, as part of a much larger multi-year EU budget (the Multi-Annual Financial Framework, or MFF) in which the EU would gain its own tax-generated resources.

As for the EP, it still had little in the way of 'size' during the pandemic. But where it did have some remit, as with voting for the first set of funding initiatives, it was actively supportive. And it continued to push the other EU institutional actors into being innovative, and to take this opportunity to pivot towards greening the economy as they combat the health and economic risks linked to the pandemic.

In short, the EU—arguably, with the exception of the frugal four—seems to have taken on board many of the legitimacy lessons of the Eurozone crisis. But it still has some way to go, largely because output legitimacy depends on the outcomes while input legitimacy remains in question. The populist revolt that stemmed in large part from citizens' negative reactions to the Eurozone crisis in terms of governance and performance is not over. Moreover, the governing by rules and ruling by numbers of the Eurozone has only been suspended, not officially revoked, while the Eurozone still lacks many of the instruments it needs to ensure optimal performance. But the response to the Covid-19 crisis, which reverses some of the Eurozone's worst legitimacy lapses, is at least a very good start!

References

Bauer, Michael and Stephan Becker (2014). 'The Unexpected Winner of the Crisis: The European Commission's Strengthened Role in Economic Governance.' *Journal of European Integration* 36(3): 213–29.

Benz, Arthur and Yannis Papadopoulos (2006). *Governance and Democracy: Comparing National, European and International Experience*. London: Routledge.

Bickerton, Christopher J., Dermot Hodson, and Uwe Puetter (2015). 'The New Intergovernmentalism and the Study of European Integration.' In Christopher J. Bickerton, Dermot Hodson, and Puetter Uwe (eds.), *The New Intergovernmentalism*. Oxford: Oxford University Press: 1–50.

Blyth, Mark (2013). *Austerity: The History of a Dangerous Idea*. Oxford: Oxford University Press.

Coen, David and Jeremy Richardson (2009). *Lobbying in the European Union: Institutions, Actors, and Issues*. Oxford: Oxford University Press.

Council of Europe (2013). 'Safeguarding Human Rights in Times of Economic Crisis.' Issue Paper, November.

Easton, David (1965). *A Systems Analysis of Political Life*. New York: Wiley.

Enderlein, Henrik et al. (2012). *Completing the Euro: A Road Map towards Fiscal Union in Europe*. Report of the Tommaso Padoa-Schioppa Group. Notre Europe Study No. 92. http://www.notre-europe.eu/media/completingtheeuroreportpadoa-schioppagroupnejune2012.pdf?pdf=ok.

Eurobarometer (2012) "Public Opinion in the European Union: First View" *Standard Eurobarometer 87* (December). Brussels: European Commission Directorate-General for Communication.

Eurobarometer (2019) "Public Opinion in the European Union: First Results" *Standard Eurobarometer 91* – Wave EB91.5 (Spring). Brussels: European Commission Directorate-General for Communication.

European Commission (2015). 'New Guidelines to the European Parliament, the EU Council, the ECB, the EIB, the Economic and Social Committee, and the Committee of the Regions for Making the Best Use of the Flexibility within the Existing Rules of the Stability and Growth Pact.' COM(2015)12 final, 13 January.

European Parliament (2015). *The Impact of the Crisis on Fundamental Rights across Member States of the EU: Comparative Analysis*. Study prepared for the Committee on Civil Liberties, Justice and Home Affairs of the European Parliament, PE 510.021. Brussels: European Parliament.

Fabbrini, Sergio (2013). 'Intergovernmentalism and Its Limits: Assessing the European Union's Answer to the Euro Crisis.' *Comparative Political Studies* 46(9): 1003–29.

Harlow, Carol and Richard Rawlings (2007). 'Promoting Accountability in Multi-Level Governance.' *European Law Journal* 13(4): 542–62.

Héritier, Adrienne (2003). 'Composite Democracy in Europe: The Role of Transparency and Access to Information.' *Journal of European Public Policy* 10 (5): 814–33.

Héritier, Adrienne, Catherine Moury, Magnus G. Schoeller, Katharina L. Meissner, and Isabel Mota (2016). *The European Parliament as a Driving Force of Constitutionalisation.* Report for the Constitutional Affairs Committee of the European Parliament, PE 536.467. Brussels: European Parliament.

Hix, Simon and Bjørn Høyland (2013). 'Empowerment of the European Parliament.' *Annual Review of Political Science* 16: 171–8.

Hobolt, Sara B. (2015). 'Public Attitudes toward the Eurozone Crisis.' In Olaf Cramme and Sara B. Hobolt (eds.), *Democratic Politics in a European Union under Stress.* Oxford: Oxford University Press: 48–66.

Hooghe, Liesbet and Gary Marks (2009). 'A Postfunctionalist Theory of European Integration: From Permissive Consensus to Constraining Dissensus.' *British Journal of Political Science* 39(1): 1–23.

Hopkin, Jonathan (2020). *Anti-System Politics: The Crisis of Market Liberalism in Rich Democracies.* New York: Oxford University Press.

Hutter, Swen and Edgar Grande (2019). 'Politicizing Europe in Times of Crisis.' *Journal of European Public Policy* 26(7): 996–1017.

IMF (2013). 'Greece: Ex Post Evaluation of Exceptional Access under the 2010 Stand-By Arrangement.' IMF Country Reports, No. 13/156 (June). Washington, DC: International Monetary Fund.

IMF (2014). 'Is It Time for an Infrastructure Push? The Macroeconomic Effects of Public Investment.' In *World Economic Outlook*, October. Washington, DC: International Monetary Fund: 76–114.

Ioannou, Demosthenes, Patrick Leblond, and Arne Niemann (2015). 'European Integration and the Crisis.' *Journal of European Public Policy* 22(2): 155–7.

Joerges, Christian (2014). 'Three Transformations of Europe and the Search for a Way Out of Its Crisis.' In Christian Joerges and Carola Glinski (eds.), *The European Crisis and the Transformation of Transnational Governance: Authoritarian Managerialism Versus Democratic Governance.* Oxford: Hart Publishing.

Laffan, Brigid (2014). 'Testing Times: The Growing Primacy of Responsibility in the Euro Area.' *West European Politics* 37(2): 270–87.

Mair, Peter (2013). *Ruling the Void: The Hollowing of Western Democracy.* London: Verso.

Mody, Ashoka (2018). *Eurotragedy: A Drama in Nine Acts.* Oxford: Oxford University Press.

OECD (2016). 'Using the Fiscal Levers to Escape the Low-Growth Trap.' In *OECD Economic Outlook.* Issue 2. Paris: Organization for Economic Cooperation and Development.

Puetter, Uwe (2014). *The European Council and the Council: New Intergovernmentalism and Institutional Change*. Oxford: Oxford University Press.

Scharpf, Fritz W. (1999). *Governing in Europe*. Oxford: Oxford University Press.

Scharpf, Fritz W. (2010). 'The Asymmetry of European Integration, or Why the EU Cannot Be a Social Market Economy.' *Socio-Economic Review* 8(2) 211–50.

Scharpf, Fritz W. (2012). 'Monetary Union, Fiscal Crisis and the Pre-emption of Democracy.' *Zeitschrift für Staats- und Europawissenschaften* 9(2): 163–98. http://www.zse.nomos.de/fileadmin/zse/doc/Aufsatz_ZSE_11_02.pdf.

Schimmelfennig, Frank (2015). 'Liberal Intergovernmentalism and the Euro Area Crisis.' *Journal of European Public Policy* 22(2): 177–95.

Schmidt, Vivien A. (2006). *Democracy in Europe*. Oxford: Oxford University Press.

Schmidt, Vivien A. (2013). 'Democracy and Legitimacy in the European Union Revisited: Input, Output *and* "Throughput".' *Political Studies* 61(1): 2–22.

Schmidt, Vivien A. (2015) "Forgotten Democratic Legitimacy: 'Governing by the Rules' and 'Ruling by the Numbers'" in *The Future of the Euro*, eds Matthias Matthijs and Mark Blyth. New York: Oxford University Press.

Schmidt, Vivien A. (2016). 'Reinterpreting the Rules "by Stealth" in Times of Crisis: The European Central Bank and the European Commission.' *West European Politics* 39(5): 1032–52.

Schmidt, Vivien A. (2018). 'Rethinking EU Governance: From "Old" to "New" Approaches.' *Journal of Common Market Studies* 57(7): 1544–61.

Schmidt, Vivien A. (2019). 'Politicization in the EU: Between National Politics and EU Political Dynamics.' *Journal of European Public Policy* 26(7): 1018–36.

Schmidt, Vivien A. (2020). *Europe's Crisis of Legitimacy: Governing by Rules and Ruling by Numbers in the Eurozone*. Oxford: Oxford University Press.

Tooze, Adam (2018). *Crashed: How a Decade of Financial Crises Changed the World*. New York: Viking.

Tsoukalis, Loukas (2016). *In Defence of Europe: Can the European Project be Saved?* Oxford: Oxford University Press.

Varoufakis, Yanis (2016). *And the Weak Suffer What They Must? Europe, Austerity and the Threat to Global Stability*. London: The Bodley Head (Vintage).

Zürn, Michael (2000). 'Democratic Governance Beyond the Nation-State.' *European Journal of International Relations* 6(2), 183–221.

6

The East–West Divide Revisited
30 Years On

Jacques Rupnik

1989 and the fall of the Soviet empire cleared the way for a recasting of the European order and the reconnection of the two hitherto separated parts of the continent known as eastern and western Europe. The accession to the European Union (EU) 15 years later of ten former Warsaw Pact members was seen as the completion of this process, which for the new members constituted a 'return to Europe' and for most old members constituted a European version of the 'end of history'.

However, 30 years after the end of the Cold War and the division of the continent, recriminations have eclipsed commemorations, raising questions about a renewed form of east–west divide in Europe. Fifteen years following the accession to the EU of the countries of central and eastern Europe, is a re-emergence of political differences between the 'old' and 'new' Europe, to use Donald Rumsfeld's terminology from the war in Iraq, a temporary political sideshow or is there a deeper divide between EU member states on issues as fundamental as democracy and the rule of law, the rise of nationalism and sovereignism? The triggering of Article 7 of the Lisbon Treaty against Poland and Hungary for breaches of the rule of law, which could in theory result in these countries losing their voting rights, suggests the latter. This also tends to be the interpretation favoured in the media and in statements made by political figures on both sides about a newly restored dividing line. In the west of the continent, this is seen as undermining political cohesion—or, indeed, the European project—and sometimes as a belated justification of reservations with regard to the EU's eastern enlargement (considered 'premature'). In the east, there are claims of being treated as second-class members of the EU, resentment over alleged double standards, and even comparisons between present interference from Brussels and past control by Moscow.

To what extent are we dealing here with perceptions and narratives, and to what extent do the realities of the divergences represent a major challenge for the Union? Are we dealing with a transient divergence relating to recent developments, such as the migration crisis and the coming to power of populist parties in the countries of the Visegrád Group? Or is it a recent expression of older and

Jacques Rupnik, *The East–West Divide Revisited 30 Years On* In: *Europe's Transformations: Essays in Honour of Loukas Tsoukalis.* Edited by: Helen Wallace, Nikos Koutsiaras, and George Pagoulatos, Oxford University Press. © OUP 2021.
DOI: 10.1093/oso/9780192895820.003.0006

deeper differences concerning values, priorities, and even the very purpose of the European project? After all, only five or ten years ago, the great transformation in the east was deemed a success, highlighted by EU accession and the choice of a Polish prime minister, Donald Tusk, for president of the European Council. And political change (a defeat of PiS, the Law and Justice party) in a pivotal country like Poland would have changed the way the region was viewed. If there is indeed a renewed east–west divide, is it more serious than the north–south divide, which emerged within the Eurozone after the financial crisis a decade ago and resurfaced in the response to the Covid-19 pandemic? It could be suggested that it is precisely the coexistence of these two divides which qualifies as a European crisis and gives the divergences analysed here a context and particular relevance. Last but not least, Brexit has shown that concerns about centrifugal forces weakening or deconstructing the EU from within are very real indeed and by no means confined to an east–west dimension. In other words, the subject must be considered from a transeuropean perspective.

Recent Divisions and Old Misunderstandings

'Illiberal' Democracy

2015 was undoubtedly the year in which an east–west divide emerged once again as Europe found itself facing the most serious migration crisis since the end of the Second World War. In symbolic terms, Hungary, the country which led the way to the bringing down of the Iron Curtain in the summer of 1989, hurriedly put up a fence along its border with Serbia to stem the flow of migrants. In political terms, on 5 September 2015, the leaders of the Visegrád Group (Poland, Hungary, the Czech Republic, and Slovakia) declared that they were firmly opposed—a position that has not changed since—to the opening of borders advocated by Angela Merkel, and later to the European Commission's decision to distribute the migrants according to a quota system. The decision taken by the Slovakian and Hungarian governments at the end of 2015 to bring an action against the European Commission before the European Court of Justice[1] in relation to this issue crystallized their distrust of Brussels. Behind the legal arguments on non-compliance with the Schengen and Dublin agreements lay two different political

---

[1] The action was based on the idea that the Commission had acted illegally in adopting a set of measures which jeopardized the sovereignty and security of member states by dispensing with the unanimity vote required in the European Council, where heads of state and government are represented, and opting for a qualified majority vote. The European Court of Justice dismissed the action in June 2017. The ruling, however, was not followed up as the Commission itself had abandoned the quota policy in the meantime. This could have consequences for the EU's future, as it meant that a court ruling could be ignored for political convenience.

visions and two different European responses to the crisis: that of the Commission (supported by most member states), which viewed the Visegrád Group's refusal as a serious breach of European solidarity, and that of the Visegrád Four (V4), which viewed the redistribution of migrants according to quotas set in Brussels as a challenge to their sovereignty and an attempt to force on them a multicultural model of society.

The Polish election of 2015 brought to power Jarosław Kaczyński's PiS party, with a stated ambition of having 'Budapest in Warsaw'. This meant that breaches of the rule of law and the restrictions on pluralism in the media under Viktor Orbán's government could no longer be considered as an anomaly or isolated case. The election of Robert Fico's SMER party in Slovakia in March 2016, following a xenophobic anti-migrant campaign,[2] which led to a government coalition including the nationalist SNS party, seemed to confirm the trend. The coming to power in Prague of a populist entrepreneur, Andrej Babiš, and in Croatia of a coalition dominated by a national-conservative party (HDZ) completed the picture. National populism was certainly not confined to central Europe, but that is where it gained power.

This general observation requires two caveats. First, although the focus of this study is the 'core' of east-central Europe, namely the Visegrád Four, the region is obviously not a bloc and the populist or illiberal trends are present beyond the V4. They extend to the Baltic states, and particularly Estonia, where in the March 2019 elections the far-right anti-immigrant and Eurosceptic Conservative People's Party (EKRE) won 18 per cent of the vote and entered the government with five ministers.[3] Similarly, Slovenia, the first of the ex-Yugoslav republics to join the EU in 2004 and long considered a successful liberal democracy, witnessed the collapse of its governing centrist coalition in the spring of 2020 and the coming to power of Janez Jansa, a nationalist populist closely associated with Hungary's Viktor Orbán.

The second observation concerns the Balkans, which provide a contrast with the post-1989 trajectory of central Europe. For historical reasons—some going back to the legacies of the Ottoman empire, others to the totalitarian features of communist regimes in Romania, Bulgaria, and Albania—the transitions to democracy were either thwarted or delayed. With the violent break-up of Yugoslavia, nation-state building took precedence over democratization. No less importantly, 30 years after the fall of the old regimes, the perspective of EU accession in the western Balkans cannot be presented (as was the case in central Europe) as a

---

[2] Orbán spoke of an 'invasion', Kaczyński of 'risks of epidemics', Fico of an incompatibility with Islam: 'I will never allow a single Muslim immigrant under a quota system', stated the Slovak prime minister before taking up the presidency of the EU Council on 1 July 2016. Cf. Henry Foy, 'Anti-migrant Rhetoric Dominates Slovakia Vote', *Financial Times*, 4 March 2016.

[3] The party leader Mart Helme became minister of the interior and his son Martin Helme, minister of finance. Both celebrated their election success with white supremacist gestures in front of Parliament. For further analysis, see Braghiroli and Petsinis (2019).

'return to Europe'. It needs a different narrative: on the one hand, that of post-conflict reconciliation, which was the founding moment of European integration; on the other, that of a geopolitical imperative for an EU which is facing the growing influence of both Russia and Turkey in the region, not to mention China and actors from the Middle East.

The most significant recent development concerns the diversion, or even the reversal, in the political trajectories of some of the countries deemed the success story of the post-1989 democratic transitions, which are now at the forefront of a democratic regression. This was not only the opinion of a European Commissioner (Franz Timmermans), or of 'malicious' reports adopted at the European Parliament (e.g. the Sargentini report on Hungary).[4] Recent years have seen the 'Nations in Transit' democratic assessments prepared by Freedom House[5] downgrade Hungary consistently and it is now ranked behind Romania and Bulgaria. Poland is displaying a similar trend.[6] In fact, the 2020 report no longer considered Hungary to be a democracy. The country 'experienced the largest drop ever recorded in the *Nations in Transit*' and was downgraded from a semi-consolidated democracy to a hybrid regime. 'Prime Minister Viktor Orbán's government in Hungary has dropped any pretence of respecting democratic institutions', the report stated. Having been one of the three democratic frontrunners for some 20 years, it 'became the first country to descend by two regime categories and leave the group of democracies entirely'.

The Bertelsmann Foundation report ranked Hungary 40th out of 41 European and OECD countries.[7] Similarly, in terms of the corruption assessed by Transparency International, Hungary is on a par with its neighbours in the Balkans. According to the *World Press Freedom Index*, media freedom is under threat and Hungary under Orbán ranks 89th worldwide[8] and Poland 62nd, a situation comparable in Europe only to that of Serbia or Kosovo. While the EU was otherwise engaged, the adoption during the Covid-19 pandemic of a law giving the Orbán government the option of ruling by decree without a sunset clause can be seen as confirmation of this authoritarian drift (Halmai and Scheppele 2020).

It is rare for politicians to borrow a concept from political science. Yet this is what Viktor Orbán did with Fareed Zakaria's 'illiberal democracy'. In an article published more than 20 years ago, Zakaria expressed concern about the

---

[4] 'Report on a proposal calling on the Council to determine, pursuant to Article 7(1) of the Treaty on European Union, the existence of a clear risk of a serious breach by Hungary of the values on which the Union is founded.' https://www.europarl.europa.eu/doceo/document/A-8-2018-0250_EN.pdf?redirect.

[5] Freedom House, https://freedomhouse.org/country/hungary/freedom-world/2020; on Orban's use of the Covid-19 crisis for a power grab, see Halmai and Scheppele (2020).

[6] Freedom House, https://freedomhouse.org/country/poland/freedom-world/2020.

[7] Ranking by the Bertelsmann Foundation: 'Quality of democracy?' Bertelsmann Stiftung's Transformation Index (BTI), 2020.

[8] Ranking by Reporters without Borders, 2020, https://rsf.org/en/hungary.

proliferation of regimes which gain legitimacy through elections but do not respect the rule of law. Orbán used the notion, in a speech made in July 2014, to reject criticism of his authoritarian drift: 'We had to state that a democracy does not necessarily have to be liberal. Just because a state is not liberal, it can still be a democracy.'[9] This is central to the European debate on populism: the link between populism and neo-authoritarianism or, stated differently, between democratic regression and the invocation of the 'sovereign people', which is precisely the foundation of democracy. Borrowing from Carl Schmitt's famous quote, a PiS MP (the father of the Polish prime minister, Mateusz Morawiecki) claimed in Parliament that 'The good of the nation is above the law.' Along the same lines, Kaczyński called for an emancipation from 'legal impossibilism': that is, from the constitutional and institutional straitjacket that guarantees the separation of powers. This is the core justification of the populist challenge to the checks and balances and the rule of law on which the very existence of the European Union is founded. It also provides the backdrop to the conflict between Poland and Hungary, on the one side, and the European Commission, on the other.

This critique of liberal democracy in east-central Europe is also extended to the societal liberalism which the EU allegedly promotes, owing to the 'hegemony of the liberal left' within it. The former Polish minister for foreign affairs, Witold Waszczykowski, mocked those who are convinced that history tends towards 'a new mixture of cultures and races, a world made up of cyclists and vegetarians, who only use renewable energy and oppose all signs of religion'. This, he said, was contrary to 'Polish values' shared by most of the population, such as 'tradition, historical awareness, love of country, faith in God and normal family life between a woman and a man'.[10]

Ryszard Legutko, a historian of ideas and PiS MEP,[11] is equally critical of the European Union for allegedly transcending the field of jurisdiction defined for it by the treaties in order to act increasingly openly in the areas of culture, religion, and morals. For him, the new 'totalitarian temptation' is no longer that of communism, but of liberalism, while both ideologies share the same objective: to dissolve the family, the nation, and the Church. In western Europe, European values are presumed to be liberal and are, according to Legutko, identified with a proliferation of rights which amount to 'social engineering'. The political message of this is that if even conservatives like David Cameron or Angela Merkel's CDU can adopt gay marriage, then we (in the east) are the last 'real conservatives' in Europe.

---

[9] V. Orbán, Address at the Bálványos Free Summer University and Youth Camp, Băile Tuşnad. 26 July 2014, http://budapestbeacon.com/public-policy/full-text-of-viktor-orbans-speech-at-baile-tusnad-tusnadfurdo-of-26-july-2014/10592.

[10] Interview with minister W. Waszczykowski conducted by Hans-Yörg Vehlewald, *Bild*, 3 January 2016.

[11] R. Legutko is the author of *The demon in democracy: totalitarian temptations in free societies*, Encounter books, 2016.

While, in western Europe, there is currently a tendency to view central Europe through the prism of 'illiberalism' and a rise in nationalism and Euroscepticism, in central Europe there is growing resentment among a significant part of the elites towards a Union allegedly dominated by the Franco-German tandem which promotes a society that is open to all, permissive, individualist, and lacking bearings. In this respect, we are not that far from the Putin-style discourse on a decadent and weak Europe.

Kaczyński and Orbán's answer to this is to defend a 'Europe of nations' and a Christian Europe. In Orbán's words: 'On the eve of the European parliamentary elections, Europe finds itself in the position that we must stand up again for our Hungarian identity, for our Christian identity.'[12]

The Misunderstandings of EU Enlargement

How can we account for this triple divide on democracy, migration, and societal issues—three aspects of European liberalism—after 25 years of unprecedented economic, political, and institutional convergence? One place to start would be to trace the misunderstandings over the process of, and meaning assigned to, the eastern enlargement of the EU. There are also deeper historical and cultural differences that have to be understood, if we are to prevent recent divisions from becoming actual fault lines. Members have different expectations of the European project and of the role they wish to play in it.

Are we dealing with an enlargement or unification of Europe? This is more than a semantic nuance. The term used by the EU is 'enlargement', which suggests that an institutional and normative system is being extended to the new members; some 100,000 pages of the *acquis communautaire*, which had to be incorporated into the legislation of candidate countries in the pre-accession phase, transformed their parliaments into "photocopiers" of European legislation. The term 'accession negotiations' became somewhat misleading: in place of 'give and take', it was more 'take it or leave it'. The concept of asymmetrical integration seemed appropriate.

'Reunification' was the term preferred in acceding countries by some of the founding fathers of the new democracies, such as Bronisław Geremek (Polish minister of foreign affairs) or the Czech president, Václav Havel (Geremek 2004). Both insisted on mutual contributions whereby the ideas and experiences of both sides would be shared. What central Europeans would bring to the EU was their rediscovery of democracy amidst conditions of unfreedom, their commitment to the values of human rights, and a sense of belonging to a shared European culture, which had been central to their nations' resilience in the face of a totalitarian

---

[12] V. Orbán, State of the Nation address, Budapest, 10 February 2019. The European election is the 'final struggle', 'the stronghold of the new internationalism is in Brussels, and its means is immigration'.

empire. For them, Europe was no mere 'common market'. They preferred a 'return to Europe' rather than an 'accession' to it: after all, they had never left Europe, so this was a return home rather than an inclusion. Yet Europe had changed in the meantime and no longer quite corresponded to the image they had of it. The gap was twofold: first, between the discourse on return and the more prosaic reality of an accession process broadly dominated by experts and techno-crats on both sides; and secondly, in relation to the two sides' expectations and illusions with regard to the future. Thus, while the new members that had regained a voice emphasized equality between members and economic catch-up, some of the founding countries succumbed to the illusory belief that an enlarged Europe would be the same but bigger. The EU had to contribute significantly to trans-forming central and eastern Europe, but with the doubling of the number of member states and the eastward shift of its centre of gravity, the EU itself was actually transformed. After the Europe of the post-war founding fathers, which resulted in the Treaty of Rome, followed by the Europe of the single market and the single currency consolidating peace through interdependence, 2004 ushered in a third Europe, this one enlarged to the east, which was 'not quite the same, nor quite another', to borrow from Paul Verlaine.

As latecomers to the EU, the new members expected a new balance within the Union, but often underestimated the tensions that this could give rise to. They took the EU for granted, an anchor for their budding democracies, while retaining a diffuse resentment towards a project that had been conceived and built without them. Conversely, in the founding countries (and France, in particular) there was an ownership reflex: a project that they had invented and conducted successfully could fall victim to its success and move beyond (their) control. This reticence towards enlargement explains, in part, the negative votes in the Netherlands and France in the 2005 referenda, which put an end to the European constitution and the prospect of a deepening of EU integration associated with it. The vote expressed an ambivalence, between a nostalgia for a smaller, Carolingian Europe and the feeling of being on a train while new carriages are being added, heading for an unknown destination and in which it is impossible to get off without setting off the alarm signal.

Migrations, Nations, Europe

The recent migration crisis led to a clash between two visions of the nation, of sovereignty and of Europe. On the one side, western Europe, following Germany's lead, would emphasize solidarity with migrants and among European nations as the way to tackle the challenge. Angela Merkel said at the time that migrants should be welcomed in the name of European values, and everything they entailed for human rights. This universalist discourse was opposed by the vision prevailing in central and eastern Europe, whose focus was on protecting the nation, its culture, and its way of life in the name of a different vision of Europe.

Unlike in France, where the state built the nation for over a thousand years, completing, with the 1789 revolution and the republic, the emergence of a civic concept of the nation, in the eastern part of the continent, there are old nations but the states are relatively recent. Their nation building within the Habsburg, Ottoman or Russian empires was based on the German model of *Kulturnation*. An ethno-linguistic concept of the nation based on language, culture, and religion prevails in central and eastern Europe. For historical reasons, these countries also considered themselves to be Europe's bulwark against the Ottoman and Russian empires. This difference in terms of the definition of the nation and its identity is therefore far reaching and will prove very difficult indeed to overcome. The irony of history, however, is that just as Germany abandoned the concept and shifted to a civic concept of the nation and a universalist interpretation of European values, its eastern neighbours, which had inherited the 'German' conception of the nation in the nineteenth century, transposed it onto the European level, justifying the closure of their borders to migrants entering Europe via the 'Ottoman route' (Turkey and the Balkans) in terms of protecting their nation and 'European civilization'.

In a second contrast, most of the nation-states created in 1918 in multi-ethnic east-central Europe became 'homogenous' post 1945. Following on from Hitler's Holocaust, Stalin's eastwards expansion helped to expel the Germans from the region at the end of the war. Border changes followed by the descent of the Iron Curtain and the Cold War completed the process: nobody could leave, but nobody could enter either. The migrations to western Europe from the 1960s onwards did not affect central and eastern Europe. The migrants who have moved to central Europe since the 1990s, mainly from the former Yugoslavia and later from Ukraine (there are over a million such migrants in Poland and 200,000 in the Czech Republic), sparked no political debate on their integration, which was not deemed problematic.

The issue of migration relates to the broader issue of the complex relationship between demography and democracy. Faced with demographic stagnation in Europe, immigration is often considered by experts in the OECD or in western European economic circles as a necessity which meets the needs of the labour market. In the east of the continent, it is more adequate to speak of demographic decline or even collapse, rather than stagnation.[13]

While the population in western Europe rose by 11 per cent between 1990 and 2015, that of eastern European countries fell by 7 per cent. Bulgaria and Romania

---

[13] This is part of a more general problem for the region, although it is more acute in the Balkans than in central Europe. See Ivan Krastev, 'Depopulation Is Eastern Europe's Biggest Problem', *Financial Times*, https://www.ft.com/content/c5d3e0ae-36eb-11ea-ac3c-f68c10993b04.

lost between a fifth and a quarter of their populations, and one million Polish nationals now work in the United Kingdom. The projections for the next 30 years show this gap widening. Concerns for the nation inherited through history are coupled with a 'demographic panic': the fear of the dissolution or even the disappearance of the nation. The powerful reluctance, confirmed in opinion polls, with regard to welcoming migrants should be analysed against this back-drop. The media and political elites have successfully propagated this pervasive anxiety by presenting the European Commission's desire to allocate migrants via a quota system as a de facto imposition of a multicultural society model which, in addition, has proved a failure in the west. After all, at the CDU congress in December 2010, Angela Merkel deemed multiculturalism to have 'utterly failed'. This in no way minimizes the expression of xenophobic discourse in the public arena and in political debate,[14] but it does help explain its echoes in society.

Which European Values?

Faced by the migration crisis, all sides have referred to European values, but each with very different content: humanitarian universalism, openness, and multicul-turalism in the west; the politics of closure, the protection of a cultural identity, and Christian-European civilization in the east.

When discussing this contrast and its implications, one must first of all point out their blatant political instrumentalization by Orbán, Kaczyński, Fico, and Zeman: the politics of fear and a hardening of attitudes around identity issues, leveraged for electoral purposes. Here, the reference to Christian values should be seen as a marker of identity rather than a quest for spirituality or an indication of religious fervour.

Yet the question cannot be reduced to its uses and abuses. It was already dividing Europeans during the Convention which produced a draft constitution for the EU. Reading the contributions of the delegates from the new member states with regard to the constitution's preamble, one notes that none of these countries considered European values without reference to Europe's Christian heritage. On this subject, the great historian and humanist intellectual Bronisław Geremek (2006) said that Europe is a community based on law and a 'common denominator' to which various cultural traditions can relate. For him, this com-mon denominator was human dignity, unthinkable without the Judaeo-Christian

---

[14] According to Orbán, if he had not put up the barrier, Hungary as a whole would have become a large-scale Marseille (*sic*). The Czech president Miloš Zeman, in his re-election campaign, even equated his rival, Jiří Drahoš of the Czech Academy of Sciences, with the migrant threat in posters stating: 'Stop immigration, stop Drahoš'.

heritage in Europe, which constituted the 'first European unification':[15] 'In European discourse...the historical tradition separates the religious factor from the humanist factor, which is considered to be secular. I am among those who believe that it is important to combine both strands in European traditions.'

Václav Havel, another figure associated with human rights and the democratic changes of 1989 in east-central Europe, and a vocal opponent of the Eurosceptic nationalism of the conservative prime minister (then president) Václav Klaus, was the first to call for a European constitution as early as the 1990s ('a short text, understandable by all'), which would define its institutions and their competences, and have a 'fine preamble' devoted to the meaning of the Union and its project. For Havel, the project relates to what he calls a 'European identity or soul', a distinct 'cultural, spiritual and civilizational space'.[16]

In other words, it would be simplistic or misleading to rigidly oppose either the western advocates of a Europe based on 'constitutional patriotism' (J. Habermas), legal standards, and the universalism of human rights, or eastern advocates of an identity-based nationalism draped in the defence of 'Christian Europe'. The east–west debate on European values and identity precedes and exceeds the debate on nationalist populism.

Legacies of Empires

To understand the differences in the relationship with the nation and with Europe against the backdrop of the migration crisis, the weight of history must be taken into account.

In western Europe, the integration project stemmed from the drive to overcome nationalism and to contain the nation-state. In central and eastern Europe, the nation and its culture were in a defensive posture first within former empires (Habsburg, Ottoman, Russian) and later within the Soviet bloc. Literature on European integration in the west spoke of a post-national project, while in the east the new member states had just regained their independence after 1989, and any surrender of sovereignty was by no means a self-evident proposition. György Schöpflin, MEP for the Hungarian Fidesz party, attributes these differences to the fact that 'the West has unilaterally declared itself post-national' (Schöpflin 2018: 14).

[15] 'The European idea has been based on the community's awareness of Christian values since the 14th century' (Geremek 2006: 31, translated from French). He continues: 'I say with Voltaire that Europe is Christian. It became a community in medieval times around Latin and Greek, in the Graeco-Roman heritage and with Latin in Church practices.'
[16] V. Havel, address to the French Senate in Paris, 3 March 1999. The Union should be separate from other 'civilization areas' with which Europe must enter into open dialogue and be respectful. This was the purpose of the annual meetings of Forum 2000, which Havel organized in Prague.

These differing conceptions of the nation and attitudes to immigration are the consequence of the contrasting heritages of empires. In western Europe, a more inclusive conception of citizenship and varieties of multiculturalism developed with the arrival over half a century of migrants from former colonies: sub-Saharan Africa and the Maghreb for France; India and Pakistan for the UK; Indonesia for the Netherlands; Angola and Mozambique for Portugal, etc. The nations of eastern Europe did not have colonies and consider themselves recently emancipated from the last colonial empire: the Soviet bloc. 'Can the West ever come to terms with those parts of Europe that were subordinated to imperial rule and, hence, have no post-colonial guilt?' (Schöpflin 2018: 15).

Convergence through the Economy or Neocolonialism?

Historians will consider the last quarter of a century as the swiftest east–west economic convergence process in the history of Europe.[17] The countries of east-central Europe, whose GPP per capita was slightly above a third of the EU average in the 1990s have been gradually closing the gap to reach about three-quarters of the EU average. For its part, Poland, whose per capita GDP was one of the lowest in Europe 30 years ago, is now placed above Greece or Portugal, while the region around Prague is the seventh most prosperous in Europe.

The process of integration of central and eastern European countries into the EU can be seen as their third 'modernization', following the unconvincing attempts of former empires and the Soviet model imposed in the post-war years, which—though this now tends to be forgotten—was presented at the time as a modernizing project for a backward and 'reactionary' part of Europe. Their economic integration with western Europe, upon their exit from the command economy of the former Comecon after 1990, has resulted in a significant inter-linking with the economies of western Europe. The percentage of exports in the gross domestic product of the Visegrád Group countries has grown spectacularly (to 80 per cent), with three-quarters of their export trade conducted with the EU. Germany's trade with the V4 exceeds its trade with France,[18] and the term economic *Mitteleuropa* adequately describes the situation.

Paradoxically, a nationalist and Eurosceptic discourse has developed against this backdrop. Countries such as Hungary and Poland, which are highly

---

[17] Over the last decade, growth in the new EU member states has been double that of the Eurozone on average. Poland was the only EU member state not to undergo a recession after 2008. The Czech Republic has the lowest unemployment rate in Europe (2.5 per cent). Both countries enjoyed a budgetary surplus in 2018.

[18] 'We thank our friend Viktor Orbán for his visit. Hungary and the Visegrád countries are close trading partners of Germany. Our trade balance with these countries is much higher than we have with France,' said Alexander Dobrindt, leader of the CSU parliamentary group in the Bundestag, in January 2018. *Le Monde*, 12 October 2018.

dependent on foreign investors, have developed rhetoric centred on 'economic patriotism', with measures hostile to foreign capital and finance. Since 2010, in the context of the financial crisis and of growing tensions with Brussels over the rule of law, a discourse of victimhood and resistance to the domination of foreign capital has emerged. When Orbán closed the IMF's office in Budapest, he claimed that it heralded 'the end of the colonial era!' 'Are we going to accept colony status as a fact?' asked Jarosław Kaczyński in a 2016 letter to PiS members. In western Europe, studies and theories on 'postcolonialism' tend to be associated with the academic left. In central Europe, in Poland or Hungary, they are adopted by the conservative right and aimed at the liberal and pro-European cosmopolitan elites which have dominated economic policy making, along with the political arena, for much of the post-1989 period. 'What we need', said Polish prime minister Mateusz Morawiecki in October 2016, 'is to build a native elite in the country around us.' After a quarter of a century of modernization through economic integration with western Europe, the 'colonized' eastern periphery of the EU is now being incited to practise economic patriotism.

Pro-Europeans and/or Atlanticists?

As the EU accession treaty was being signed in Athens by central and western European countries in April 2003 amidst speeches about European unification, Europe split openly over the US war in Iraq. To use the words of Donald Rumsfeld, US secretary of defense: the 'new Europe' was opposed to Franco-German 'old Europe'. For the first time since 1945, the US was making European division into a virtue in transatlantic relations. The division was deep-seated and left a mark, but it was misleading to seek out a divide among eastern political elites in terms of 'pro-Europeans' versus 'Atlanticists'. In fact, most of those who supported Bush were also pro-European. Support for the war in Iraq was, above all, an insurance policy ensuring a US security guarantee for the countries of central and eastern Europe. Hence the ambition to join NATO, an organization indivisible from the then unchallenged American superpower, was associated in central Europe with Western values and 'democracy promotion'; this in contrast with the European Union, which remained identified predominantly with the 'single market' and the route to prosperity. In simple terms, the central European elites shared a British vision of Europe: the nation-state was and would remain the preferred framework for democracy; security was the remit of NATO and there-fore of the USA, and Europe is a space for trade, economic development, and the legal norms required when economic interests are negotiated.

This 'Euro-Atlanticist' positioning was recently recontextualized by the election of Donald Trump and by Brexit. Trump in the White House was welcomed by Orbán, Kaczyński, and the Czech president, eager to find an ideological ally against European liberalism.[19] 'Western Europeans were pointing fingers at us as if we were backward post-communist periphery, and yet we were the vanguard of the coming populist and sovereignist wave.' The response France and more cautiously of Germany to 'America First' and Washington's unilateralism has been to propose the idea of a 'strategic autonomy' (Macron) and a 'European sovereignty' (see also Chapter 14 in this volume). Meanwhile, the Visegrád Group allowed Washington to play on the divisions in Europe in regard to certain aspects of foreign policy such as the Middle East (the Israeli–Palestinian conflict, Jerusalem as the capital of Israel), to the extent that a V4 summit was planned to be held in Jerusalem.[20] Poland combined defiance towards the EU with support for Trump's policies in the most explicit way. On a visit to the White House, the Polish president announced his 'Poland First' policy and offered to invest $2 billion for a permanent US military base in Poland to be named 'Fort Trump'.[21] In sharp contrast, but seen as no less divisive, President Macron called the NATO alliance 'brain dead' and initiated (without any results) in August 2019 a dialogue with Vladimir Putin; both provoked dismay in east-central Europe.

Faced thus with new threats, the fear of a US withdrawal, and doubts about NATO's future, Europeans offered diverging responses. Given their contrasting threat perceptions (some prioritizing security threats from the south, such as Islamist terrorism; others threats from the east in the form of Russia and its hybrid war in Ukraine), how can Europeans develop a common strategic culture as a condition for a shared security policy?

The Limits of European Divisions

As Europe was being divided by the Cold War, Polish historian Oskar Halecki published a book entitled *The Limits and Divisions of European History* (1950). It provides an appropriate perspective for our analysis of the limits of the division of Europe. What Halecki called the lands of 'East-Central Europe' were located between Germany and the Soviet Union; in the post-war era, they were seen as

[19] On the day after Trump's election to the White House, Orbán declared, 'The era of liberal non-democracy is over. What a day! What a day! What a day!', *Daily Telegraph*, 11 November 2016. The Czech president sent a letter of congratulations, stating: 'In my country, I'm known as the Czech Trump.' And, not surprisingly, they cheered for Trump's re-election in 2020

[20] The fact that the Visegrád Group was to hold its first summit outside of Europe in Jerusalem in mid-February is described by the Israeli newspaper *Haaretz* as an 'attempt by Netanyahu to erode the EU consensus on issues concerning the Palestinians and Iran'. The summit was postponed and changed to bilateral meetings following the spike in the dispute between the Polish government and that of Benjamin Netanyahu with regard to Polish complicity in the Holocaust.

[21] This is an extension of the US engagement with the missile defence shield deployed in Poland and Romania in the spring of 2016. Along the same lines, Poland, like most central European countries, procures its military equipment from the USA.

the west of the east. For the last 30 years, and especially since their accession to the EU, they have become the east of the west.

We have presented some of the east–west divides that have emerged within the EU. Now their scope needs to be put into perspective and their limits identified.

Brexit is a good example of this. It was hailed at first by the governments of the Visegrád Group as a reaction to Brussels' excessive drive for regulation in the name of an 'ever closer Union', and a sign that it was high time to restore the competences of member states. With the departure of the British, the V4 countries found themselves deprived of a precious ally, yet none made any attempt to follow suit with a 'Polexit' or a 'Czexit'. There are several reasons for this, first and foremost powerful economic factors: they are closely interdependent with western European countries, and the significant financial advantages that come with EU membership (with transfers of 3–4 per cent of their gross domestic product), has made them think twice before slamming the door shut. The UK wants to find itself a role in the world again, but this is not an option for small nations which conduct over three-quarters of their trade with the EU, and almost half of it with Germany.

Above all, the countries of central and eastern Europe do not form a bloc. Even within the Visegrád Group, which adopted common positions on some of the issues presented above, there is real diversity as regards their domestic political situation and their approach to the EU. On posted workers, a long-standing bone of contention between old and new EU member states, President Macron found some common ground in July 2017 with the leaders of the social-democrat governments then in power in Prague and Bratislava. This opening helped to pave the way for a European consensus on the issue. The Czech prime minister Andrej Babiš shows solidarity with the V4 on migrants, but will not undertake anything that may jeopardize the benefits that his country (and his company Agrofert) derive from EU membership.[22] Slovakia elected a strongly pro-European liberal lawyer, Zuzana Caputova, to the presidency in 2019. And public opinion in countries with Eurosceptic governments such as Poland and Hungary shows strong support for the EU.

We find similar diversity among the V4 countries with regard to their relations with Russia. All the countries in central and eastern Europe approved the EU's imposition of sanctions following Russia's annexation of Crimea, but there is a gulf between the hard line adopted by Poland and the good relations which Viktor Orbán is cultivating with Vladimir Putin. The Czechs and Slovaks fall somewhere between these two positions. Given the region's recent history and geographical proximity to Russia, there are in east-central Europe real geopolitical constraints

---

[22] Agrofert, the Czech agri-food flagship company, does a large proportion of its business in Germany and benefits directly and indirectly from European funding for its development. An investigation has been initiated in the Czech Republic and by the Commission on the (mis)use of these funds.

on the temptation to engage with the great power in the east, and this also places certain limits on governments' willingness to deepen their disputes with Brussels.

Last but not least, the east–west divide is very real in relation to certain issues, but must be viewed in a broader European framework. Most of the themes discussed above actually transcend the east–west divide; they are transeuropean issues. This holds for the crisis of democracy and the rise across Europe (with the exception of the Iberian Peninsula) of nationalist populism opposing the liberal elites and 'Brussels'. The double divide between 'people versus elites' and 'open society versus closure' is now affecting most European countries to varying degrees. Indeed the real divide in European politics on both scores is between big cities, with higher incomes and education levels and small cities and rural areas. The crisis of representative democracy, the demise of traditional parties, and the rise in Europhobic populism are transeuropean phenomena with multiple interactions which obviously exceed the east–west divide.

Admittedly, Orbán and Kaczyński were the first leaders of EU member states to call for a 'counter-revolution' in Europe, but they have since found partners who share similar aims. One of them is Salvini, the leader of the Lega Nord in Italy, who in August 2018 joined Orbán in a joint challenge to Emmanuel Macron's European initiatives. Their ambition has been to reshape politics in the EU with the opposition between nationalist-populist and progressive-Europhiles replacing the traditional right/left cleavage. Salvini travelled to Warsaw ahead of the 2019 European elections to announce a common platform with Kaczyński's PiS, which could be summed up as 'taking back control'. The aim of Orbán and Kaczyński is not to leave the EU, but, one could say, to have the EU leave Poland and Hungary. In association with other populists across Europe, they want to transform the EU from within.

The east–west divisions in the EU are undoubtedly a significant obstacle to the pursuit of the European integration process, but this new transeuropean dimension poses a more serious threat. Viktor Orbán understands this: '[In 1989], here in central Europe, we thought that Europe was our future; today we feel that we are Europe's future.'[23]

The response to this ill-fated prophecy will mainly depend on two issues. First, the general public is extremely mistrustful of liberal elites; but while it often votes for Eurosceptic parties, it is definitely not in favour of leaving the EU.[24] It is as if,

---

[23] Viktor Orbán's speech at the 28th Bálványos Summer Open University, 22 July 2017, Tusnádfürdő (Băile Tuşnad, Romania): V. Orbán: Will Europe Belong to Europeans?" *Visegrád Post*, 24 July 2017, https://visegradpost.com/en/2017/07/24/full-speech-of-v-orban-will-europebelong-to-europeans.

[24] As demonstrated by a major European opinion survey conducted in 2018 by Fondapol on all the major issues concerning democracy and Europe. Two elements should be noted: while the basic trends are similar in the western and eastern parts of Europe, they are clearly more pronounced in the latter; paradoxically, attachment to EU membership is strongest in countries where democracy is under the greatest threat (around 75 per cent in Poland and 67 per cent in Hungary).

faced with the illiberal drift and divided by the crisis of faith in democracy, eastern Europeans have come to view the Union as the ultimate safeguard against their own demons.

Ultimately, the capacity to contain an east–west divide within the Union will depend not just on shared interests and the interpenetration of economies and societies, but also on the resilience of European institutions and, perhaps most importantly, on the Union's political capacity to defend the values and principles on which it was founded.

References

Braghiroli, Stefano and Vassilis Petsinis (2019). 'Between Party-Systems and Identity-Politics: The Populist and Radical Right in Estonia and Latvia.' *European Politics and Society* 20(4), 431–49.

Geremek, Bronisław (2004). 'De l'élargissement à la réunification. Qu'allons-nous apporter à l'Europe?' In J. Rupnik (ed.), *Les Européens face à l'élargissement*. Paris: Presses de Sciences Po.

Geremek, Bronisław (2006). 'L'humanisme européen, creuset du laïc et du religieux.' *Rue Saint-Guillaume*, issue 144 (September).

Halecki, Oskar (1950). *The Limits and Divisions of European History*. London: Sheed & Ward.

Halmai, Gábor and Kim Lane Scheppele (2020). 'Don't Be Fooled by Autocrats! Why Hungary's Emergency Violates Rule of Law.' *VerfBlog*, 22 April. https://verfassungsblog.de/dont-be-fooled-by-autocrats/.

Schöpflin, György (2018). 'What If.' *Hungarian Review* 9(6).

7

Liberal Democracy and Its Discontent

Yves Mény

Liberal democracy is a baroque construction, a never-ending process permanently subject to criticism, celebration, and challenges. In a recent book on democracy and populism (Mény 2016) I used the word 'bricolage' to characterize the endless transformation of a political regime which is based on vivid contradictions, but which survives or prospers through the dynamics of these internal tensions. During these historical developments, moments of stability and equilibrium alternate with moments of crisis. To tell the truth, the periods of peace and serenity are less frequent than the periods of turbulence and confrontation.[1]

This permanent state of uncertainty and instability has long-term causes and must be identified with the critical juncture of the American and French revolutions. Two visions of the world dominate the scene. The first, inherited from the past and from tradition, presents a hierarchical world dominated by the idea of unity under the direction of a monarch of divine origin. The second— revolutionary—vision rejects this vertical organization in which the multitude is subject to a single authority and reverses the perspective: the origin of power is to be found in the many, who are the source and foundation of sovereignty. In the first case, sovereignty stems from the top; in the second, it stems from the bottom.

Actually, between these two radically contrasting visions, there is a third way which would become dominant while borrowing elements from both. Rather than a 'vision', it is a quite pragmatic approach which tries to steer its way through incremental adjustments and compromises. In the United Kingdom, where the Glorious Revolution could have triggered radical options (after all, the republican government set up by Cromwell could have been as revolutionary as its American and French successors), what prevailed in the end was a rather unique compromise. Everything seemed to have remained in place, and at the same time everything had changed. The exact opposite of the Prince of Salina's cynical observation in *The Leopard*, Lampedusa's famous Sicilian novel: 'Everything must change for everything to remain the same.' At the end of the nineteenth century, the situation would be summarized by the most famous commentator on the British constitution, Bagehot, who underlined the fact that the Fundamental Laws of the British

---

[1] The recent period has been marked by an impressive flow of publications about the crisis of democracy. Among the recent titles, see Urbinati and Mény (2004).

Yves Mény, *Liberal Democracy and Its Discontent* In: *Europe's Transformations: Essays in Honour of Loukas Tsoukalis*. Edited by: Helen Wallace, Nikos Koutsiaras, and George Pagoulatos, Oxford University Press. © OUP 2021.
DOI: 10.1093/oso/9780192895820.003.0007

system were made up of two components, which he called the efficient part and the dignified part. While the UK remains a monarchy, it possesses all the attributes of a democracy. For a long time, this internal contradiction did not raise much concern. Pragmatism and tradition prevailed over logic and formal, rational design. It is only recently, as the Brexit saga has revealed, that these contradictions have become so glaringly obvious and counterproductive. The tension between parliamentary sovereignty (see also Chapter 10 in this volume)—which is still, in theory, the prevailing value—and popular sovereignty—which emerged by accident with the setting up of a *consultative* referendum—was obvious and its enduring implications not fully appreciated.

This shows how much 'liberal democracy' is an elusive concept whose content and meaning have never stopped adjusting to social and political demands or circumstances. The present crisis facing democracies is both worrying, given its universality and its depth, and at the same time a sign of vitality and of a potential capacity to address issues and identify solutions. The bad news is that democracies are in crisis; the good news is that democracies have always been confronted by crises of all kinds: crises of institutions, crises stemming from the nature and extent of public policies; crises relating to the relative weighting of democracy's core values, equality versus liberty; crises about its very legitimacy vis-à-vis alternative regimes or forms of government.

Some of these issues or problems relate to a basic constitutive element of what we call 'democracy' or more precisely 'liberal democracy'. The regimes in this category have actually been created in a very incremental and inventive way, and are a kind of political chimaera. In the same way that the animal from Greek mythology was a composite of components from a goat, lion, snake, etc., the modern democratic construct is the unexpected outcome of various components assembled together over the course of its historical evolution. Each country—since democracy was imagined within the borders of individual states—constructed its own 'democratic' system on the basis of historical choices or constraints and according to a set of preferences expressed by social or political groups, vested interests, and also philosophers, thinkers and/or political intellectuals. This means that every democracy is singular and particular, even when institutions have been copied from more advanced or innovative counterparts. Ever since the Greek philosophers set down their contributions, there has been a flourishing market in ideas, debate, and mimicry around different forms of government and their classification from 'ideal' to 'bad' or 'worst'.

However, one can talk about 'democracy' beyond the variety of 'democracies', since most of them have attempted over the past two centuries to reconcile two antagonistic sets of values: on the one hand, placing the source and legitimacy of power in the hands of the 'people' conceived as a single 'whole', and, on the other, trying to limit the drawbacks of this ideological construct, here and elsewhere, by relying upon its opposite alternative, liberalism, which is centred around the individual, the single person with their rights and entitlements. Since the unfolding of the British, American and French revolutions, the democratic construction can be seen as an ongoing struggle between these two poles in search of a better, albeit changing and unstable, equilibrium between opposing trends. The aim has been, on the one hand, to ensure that the sovereign is not reduced to a symbolic role and, on the other, to prevent the sovereign from ruling unchecked and acting *ultra vires*. Every democratic system, even at the most primitive stage, is a 'blend' of these two unstable and conflicting objectives. Actually, what we call 'crisis' is the attempt by some social or political groups and elites to modify the balance secured by previous constitutional rules, conventions or political settlements. Some of these pressures may be successful, many fail; some periods or some countries are characterized by stability or by quasi-invisible and pragmatic adjustments, while others are more prone to change or revolution. The period from the 1980s to 2020 was characterized by a swift and unexpected U-turn in relation to 'the state of democracy': within a 40-year span, the mood and perception has moved from utopian euphoria to a sinister prospect for democracy (Mastropaolo 2009). How are we to explain such a radical transformation?

The causes are manifold and difficult to disentangle. However, I will suggest three explanations for the present state of affairs; they are not exhaustive, but they do complement each other. The first explanation is to be found in the creeping but continuous transformation of the post-1945 democratic settlement; the second relates to the growing imbalance between the popular and the liberal components of the democratic fabric; and the third derives from the contradiction between the space of politics and the space of policies. In my conclusion, I will suggest possible ways out of the present impasse.

Surreptitious Processes, Striking Outcomes: The Transformation of Democracies

The post-1945 settlement promoted in particular by the USA and UK explicitly sought to avoid the mistakes of the post-1918 reorganization of Europe and to secure the success of democracy in the former authoritarian regimes. The strategy was based on a mix of internal reforms and supranational arrangements guaranteeing both economic and political stability. The ingredients are well known: on the one hand, US economic support (Marshall Plan) combined with the setting up of collaborative organizations (OEEC later OECD), military integration under an American umbrella (NATO) and legal cooperation and supervision (Council of Europe); on the other hand, strong incentives to build new constitutional frameworks capable of securing democracy where previous attempts had failed. Under the influence of the American administration, as well as of powerful private foundations (Rockefeller, Carnegie, Ford, Fulbright, and so on), a new set of values were emphasized: universal suffrage (extended to women in countries such as France and Italy which still lagged behind in this regard); the rule of law; constitutional checks and balances; liberal principles such as free speech, a free press, party and social organizations as necessary political tools; the territorial and functional division of powers and so on. Furthermore, the British domestic debate after the war contributed additional elements to the substantive meaning of democracy: the development of a fully -fledged welfare system was theorized by Marshall and implemented by the Labour government. Social citizenship was conceived as a necessary addition to the civic and political dimensions. This 'universal' approach to social issues was then emulated in every European democracy, according to its social traditions and political choices. There is no single blueprint, rather nationally distinct systems divided by policy choices but united by common purposes.

The American influence was particularly strong in the defeated countries, Germany and Italy, where the occupying forces could keep an eye on political developments. In Greece, the conflict between the former allies over the future of the country triggered a bloody civil war and, in the end, a rather imperfect form of Western-type democracy was put in place. In contrast, the Western capacity to exert influence and pressure was reduced to nothing in the countries occupied by the Soviet army. As a consequence, a model (viewed as ideal) and its negative counterpart became the structural forces driving the continuing transformation of Europe. This black and white world would last until 1989 and the fall of the Berlin Wall. The deficiencies and flaws of the 'good' model were forgotten or forgiven when viewed from the bleak perspective of the Soviet Union and its subdued allies. For the next 40 years, the potentiality of the new rules of the game would unfold step by step and become part and parcel of a new definition of democracy.

Democracy everywhere took the shape of the British model, being centred around parliamentary prerogatives, the enforcement of the rule of law, the effectiveness of civil liberties and the growing influence and role of political parties. Parties became the pillars of the democratic system to the point that each system was characterized by the particular features of its party system: two-party system, *parteienstaat, partitocrazia, régime des partis*. Obviously their contributions to establishing of the new democratic systems were framed by local traditions and practices inherited from previous regimes, such as ideological and organizational fragmentation in Italy, France, Belgium, and the Netherlands, and the presence or absence of strong social-democratic parties. In some countries, the democratic framework and its workings were heavily conditioned by the influence of a strong communist party legitimized by its resistance to the Nazi or fascist regimes. This was the case in Italy, France, and Greece in particular. There was a de facto 'conventio ad excludendum', to use the expression adopted by the Italian elites, which lasted into the 1980s. In addition, some crucial innovations foreign to European traditions and imported from the American experience were inserted into the Italian and German constitutions: namely, the control of any legislation or regulation vis-à-vis the fundamental principles included in the national constitution. These spread to practically all the democracies in Europe with the (partial) exception of the UK and the Scandinavian countries. While both the old and new democratic systems referenced well-established principles, major innovations were inserted which came to fruition only in the 1960s and 1970s or even later. The systems which were democratized at a later stage (Spain, Portugal, Greece, then the former Soviet-dominated countries of eastern Europe) were presented with the entire democratic kit, consisting of a 'bricolage' of old and new from which they picked those elements that best fit their national preferences in accordance with cultural or historical traditions. In 1993, the process was streamlined and completed with the European Council's Copenhagen declaration, whereby EU members made access to the club contingent on respect for the so-called 'democratic principles'. In many ways, the Europeans were making their own the set of values, rules, and institutions that the winners of the Second World War had attempted to promote half a century before, while mimicking the innovations of their neighbours or partners (for instance, the Freedom of Information Act, the Ombudsman). The triumph was apparently complete.

However, most observers had paid insufficient notice to the long-term consequences of these major innovations and/or of the on-going transformation of the political contexts. For instance, political parties were more than ever the central pillars of the system, but only a few observers underlined the internal dynamics at work. Peter Mair (2009), an acute analyst of party systems, was one of the few to underscore that the expected competition between political forces had receded and given way to the 'cartellization' and 'étatisation' of parties. In other words, due to the penetration and control of the state apparatus, political parties were more interested in securing their survival than in winning support from voters by listening to their claims and proposing reforms in line with their expectations. Through the control of access (electoral systems, public funding, clientelism), parties were able to deprive any newcomers of the chance to win and thus replace the incumbents. The first cracks appeared in Austria, where the two dominant parties had managed to alternate from the post-war period through into the 1990s. In 1986, Haider, a populist leader from the radical right, took over the leadership of the old Freedom Party, transforming it into a populist movement capable of breaking the duopoly of the 'Reds' (social democrats) and the 'Blacks' (Christian democrats). The changes came later in other democracies, but there were increasing signs of profound changes in the workings of the system: electoral volatility, the emergence of new parties or movements, and the diminishing capacity of parties of government to together attract between 70 per cent and 90 per cent of the votes, as they had done before. On the surface, it appeared that not much had changed, since the dominant cartelized parties were still able to maintain their grip on power and institutions, but the worm was already in the fruit in Italy, France,

Belgium, and the Netherlands, as well as the Scandinavian countries and, later on, eastern Europe. No political system escaped the creeping influence of populist parties fighting political elites and bureaucratic experts as well as supranational institutions. The final blow was the coming to power, for the first time in American history, of a populist candidate: Donald Trump.

Another creeping evolution was transforming the nature of democracies year after year: the inability of most parliaments to develop legislation of their own meant they were reduced to approving bills drafted by executives, meaning in fact their bureaucracies. In parallel, the constitutional courts were exerting a growing influence on past and future legislation. They adopted a broad definition of their role and transformed norms and policies in the domain of party politics into non-negotiable and inflexible rules (Grimm 2015). By the end of the 1970s, European democracies were in a situation that matched the diagnosis formulated by Bagehot in relation to the British constitution at the end of the nineteenth century: there was still an efficient part, but the key features of democracies in the past had become 'dignified'. Democracies were increasingly relying more on executives and bureaucracies than on parliaments; independent agencies of all types (from minority protection bodies to central banks) were substituting experts' preferences for political choices; parties of government were more interested in perpetuating their control over institutions than in taking on new claims and demands made by society; policies were more and more constrained by broad and creative jurisprudence stemming from supreme courts. Last but not least, the supremacy of rules stemming from the European Union was felt in every domain related to economic or regulatory policies through the twin influence of (national) deregulation and (supranational) reregulation. There came the time when 'democratic deficit' was the motto of the day as more and more movements of diverse political leanings expressed doubts about the substance and legitimacy of decisions adopted by unaccountable authorities. Peter Mair's assessment was brutal: states were 'ruling the void'(2013).

The Shaking Up of Democratic Creeds

As we know well, democratic systems are quite different from the ideals or dreams prevailing in the minds of attentive citizens. If asked their opinion, many if not most would spontaneously subscribe to Lincoln's definition: democracy is 'the government of the people, by the people, for the people'. The first part of the declaration is not an issue, and the last one should be the natural outcome of any regime claiming that it is 'democratic'. However, as we shall see, this aim has been increasingly contested by those concerned. Finally, the central 'by the people' is the most problematic of all, as no government fully corresponds with this utopian wishful thinking.

The evolution of democracies testifies to the ways and means put in place to address these three components of the most celebrated form of democratic government. The first one attempts to make two images coincide which do not fully overlap: the sociological and political composition of the people. A long story unfolded over the nineteenth and twentieth centuries which has permitted the move from a very narrow popular base (in the 1830s, Tocqueville was elected by a few hundred voters and rotten boroughs still survived in Britain) to systems granting the vote to every citizen over 18. The myth of a people constituted as a single 'whole' could finally acquire more substance. Actually, this remains a convenient ideological and political convention which helps to mobilize public opinion and voters, but remains impossible to translate into a concrete reality. One can talk of a majority, of public opinion, of crowds, masses or people in the street. The people does not exist as such (Rosanvallon 2018). However, the concept has the great advantage of attributing to a single abstract entity the sovereignty once embodied in a single individual, the king. No constitution has better used this fiction that the American one: 'We, the people...', claimed the small group of state representatives at the Philadelphia convention. It also has drawbacks, since it allowed the leaders of groups or parties to claim to speak on behalf of the people or to be 'the' people. The claim of a part to be the whole is not new. In the first democracy worthy of the name, the Athens of the fourth/fifth centuries BC, the *demos* was composed of a few thousand males governing a city of 350,000 to 400,000 inhabitants. The irony is that the very same terms and concepts have been used over the past 30 years to underline the non-existence of a European people, as if the concepts were not an intellectual creation beyond and above an extremely diverse sociological reality.

It remains the case that, in the collective representation of what democracy is about, public opinion focuses virtually exclusively on the voice, the will of the citizens, and in addition on the entitlements they have vis-à-vis those who govern. Over the past 40 years, many citizens have felt that their claims and demands were not being taken into consideration. This indifference had many different causes. The first was the incapacity, after the collapse of the Soviet Union, to present voters with a convincing ideological framework. It is true that the social bases for such an ideological compact were also missing. The traditional working class was disappearing together with the collapse of old industrial sectors; the remaining jobs, once occupied by nationals, were increasingly being taken on by foreigners, who were not allowed to vote; the new service sectors provided the biggest share of economic output, but their employees were dispersed among smaller working units and were thus less prone to become members of trade unions. The weakening of intermediary groups was also linked to the growing individualism of workers or citizens facilitated by new technology and social networks. Finally, in order to secure a majority or the possibility of forming a grand coalition, the governing parties tended to compete for the votes of the centre right or centre left, neglecting the more radical voters of the right or left. This strategy worked for a long time, seemingly guaranteeing some parties quasi-permanent control over the executive: the Austrian parties, the CDU-CSU in Germany (alone or in coalition with the social democrats), and the moderate right and socialist party in France or Spain were all examples of this continuity or of alternating between parties whose offerings were indistinguishable. Each of these parties had made its platform a version of the Margaret Thatcher dictum: 'There is no alternative.'

However, voter disenchantment continued to grow election after election, since the political systems were deaf to the mounting discontent of a large share of the electorate (Betz 1999). This unease with the political supply on offer from the dominant parties manifested itself in ever stronger forms of protest: electoral abstention, electoral volatility from one party to the other and election after election, single-issue or anti-system movements which attracted many votes one day and disappeared the day after. Increasingly, parliamentary majorities were the by-product of a sociological minority deliberately favoured by electoral systems. Electoral engineering was able to secure governability, but unable to provide sufficient legitimacy for the approval of policy choices. Despite the political rhetoric, many citizens in nearly every country felt they had no voice. In particular, the acceptance of neoliberal economic policies by most social-democratic parties as well as by Labour in Great Britain has deprived the workers or the poorest of their traditional voice. They feel abandoned and have turned to protest movements more in tune with their feelings and claims.

As already mentioned, democracies constitute a delicate and unstable mix of popular input and checks and balances aimed at channelling, or fencing off, the unpredictable and sometimes wild manifestations of masses pretending to be 'the' people. The 'tyranny of the majority' was already feared by the liberal American founding fathers and would become a dramatic reality in France during the Terror of 1793. The liberal input aimed at avoiding these excesses was crucial, since it permitted the evolution from republican or monarchical regimes towards dem- ocracy (Tocqueville 1967). In spite of a suspicious and reluctant attitude vis-à-vis the intrusion of the people into governing institutions, it is actually liberalism which made democracy feasible: by underlining the necessity of representation; by favouring the aggregation of individual opinions within party organizations; by promoting an aristocracy of merit in order to legitimize power and authority; and by defending individual rights against state or governmental infringements. From this perspective, fundamental rights and the rule of law were as important, to say the least, as the power of the people. This is why the second dimension of the Lincoln definition is wrong or at least misleading. 'Government by the people' is an illusory dream, or a nightmare, if it is understood as the direct, continuous, and unlimited involvement of the people in public affairs.

However, when the balance between the popular voice and liberal components is lost to the detriment of the former, there is a risk that vocal protesters will use and abuse this attractive catchword and demand its literal application. Another version—'by the people, for the people'—was coined at the end of the nineteenth century in the USA under pressure from the People's Party, the first populist movement ever, and has now become the favourite motto of the protest parties that have mushroomed everywhere in Europe, and not only over the past 40 years (Mény and Surel 2000). Recent research under the direction of Matthijs Rooduijn Rooduijn (2020) shows, for instance, that the vote for Eurosceptic parties (which are usually populist parties) has more than doubled in the two decades since 2000, and accounts for one-third of the total votes in 2020. The favourite targets of the protest and populist movements are those liberal components which have become part and parcel of democracy as we know it: private and public elites, central bankers, courts, national and European bureaucrats and technocrats, experts in general. There is a general distrust of and contempt for those who are not considered part of the 'people', and an uncompromising bias in favour of the 'people on the street', who have a better idea what is needed, since they possess a quality the so-called experts lack: 'common sense'. As the Five Stars Movement in Italy repeated ad nauseam, 'uno vale uno', transforming the principle of political equality into the recognition of equal and universal competence, whatever the issue may be (Cassese 2019). The solutions advocated by the populist movements are often naïve, inconsistent or inapplicable and they have shown, every time they come to power, that their rhetoric is mere demagogy. But they have a point. While the 'popular' element has remained identical since the post-war period (the only improvement being the lowering of the voting age to 18 in most cases), the 'liberal' element has expanded to its limits, giving the correct impression that democratic institutions are not responsive to the people and are merely 'dignified' bits and pieces, while the decisions that matter are taken elsewhere (Mény and Surel 1998). This negative evaluation has been further exacerbated by the growing influence of Europeanization and globalization on national issues and policy choices.

Scapegoats and Invisible Hands

Democracy suffers from a major genetic defect: it has been thought about and developed within the shell of the nation-state. There are few exceptions to that iron rule: at the local level, democracy is and has been a lively reality but its development is or was conditioned by the existence of a national democratic framework. Beyond the nation-states, there are examples of democratic developments within empires (for instance, both the Prussian and Austro-Hungarian empires relied on restricted elections and ample decentralization), but what was crucial was the definition of any internationally recognized political entity as a state. The Westphalian frame of reference was the only political space within which democracy could be put in place in lieu of authoritarian or monarchical regimes. With the passing of time, democracy came to be equated with a regime that can only develop within the nation-state. The possibility that 'democracy' might be established beyond the nation-state is generally perceived as a romantic or utopian dream. While it has been possible to transfer some features of institutional liberalism to the international institutions (for instance, the separation of powers among assembly/executive/tribunal or the principle of the rule of law), stating that there is no such thing as a 'European people' seems obvious. For 40 years, the catchphrase when referring to the European transnational construction has been 'democratic deficit'(Marquand 2003).

This dichotomy, however, underlines a problem which, year after year, is becoming ever more acute and relevant: more and more decisions which have an impact on individuals' lives are being taken at a level beyond the borders of the nation-state, or result from international cooperation or commitments. Neither national governments nor national courts can be held accountable for such policies, nor can they adjudicate on cases which are crucial for their citizens' lives. This is because they are dependent on private or public bodies that are beyond their jurisdiction. Governments might still claim they are in charge, make firm commitments during electoral campaigns, promise they will not accept such or such regulation, but in actuality, the 'emperor has no clothes'. Faced with this situation, citizens become less and less tolerant vis-à-vis this shrinking of their capacity to evaluate, punish or reward those governing on their behalf. In the present climate of exasperation and hatred, private companies and public organizations beyond the state become easy scapegoats: McDonald's restaurants, international banks, and investment funds have become the target of stiff criticism, and governments are accused of letting them get away with it, being complicit or corrupt. Pressure is exerted on companies that are perceived to be neglecting human rights, exploiting workers—and in particular, children—damaging nature, polluting or over-exploiting natural resources. However, national governments are unwilling or unable to take serious action, even when they share the views of the protesting groups.

More critical still are the consequences of international multilateral treaties signed and ratified by national governments. This is particularly true in the case of trade treaties, whose content relates less and less to tariffs and customs duties, and more and more to health, environmental or social norms, and technical standards. As the last half-century in Europe has made clear, the loosening or elimination of standards has had a huge impact on the capacity of a state to initiate or continue the production of certain goods when differences in production costs or productivity provide a comparative advantage to one or several trading partners elsewhere in the world. On the basis of these trade agreements, entire production processes can be transferred from one country to another within a short period of time. No public authority is in a position to stop the haemorrhaging once the treaty is in force. This situation appears unacceptable to workers, who do not understand why their government cannot protect them. Such trade treaties are even more contested when they are negotiated by an unelected and apparently unaccountable body such as the European Commission.

The democratic creed is further damaged when direct expressions of the people's will are ignored or bypassed, as happens when popular referenda return results which emphasize options which seem unrealistic or counterproductive to the ruling elites. This occurred on several occasions in Denmark and Ireland in relation to the approval of EU treaties, when their electorates were asked to rethink their position in a repeat referendum. A similar phenomenon occurred when the Dutch and French electorates rejected the constitutional treaty in 2005. On the surface, it appeared that the voices of the majority were being heard, but actually the disputed substance was transferred into a new treaty with a more modest title and the same content. It was the case once again with the victory of the parties objecting to the austerity policies imposed on Greece by the Troika,[2] but the Greek population was subsequently forced to swallow the bitter pill. Finally, the Brexit saga has demonstrated just how difficult it is to reconcile popular democracy and parliamentary democracy.

Actually, the Brexit option (see also Chapter 10 in this volume) preferred by a majority of British voters has the merit of logic: since democratic government in traditional terms is feasible only at the national level, it seems rational and legitimate to repatriate decision-making power and accountability to the national level and to recover 'full' control over the decisions, positive or negative, that affect the country. However, this is only one side of the coin, given that no country today can live alone and make credible the illusion that 'splendid isolation' is the best option. It is surely beyond question that the UK will very soon realize through experience that national sovereignty and the freedom to act by itself, without the impedimenta of international cooperation, are not an easy road. Compromises and negotiations, as well as the need to accept forms of trade-off, will be the unavoidable consequences of going it alone in an interdependent and intermingled world.

To conclude, it might seem that, in order to rescue the liberal-democratic paradigm, one should go back to the comfort of the old nation-state before it was challenged and shaken by the last 40 years of radical change. This is, however, a dubious solution. The indisputable supremacy of nations in the past was linked to international regimes such as the 'concert of nations', imperialistic domination or Cold War antagonism, and its 'achievements' were rather dubious. The attempt

---

[2] The so-called Troika was made of experts setting up the conditions and the required reforms imposed on a country applying for international support in order to get acceptable lending conditions. Greece was the first country that asked for help in 2010 since it was unable to borrow at normal conditions on the market. The Troika, composed of representatives of the European Commission, the Central Bank, and the IMF, imposed drastic conditions which triggered violence, protest, and political frustration.

to pool state sovereignty within Europe was and still is a valid project, provided that the balance is readjusted between member states and the EU, between democracy and technocracy, or between popular input and liberal components. This is a demanding task, but not impossible provided we do not look for a ready-made solution born of an intelligent mind—such as Zeus's solution of giving birth to a fully armed Athena. Finding the appropriate solution will require time, patience, and creative tinkering of the sort which succeeded in giving democracy a content which extends far beyond its initial narrow meaning. A major reordering of democratic systems, including their supranational dimension, is unavoidable, particularly in the light of the Covid-19 epidemic storm which has impacted on every dimension of life and institutions nationally and internationally. There are still very few clues as to the direction to take, but one element is crucial: achieving a new balance between a currently sketchy popular and an inflated 'liberal' component. The patient and incremental construction of two centuries is at risk. However, the present circumstances offer a unique opportunity to rethink and reframe the post-war settlement. The old arrangements are obsolete and falling apart under attacks from the American leadership(?), while China is becoming a powerful and possibly dangerous world power. Within this context, Europe's role and contribution will be crucial, in spite of its internal divisions and tensions. If adopted, the recent post-coronavirus programme proposed by Macron and Merkel would constitute a decisive leap. Indeed, the acceptance of the solidarity principle would have two consequences: first, it will require the clearer and more decisive political involvement of the people as a 'community'; secondly, it implies the setting up of institutions and rules of a federal nature. It might be disturbing to many, but these two consequences are the unavoidable implications of the principle of solidarity between the components of the EU system. At this point, there is little need to increase the liberal dimension within the EU institutions, since it has already been taken to its limits. Instead, new forms of public involvement, participation, and control will have to be invented pragmatically and put in place. This is a daunting task, but an indispensable one if we want to reduce the growing gap between voters and citizens at large, on the one hand, and a political community in the making, on the other. As Renan noted in his Sorbonne Lecture of March 1882 when analysing the concept of nation: 'A zollverein is not a polity.' The European 'zollverein' is there now. The polity is still in its infancy.

References

Betz, Hans Georg (1994). *Radical Right-Wing Populism in Western Europe*. New York: St. Martin's Press.

Canovan, M. (1999). 'Trust the People! Populism and the Two Faces of Democracy.' *Political Studies* 47(1): 2–16.

Cassese, Sabino (2019). *La Svolta, Dialoghi sulla politica che cambia.* Bologna: Il Mulino.

Crouch, Colin (2004). *Post-Democracy.* Cambridge: Polity Press.

Grimm, Dieter (2015). 'The Democratic Costs of Constitutionalization: The European Case.' *European Law Journal* 21(4): 460–73.

Mair, Peter (2009). 'Representative vs Responsible Government.' MPIfG Working Paper, 09/8. Köln.

Mair, Peter (2013). *Ruling the Void: The Hollowing Out of Western Democracy.* New York: Verso.

Marquand, David (1979). *A Parliament for Europe.* London: Jonathan Cape.

Mastropaolo, Alfio (2009). *Democracy: A Lost Cause?* Colchester, UK: ECPR Press.

Mény, Yves (2019). *Imparfaites démocraties.* Paris: Presses de Sciences Po (English edition, *Imperfect Democracies*, ECPR Series, London: Rowman & Littlefield, 2021).

Mény, Yves and Yves Surel (2000). *Par le peuple, pour le peuple. Le populisme et les démocraties.* Paris: Fayard.

Mény, Yves and Yves Surel (eds.) (2002). *Democracies and the Populist Challenge.* Basingstoke: Palgrave Macmillan.

Prezworski, Adam (2019). *Crises of Democracy.* Cambridge: Cambridge University Press.

Renan, Ernest (1992). *What Is a Nation?* Paris: Press-Pocket.

Rooduijn, Matthijs (2020). 'Immigration Attitudes Have Barely Changed—So Why Is Far Right on Rise?' *The Guardian,* 2 March (available online at https://www.theguardian.com/world/2020/mar/02/immigration-attitudes-have-barely-changed-why-far-right-on-rise).

Rosanvallon, Pierre (1998). *Le peuple introuvable. Histoire de la représentation démocratique en France.* Paris: Gallimard.

Scharpf, Fritz (1998). *Governing in Europe: Effective and Democratic.* Oxford: Oxford University Press.

Tocqueville, Alexis de (1967). *De la démocratie en Amérique.* Paris: Gallimard.

Tsoukalis, Loukas (2003). *What Kind of Europe?* Oxford: Oxford University Press.

Urbinati, Nadia (2019). *Me, The People,* Cambridge, MA: Harvard University Press.

PART II
LOPSIDED INTEGRATION

8

The European Council as a Transformative Force

Wolfgang Wessels

Upheavals in History and an Astonishing Transformation of the EU

The author met Loukas Tsoukalis in the late 1970s and early 1980s when we were both working as directors of studies at the College of Europe in Bruges. Since then, the world and our Europe have changed in a way and to an extent we could never have anticipated. We saw both the global bipolarity and the division of Germany and Europe as features that would be frozen forever. After 'trente glorieuses années' (Fourastié 1979: 45), the European welfare state was challenged by the collapse of the Bretton Woods system and by oil embargos. These developments affected the domestic economies of member states and thereby also their political systems. The zeitgeist in western Europe was dominated by an *Endzeitstimmung* or 'Eurosclerosis'. The gloom and doom were caused by a new phase in the Cold War, the result of the installation of SS-20 middle-range missiles; by an economic downturn; and by new Eurosceptic heads of state or government (Thatcher, Papandreou, the early Mitterrand). Academic assessments were often oriented towards maintaining the status quo. Treaty changes were not seen as a realistic option; they might even be risky, as they could open a Pandora's box, weakening the *acquis* and leading to disintegration. Many actors and observers saw the Solemn Declaration of Stuttgart (1983) as the absolute furthest institutional engineering could be taken.

Looking back, we can see the many dramatic changes to the international system since then, with the collapse of the Soviet Union and the rise of China. In the Union's neighbourhood, we were shocked by wars in the Balkans, in Ukraine, and in Syria. Economic interdependencies have increased and changed in nature. The international financial system changed fundamentally and nearly collapsed in 2007–9. In member states, traditional party systems were replaced by new political constellations. We have also witnessed the evolution of basic features of our European societies.

Given these fundamental exogenous changes in the Union's environment, from a long-term (Braudel 1969) perspective and viewed from the context of the 1970s

Wolfgang Wessels, *The European Council as a Transformative Force* In: *Europe's Transformations: Essays in Honour of Loukas Tsoukalis.* Edited by: Helen Wallace, Nikos Koutsiaras, and George Pagoulatos, Oxford University Press. © OUP 2021. DOI: 10.1093/oso/9780192895820.003.0008

we observe a remarkable and surprising transformation of the early Communities into the multi-level system we now call the European Union (EU). Major developments of this sort are often characterized by three processes: 'widening', 'deepening', and 'broadening'.

With regard to 'widening', the number of member states has increased from six (1951) to 28 (2013). The political map of Europe in 2019 looks quite different from its counterpart back in the 1950s. Even in the shadow of Brexit, other European states express a preference to remain or become members of the EU—as in the case of the western Balkans.

As for 'deepening', the EU member states, as 'masters of the treaties' (Bundesverfassungsgericht 2009: §150), have transferred multiple competences and public policy instruments to the EU level by means of eight main and various 'satellite' treaties (Gerards and Wessels 2019). In more detail, they have transferred a number of key policy areas such as trade and monetary policy to the exclusive competence of the EU (Articles 2 and 3, Treaty on the Functioning of the European Union (TFEU)). The treaty architects have also allocated several core state powers (Genschel and Jachtenfuchs 2018)—such as the area of freedom, security and justice (AFSJ)—to competences shared between the member states and the EU (see Articles 2 and 4, TFEU). In some areas, such as health policy, the Union is given only the competence to 'support, coordinate or supplement the actions of member states' (Article 2(5), Treaty on European Union (TEU)). Other areas remain the 'sole responsibility of each member state' (Article 4(2), TEU).

In terms of 'broadening', a glance at Article 3 of the TEU and Articles 2–6 of the TFEU tells us that the masters of the treaties have pushed the scope of policy fields towards a 'state-like agenda' (see also Bundesverfassungsgericht 2009: §264). As further indicators of this evolution, nearly all national ministers participate in the ten configurations of the Council, and the leaders' agenda in the European Council has covered a considerable and comprehensive range of public policies during its existence.

The European Council as the Driver of a Fusion Process

By analysing and assessing the Union's growth, Loukas Tsoukalis and the author have contributed to a lively academic debate: our academic community has seen the rise and fall of multiple approaches, various turns, often in reaction to political events, and a number of U-turns involving numerous 'neo-' labels. To explain the process that has brought us to this stage in the evolution of the EU system, this chapter argues that the European Council—the regular summit forum for national and European leaders—has taken on the role of an active constitutional architect, transforming the EU's multi-level polity in respect of three fundamental developments. We shall approach these trends using the 'fusion model' (Wessels 2016: 18–20).

Conventional wisdom views the European Council as the incarnation of 'l'Europe des Patries' (de Gaulle 1962, in de Gaulle 1970: 406), as a European 'association of sovereign states' (Bundesverfassungsgericht 2009: §148), and as being 'intergovernmental *par excellence*' (Quermonne 2002: 3). In contrast, I would argue that the institution, in reacting to different forms of crisis, has been the driving force in transforming the Union away from a confederal union of states. The intended or unintended consequences of the European Council's historic decisions at critical junctures have steered a dynamic fusion process by which the heads of state or government have increasingly pooled and merged national and EU agendas and competences—in a vertical direction. With the short term constrained by decisions on immediate practicalities, the European Council has nonetheless proved to be a transformative force in shaping the EU's multilevel system from a long-term perspective.

In relation to this transfer of competences towards the Union, we see that the members of the European Council are often caught in a dilemma between, on the one hand, a strong inclination towards having the EU deal with significant topics on their national agenda (which I call the 'problem-solving instinct'), and, on the other hand, an inbuilt propensity to protect their national autonomy (which I call the 'sovereignty reflex'). In the Lisbon Treaty, the masters of the treaties have themselves signalled such a dilemma: in particular, Articles 4 and 5 of the TEU embody member states' preference to limit the conferring of competence on the Union, whereas Articles 2–6 of the TFEU indicate that member states want potentially to use the Union for nearly all the issues on their political agenda.

In taking successive treaty decisions, the European Council has not shifted the institutional balance in a clear intergovernmental direction, as several (neo-) intergovernmental schools of thought might have expected (see Puetter 2015: 410–14; Bickerton et al. 2015); nor has there been a clear shift towards a 'communitarization', as an extrapolation of neofunctionalist assumptions about 'spillover' (Niemann and Schmitter 2009: 57–61) or '*Sachlogik*' (Hallstein 1979: 322) might have predicted. Instead, from a long-term perspective, we see significant shifts in the institutional balance towards a horizontal fusion defined by a mixture of both power sharing and rivalry, which is typical for a constitutional architecture aiming at a Montesquieuesque balance of power.

Pursuing their problem-solving instincts, but hesitant to reduce national sovereignty, the European Council members have developed an incremental process driven by shared challenges and crises. By analysing the changes to treaty provisions, I propose to test for a generalizable pattern of an ideal-type four-step transformation during the EU's history. In the four cases that illustrate this transformation, the patterns reveal both striking similarities and considerable variation.

A Four-Step Process: An Ideal-Type Model

The ideal type starts from a traditional notion of national sovereignty and leads in four steps from intergovernmental, non-binding agreements to a supranational set of rules.

In the first step in this process of transformation, national governments identify shared or common problems in a given policy area. In the light of transnational interdependencies and extraterritorial effects, they implicitly recognize their decreased ability to deal with the points on their agenda by exercising exclusively national competences and instruments. In order to confront these shared challenges, the heads of state or government agree in the European Council to the first step of non-binding informal procedures for some kinds of problem solving. They take care to protect their national sovereignty by keeping the core EU institutions out of the game as far as possible. This first set of procedures can be characterized as a pattern of 'soft intergovernmentalism' by informal cooperation.

However, in the real world, the day-to-day practice of non-binding cooperation of this sort proves ineffective in the pursuit and achievement of the agreed objectives. As a lesson learned from the 'capability-expectation gap' (Hill 1993), the European Council may then introduce legal provisions for policy making in the relevant area. However, given the sovereignty reflex, national leaders will only agree to treaty articles of an intergovernmental nature if they reserve a veto for each national government. EU institutions are awarded a limited role in the policy agenda, with no powers of co-decision making or ultimate veto. When pre-existing procedures are enshrined in a legal text, this second set of procedures is characterized by a pattern of 'hard intergovernmentalism' which relies on formal cooperation and coordination.

A possible variation at this stage would see some member states acknowledge a stronger need to solve problems together than others and create an '*avant-garde*', 'directorate', or 'core Europe' (for this discussion, see de Schoutheete 2017: 76–7; Tekin 2016: 185–8; Holm 2009). The reluctant members opt out but retain the opportunity offered to opt back in later.

However, even after a treaty-based upgrade of this kind, member states can still block each other in the real world due to the unanimity rule in the Council. Thus, even with the additional procedures, the revised rules prove inadequate for problem solving. In view of this inadequacy, the political leaders agree in a third step on a set of procedures characterized by a '(dirty) incomplete communitarization'. They institute a set of supranational procedures, but maintain a say for the European Council, which is granted ultimate veto power.

This set of upgraded treaty procedures might also be seen as ineffective for the challenges on the agenda. Subsequently, in a fourth step, the members of the European Council may agree to introduce supranational provisions for a 'complete communitarization' for which the Ordinary Legislative Procedure (OLP) is a valid indicator. This assigns a strong co-decision power to the European Parliament (Article 294, TFEU). The third and fourth steps may overlap, as the regulations developed by the avant-garde may be partially or fully integrated into the Union's framework.

Empirical Tests: A Variety of Cases

Towards Incomplete Communitarization: From the TREVI Group to the AFSJ

The European Council's agreements on constructing the area of freedom, security, and justice (AFSJ) can be taken as an illustrative case for the step-by-step pattern of the fusion model. Since its creation in 1974, the European Council has frequently dealt with issues of justice and home affairs, even though these issues have traditionally been considered 'domestic affairs' in which the Union 'shall respect essential state functions, including ensuring the territorial integrity of the state, maintaining law and order and safeguarding national security' (Article 4(2), TEU). Table 8.1 lists the main decisions.

As a first step towards establishing procedures for cooperation, the European Council established in 1975 an informal, purely intergovernmental grouping of senior officials from ministries of justice and home affairs. The so-called TREVI Group was given a mandate to work on international issues relating to terrorism, radicalism, extremism, and international violence. In 1985, five member states reached the separate Schengen Agreement to eliminate border controls on persons crossing the frontiers between them.

In the first relevant treaty revision, the Single European Act of 1987, although the heads of state or government did not include any issues of justice or home affairs in primary law, they did continue to introduce and support several specific non-binding forms of administrative cooperation (see e.g. Lavenex 2015: 369–70).

The Maastricht Treaty then introduced a new 'third pillar', which labelled the legal provisions as 'cooperation in the fields of justice and home affairs' (Title VI, TEU (Maastricht)). This legal upgrade marks the step from soft to hard intergovernmentalism.

In the Amsterdam amendments, the European Council adopted provisions in relation to issues that have since then been called the 'area of freedom, security and justice' (see Titles VI and VII, TEU (Amsterdam)). The Schengen Agreement was partially integrated into the treaty with opt-outs for unwilling member state. Retrospectively we might argue that the Schengen group served as an avant-garde The amendments in the Nice Treaty (2001) formalized this variation by adding procedures for enhanced cooperation which included this policy field.

Table 8.1 The European Council's agreements on justice and home affairs, 1975–2019

Year and place	Topic
December 1975Rome	Launch of the TREVI Group of senior officials of justice and home affairs ministries
June 1985Schengen	Schengen Agreement: creation of the Schengen Area abolishing internal border checks between the participating European states
July 1987Single European Act (SEA)	No provisions
1993Maastricht Treaty	Creation of the (intergovernmental) 'third pillar': 'cooperation in the fields of justice and home affairs'
May 1999Amsterdam Treaty	Revision of Maastricht provisions and partial communitarization: creation of the 'area of freedom, security and justice'
October 1999Tampere	The Tampere Milestones: 'Towards a Union of Freedom, Security and Justice'
2003Nice Treaty	Introduction of the flexibility procedure of enhanced cooperation
November 2004Brussels	The Hague Programme: 'Ten priorities for the next five years'
December 2009Brussels	The Stockholm Programme: 'An open and secure Europe serving and protecting citizens'
2009 LisbonTEU/TFEU	Abolition of the pillar structure: the AFSJ as 'shared competence'
June 2014Brussels	Definition of the strategic guidelines for legislative and operational planning for the AFSJ in the years to come

Source: Compiled by the author. Adapted from treaty articles, presidency conclusions and conclusions of the European Council. See also Wessels (2017: 229).

As the last stage in this step-by-step process, the heads of state or government developed a set of new provisions in the Lisbon Treaty. The High Contracting Parties placed the area of freedom, security, and justice higher than before on the list of the Union's priorities (Article 3(2), TEU) and categorized it as a 'shared competence' (Article 4, TFEU). Pursuant to this category of competence, 'the Union may legislate and adopt binding legal acts' (Article 2(2), TFEU) in key areas of justice and home affairs. The EU institutions decide on legal acts in accordance with the OLP.

At the same time, the member states agreed on some remarkable exceptions. These included an 'emergency brake' (Piris 2010: 185–7) that grants national veto rights on judicial cooperation in criminal matters (Articles 82(3) and 83(3), TFEU), in which context the Council could decide by a qualified majority vote. They also envisaged the right of initiative for a group of member states (Article 97(3), TFEU). Even more remarkably, Article 68 of the TEU empowers the European Council *de jure* '[to] define the strategic guidelines for legislative and operational planning within the area of freedom, security and justice'; the European leaders thus retained strong pre-legislative power, reducing both the autonomy of the Commission in the submission of legal acts and the co-decision role of the European Parliamenr in the

OLP. Due to strongly differing opinions on this particular competence of the EU to reach agreements, the heads of state or government have allowed specific forms of opt-out (see Tekin 2012).

Viewed overall, we can observe three steps, each of which is framed and concluded by the European Council as it drives the process within the current constellations. Thanks to its power as constitutional architect, the European Council has reached a stage of integration that can be characterized by the notion of vertical and horizontal fusion: since the 1970s, the masters of the treaties have shifted core areas of national sovereignty to the EU level by granting strong powers to supranational institutions. At the same time, the European Council has been empowered to retain the national influence.

Towards Hard Intergovernmentalization: From EPC to the CFSP

A second case for studying the patterns of European Council actions concerns another area of national sovereignty: the evolution from the European Political Cooperation (EPC) of the early 1970s to the Common Foreign and Security Policy (CFSP) and Common Security and Defence Policy (CSDP) contained in the Lisbon Treaty of 2009 (see Table 8.2). How did national leaders resolve the dilemma between the problem-solving instinct and the sovereignty reflex in this 'high politics area' (Hoffmann 1966: 874)?

After the Second World War, many western European governments quickly realized the benefits of cooperating in foreign, security, and military affairs. There were failures ahead in the form of the more supranational plans of the European Defence Community in the early 1950s and then also of de Gaulle's intergovernmental Fouchet plan in the early 1960s (Wessels 2016: 211). However, the then six EC member states agreed at the Hague summit of 1969 to launch a process of informal cooperation in foreign affairs. In reacting to three reports, and in the Solemn Declaration of Stuttgart in 1983, the heads of state and government formulated vague commitments, steering clear of addressing the eventual form such a cooperation might take. This first set of informal procedures could be characterized as a typical case of soft intergovernmentalism.

By creating the second pillar of the Maastricht Treaty, member states took the decision to upgrade EPC into a 'Common Foreign and Security Policy'. Having analysed the relevant treaty articles, one can characterize these provisions as a typical form of hard intergovernmentalism based on binding rules that retain the power of veto for member states' governments while assigning only weak powers to EU institutions.

To improve the efficiency of their procedures, the masters of the treaties established in the Amsterdam Treaty the office of a 'High Representative for Common Foreign and Security Policy'; based in the Council as its most senior

Table 8.2 European Council agreements on the EPC/CFSP architecture

Year and summit/treaty	Topic
December 1969 The Hague Summit	Launch of (European) Political Cooperation
October 1970 Luxembourg Summit	First report on (European) Political Cooperation (the Luxembourg or Davignon Report)
December 1973 Copenhagen Summit	Second report on (European) Political Cooperation in Foreign Policy Matters (the Copenhagen Report) Declaration on European Identity
November 1981 London	Report on European Political Cooperation (the London Report)
June 1983 Stuttgart	Solemn Declaration on European Union
1987 Single European Act	Provisions on European Cooperation in the Sphere of Foreign Policy
1993 Maastricht Treaty	(Second Maastricht Pillar on) Common Foreign and Security Policy
1999 Amsterdam Treaty	Creation of the High Representative for the Common Foreign and Security Policy
June 1999 Cologne	European Security and Defence Policy (ESDP)
2003 Nice Treaty	Provisions for enhanced cooperation within the Common Foreign and Security Policy
2009 Lisbon Treaty	Specific provisions on the Common Foreign and Security Policy (including the Common Security and Defence Policy)

Source: Compiled by the author. Adapted from presidency conclusions and conclusions of the European Council and relevant articles from the treaties; see also Wessels (2016: 212).

civil servant, the new office was clearly under the control of the rotating presidency of the member states.

Another informal step was taken at the European Council session in Cologne in 1999: in the shadow of their inability to respond coherently to the civil wars in the former Yugoslavia, the leaders agreed on increasing their efforts to develop a 'European Security and Defence Policy' (ESDP).

The next constitutional step was taken in the Lisbon Treaty of 2009, in which the member states revisited and revised the CFSP provisions. Among other things, they added a long chapter on the 'Common Security and Defence Policy' (Articles 42–6, TEU), which framed ambitious goals. However, an analysis of these procedures reveals that the member states did not take a step towards more supranational forms. Article 24(1) of the TEU clearly states that the CFSP follows a different procedure from other policy areas of the Union, restating the veto rights of the member states and the weak role of the European Parliament and—especially—keeping the Court of Justice of the European Union (CJEU) out of this set of procedures.

Although the legal position of the High Representative of the Union for Foreign Affairs and Security Policy was upgraded, and a European External Action Service (EEAS) created, member states stressed that these provisions would 'not affect the existing legal basis, responsibilities and power of each member state in relation to the formulation and conduct of this foreign policy' (Declaration 14 annexed to the treaty). With regard to their own institution, the political leaders allotted it a pivotal position: 'The European Council shall identify the Union's strategic interests, determine the objectives of and define general guidelines for the common foreign and security policy including for matters of defence implications. It shall adopt the necessary decisions' (Article 26(1), TEU).

In their conclusion, aiming to strengthen 'the Union's action on the international scene' (Article 23, TEU), the political leaders decided to improve the efficiency of the cooperation procedures. However, they neither conferred competences upwards nor reinforced the role of any EU institution. Also, when the European Council decided in 2017 to launch a long list of projects under the treaty articles (42(6) and 46) for 'Permanent Structured Cooperation' (PESCO), a voluntary cooperation of national governments retained national control over these concrete military missions and activities.

The masters of the treaties did not go beyond a set of procedures which I would characterize as hard intergovernmentalism. In spite of the many revisions and adaptations made to treaty articles, the European Council has not driven the process towards more supranational features. In view of the limited capacity of the EU27 to act efficiently and effectively in the international arena, governments have on numerous occasions considered introducing qualified majority voting into the CFSP, too. However, the sovereignty reflex has to date proved stronger than the problem-solving instinct.

From the EMS to the EMU: Various Combinations of the Four Steps

A major case to be studied is the evolution from the creation of the European Monetary System (EMS) in the late 1970s to the founding of the Economic and Monetary Union (EMU) in 1990 and from there to the crisis measures of the last decade. The creation of the EMU is generally characterized as a history-making decision on the part of the European Council, which underlines its role as a constitutional architect (see Table 8.3).

Already, at their summit in The Hague, political leaders had declared that 'a plan in stages will be worked out during 1970 with a view to the creation of an economic and monetary union' (The Hague, December 1969). However, fundamental differences in national interests and in how these plans were conceived, plus diverging national reactions to asymmetric shocks caused by monetary turbulence in the

Table 8.3 European Council and economic governance: the main agreements on the EMU, 1969–2007

Year and place	Topic
December 1969 The Hague Summit	Plan for an EMU
December 1978 Brussels	Creation of the European Monetary System (EMS)
June 1986 The Hague	Single European Act: area without internal frontiers
June 1988 Hanover	Delors Committee to propose concrete stages leading towards the EMU
December 1991 Maastricht	Treaty provisions for the EMU
October 2007 Lisbon	Agreement on Lisbon Treaty, involving minimal changes to the provisions of the EMU

Source: Compiled by the author; see also Wessels (2016: 190).

1970s, blocked the implementation of this ambitious project. In 1978, the European Council agreed to create the European Monetary System (EMS) (see Ludlow 1982). In the Single European Act (SEA) of 1987, the heads of state or government reinforced treaty provisions so as to achieve the internal market by 1992.

Following on from the dynamic of the 'l'europe sans frontières' vision, the European Council appointed the Delors Committee, in which national central bankers were given the task of 'studying and proposing concrete stages leading towards this union' (Hanover, June 1988). The Maastricht summit agreed on provisions for monetary union and on rules for fiscal policies in the economic union (December 1991). Driven by different economic interests and considerable (geo)political pressures, national leaders agreed on a far-reaching and history-making set of decisions. The treaty provisions assigned the monetary policy of the member states of the Eurogroup to the 'exclusive competence' of the Union (see Article 3(1), TFEU). It granted opt-out status for two member states which declined to join: Denmark, after a negative referendum on the treaty, and the United Kingdom. The Edinburgh European Council (1992) confirmed these forms of flexibility. The treaty established the European Central Bank as an independent supranational institution. In the follow-up, the European Council concluded the Stability and Growth Pact (1997), revised in 2005, and also created the Eurogroup (Luxembourg, December 1997), which the High Contracting Parties later formalized in Protocol No. 14 attached to the Lisbon Treaty.

During the constitutional decade, the heads of state or government revised the provisions for EMU to only a limited degree (Umbach and Wessels 2008: 55–7); as a result, 'the (Lisbon) EU Treaty simply did not provide instruments to deal with a financial crisis' (Van Rompuy 2014: 28–9). Then, in 2012, the European Council concluded the Treaty on Stability, Coordination and Governance (the 'Fiscal Compact') and the Treaty on the European Stability Mechanism. Later agreements framed and paved the way towards a banking union. The provisions dealing with the fiscal discipline of member states and their revisions have instituted several forms of hard coordination which include the possibility of sanctions being imposed by EU institutions.

The record shows that the European Council was the driver behind different forms of the transformation process: in framing and creating monetary union, the agreements of the European leaders could be classified as leading to our ideal model's fourth step. In view of the composition of the Governing Council, on which the members of the executive board and the governors of the participating national central banks take decisions together, we can also make out some features of vertical and horizontal fusion. In the process towards the framing and creating of economic union, the steps taken by the European Council could be classified as variations on hard intergovernmentalism as well as a mixture of intergovernmentalism and incomplete communitarization.

From the Single European Act to the Lisbon Treaty and Beyond: Shifting the Institutional Balance

In order to study the role of the European Council as the constitutional architect of the Union, we analyse agreements made by the heads of state or government in the final stage of intergovernmental conferences (IGCs) in their role of 'treaty negotiators' (de Schoutheete 2012; Christiansen and Reh 2009) (see Table 8.4) The heads of state or government have taken several significant decisions since the mid-1980s.

In these constitutional steps, the masters of the treaties have not only conferred competences vertically upwards to the Union level, but also changed the horizontal balance of powers among the EU institutions. One persistent trend is the extension and strengthening of the Community method, as measured by the increase in the number of articles which enable qualified majority voting in the Council, and in the number of treaty rules which apply co-decision in respect of the Ordinary Legislative Procedure (see Figure 8.1).

However, this overview also documents the extension by the heads of state or government of the role of their European Council. The co-evolution of both trends towards supranational and intergovernmental procedures marks a horizontal fusion, which we also observe in detail in treaty provisions, especially with regard to the election of the Commission president (Article17(7), TEU) and the adoption of the Multiannual Financial Framework (MFF) (Article 312, TFEU).

Table 8.4 European Council and treaty making: main agreements, 1985–2013

Year and place	Topic and entry into force
December 1985 Luxembourg	1987 Single European Act
February 1992 Maastricht	1993 (Maastricht) Treaty on European Union
October 1997 Amsterdam	1999 (Amsterdam) Treaty on European Union
December 2000 Nice	2003 (Nice) Treaty on European Union
December 2001 Laeken, June 2004 Dublin, and October 2004 Rome	Treaty Establishing a Constitution for Europe (failed in 2005)
June and December 2007 Brussels	2009 (Lisbon) TEU and TFEU
December 2010 Brussels	Amendment of Article 136, TFEU
February 2012 Brussels	2012 Treaty Establishing the European Stability Mechanism (ESM)
March 2012 Brussels	2013 Treaty on Stability, Coordination and Governance (TSCG)

Source: Compiled by the author. Based on presidency conclusions and conclusions of the European Council; see also Wessels (2016: 164).

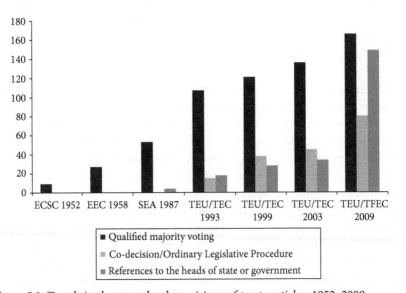

Figure 8.1 Trends in the procedural provisions of treaty articles, 1952–2009

Source: Compiled by the author. Based on an analysis of the provisions of the relevant treaties; see also Wessels (2016: 88).

Conclusions: Challenges for the Model

The analysis of the above cases has identified several different ways in which political leaders have driven the processes of vertical and horizontal fusion via the European Council. The formal decisions laid out above refer to the legal wording of the provisions, which does not determine what happens in the real world. Further studies need to analyse the historical constellations more profoundly in order to determine why several generations of national leaders have taken the final decision to agree on steps which have led to this evolution in EU polity. Other cases, such as the evolution of environmental, energy, and health policies, could offer additional insights.

Reactions to crises have been a major driving force in this process. When analysing the transformative role of the European Council in these circumstances, we should take care to avoid two methodological traps: one is taking an overly narrow view, which in this case would mean examining only the immediate outputs and the constellations at the particular historical moment; the other is extrapolating historical trends from the crisis management of heads of state or government.

Another case that presents itself for further study is the emerging package of measures taken by the heads of state or government to respond to the Covid-19 pandemic, and its socio-economic consequences in particular. The financial mega deal agreed by the European Council in July 2020 to establish the recovery fund and to draw on the Multiannual Financial Framework tells us that the problem-solving instinct of political leaders leads to a more extensive use, and innovative creation, of new Union instruments. We can identify further and significant steps in some of the measures agreed upon, which confirm assumptions and expectations relating to the fusion approach.

Overall, given its transformative power, the European Council remains a key institution to study in researching and teaching European politics and policies.

References

Bickerton, Christopher J., Dermot Hodson, and Uwe Puetter (2015). 'The New Intergovernmentalism: European Integration in the Post-Maastricht Era.' *Journal of Common Market Studies* 53(4): 703–22.

Braudel, Fernand (1969). *Écrit sur l'histoire.* Paris: Flammarion.

Bundesverfassungsgericht (2009). Judgement of the Second Senate of 30 June 2009–2 BvE 2/08. Karlsruhe. Available online at https://www.bundesverfassungsgericht.de/SharedDocs/Entscheidungen/EN/2009/06/es20090630_2bve000208en.html, accessed on 5 May 2020.

Christiansen, Thomas and Christine Reh (2009). *Constitutionalizing the European Union.* Basingstoke, New York: Palgrave Macmillan.

de Gaulle, Charles (1970). *Discours et Messages. Avec le Renouveau. 1958–1962.* Paris: Plon.

de Schoutheete, Philippe (2012). 'The European Council.' In John Peterson and Michael Shackleton (eds.), *The Institutions of the European Union*, 3rd edn. Oxford: Oxford University Press: 43–67.

de Schoutheete, Philippe (2017). 'The European Council: A Formidable Locus of Power.' In Dermot Hodson and John Peterson (eds.), *The Institutions of the European Union*, 4th edn. Oxford: Oxford University Press: 55–79.

Fourastié, Jean (1979). *Les Trente Glorieuses, ou la révolution invisible de 1946 à 1975.* Paris: Fayard.

Genschel, Philipp and Markus Jachtenfuchs (2018). 'From Market Integration to Core State Powers: The Eurozone Crisis, the Refugee Crisis and Integration Theory.' *Journal of Common Market Studies* 56(1): 178–96.

Gerards, Carsten and Wolfgang Wessels (2019). 'Enhancing "Enhanced Cooperation": Constraints and Opportunities of an Inflexible Flexibility Clause.' In *College of Europe Policy Brief* #1.19 (March 2019). Available online at https://www.coleurope.eu/system/files_force/research-paper/gerards_wessels_cepob_1-19_0.pdf?download=1, accessed on 5 May 2020.

Hallstein, Walter (1979). *Europäische Reden.* Edited by Thomas Oppermann. Stuttgart: Deutsche Verlags-Anstalt.

Hill, Christopher (1993). 'The Capability-Expectations Gap, or Conceptualizing Europe's International Role.' *Journal of Common Market Studies* 31(3): 305–28.

Hoffmann, Stanley (1966). 'Obstinate or Obsolete? The Fate of the Nation-State and the Case of Western Europe.' *Daedalus* 95(2): 862–915.

Holm, Ulla (2009). 'Sarkozysm: New European and Foreign Policy into Old French Bottles?' *DIIS Working Paper*, No. 30 (11 October 2012).

Lavenex, Sandra (2015). 'Justice and Home Affairs: Institutional Change and Policy Continuity.' In Helen Wallace, Mark A. Pollack, and Alasdair R. Young (eds.), *Policy-Making in the European Union*, 7th edn. Oxford: Oxford University Press: 367–87.

Ludlow, Peter (1982). *The Making of the European Monetary System: A Case Study of the Politics of the European Community.* London: Butterworth Scientific.

Niemann, Arne and Philippe C. Schmitter (2009). 'Neofunctionalism.' In Antje Wiener and Thomas Diez (eds.), *Theories of European Integration*, 2nd edn. Oxford: Oxford University Press: 45–66.

Piris, Jean-Claude (2010). *The Lisbon Treaty: A Legal and Political Analysis.* Cambridge: Cambridge University Press.

Puetter, Uwe (2015). 'Deliberativer Intergouvernementalismus und institutioneller Wandel. Die Europäische Union nach der Eurokrise.' *Politische Vierteljahresschrift* 56(3): 406–29.

Quermonne, Jean-Louis (2002). 'The Question of a European Government.' *Research and European Issues*, issue 20. Notre Europe.

Tekin, Funda (2012). *Differentiated Integration at Work: The Institutionalisation and Implementation of Opt-Outs from European Integration in the Area of Freedom, Security and Justice.* Baden-Baden: Nomos.

Tekin, Funda (2016). Was folgt aus dem Brexit? Mögliche Szenarien differenzierter (Des-)Integration. *Integration* 39(3): 183–97.

Umbach, Gaby and Wolfgang Wessels (2008). 'The Changing European Context of Economic and Monetary Union: "Deepening", "Widening" and Stability.' In Kenneth Dyson (ed.), *The Euro at Ten: Europeanization, Power, and Convergence.* New York: Oxford University Press: 54–68.

Van Rompuy, Herman (2014). *Europe in the Storm: Promise and Prejudice.* Leuven: Davidsfonds Uitgeverij.

Wessels, Wolfgang (2016). *The European Council.* Basingstoke: Palgrave Macmillan.

9

Core–Periphery Relations and European Integration

Brigid Laffan

Introduction

Core–periphery relations have always played an important role within nation-states, across regions, and at the global level. Politics and economic well-being are moulded by the way in which relations between cores and peripheries play out across time and space. These concepts are a vital part of the conceptual toolkit of the social sciences and are found in grand theory, world systems theory, theories of state building, and theories of economic divergence. Historians of the middle ages highlighted the significance of what they termed 'germinal' or core areas for state building in Europe (Pounds and Ball 1964; Jones 2003). Later international relations scholars, such as Deutsch, concluded that the growth of political communities was characterized by the fact that 'larger, stronger, more politically, administratively, economically and educationally advanced political units were found to form the cores of strength around which in most cases the integrative process developed' (Deutsch 1957: 130). Lipset and Rokkan's seminal work on cleavage structures identified the core–periphery cleavage as one of four cleavages that influenced centre formation and state building (Lipset and Rokkan 1967). In later work, Rokkan returned to the question of territorial politics when he and Urwin identified the characteristics of peripheries as regions which were geographically distant, culturally different, and economically dependent on the core regions (Rokkan and Urwin 1983, 13).

Given the significance of core–periphery dynamics to state building historically, we would expect these dynamics and patterns of economic convergence and divergence to matter in the process of European integration. Questions relating to convergence and divergence, the management of diversity, and core and periphery have played a central role in the Tsoukalis *oeuvre*. His background and interests ensured that this dimension of European integration would receive close attention. Loukas Tsoukalis, against the backdrop of Greece, understood what it meant to come from a small, relatively poor, and peripheral state. His long-term interest in Economic and Monetary Union (EMU) led him and many others to analyse the conditions under which EMU might work and the degree of

Brigid Laffan, *Core–Periphery Relations and European Integration* In: *Europe's Transformations: Essays in Honour of Loukas Tsoukalis*. Edited by: Helen Wallace, Nikos Koutsiaras, and George Pagoulatos, Oxford University Press. © OUP 2021. DOI: 10.1093/oso/9780192895820.003.0009

convergence necessary to have a stable currency union. As a life-long social democrat, solidarity mattered to him. In addition, underlying his work was a strong normative commitment to the project of European integration. His 2016 volume *In Defence of Europe*, written in the aftershock of the Greek and Eurozone crisis, was a plea for a new European grand bargain that would reset the EU on a better and safer path. Referring to the European project, he concluded his defence in the following manner: 'We should try to work on it and improve it, instead of throwing it away. We simply cannot afford to let it fail. Just think of the alternative' (Tsoukalis 2016: 210). Never blind to the tensions and failures of the EU, he considered it an essential part of governance in Europe.

The European Union is characterized by a core and periphery, perhaps by more than one periphery.[1] Wallace in a 1990 study of European integration identified the core of the EU in the following terms: 'Germany and its neighbours in the Rhine Valley and across the Alpine passes constitute the contemporary core of Europe, in terms of economic interaction, social interchange and security focus. Historical "Europes" have largely revolved around the same broadly defined area' (Wallace 1990: 14). Economists and economic geographers identified a 'golden triangle' linking Europe's most prosperous regions. Economic and political integration in Europe during the post-war period, and EU expansion though successive waves of enlargement, involved the gradual inclusion within the EU of a north-western, southern, and eastern periphery. From the outset, a commitment to 'harmonious development by reducing the differences existing between the various regions and the backwardness of the less-favoured regions' was contained in the Preamble to the 1958 EEC Rome Treaty, a foundational document of the Union.

This chapter traces how the EU addressed its commitment to 'harmonious development' as it deepened and widened following the original aim of the Treaty of Rome. We identify a series of significant phases in the management of the EU response to core–periphery relations. Historical institutionalism reminds us of the importance of a temporal perspective in analysing both the origins of and change in public policies (Pierson 1996; Thelen 1999; Bulmer 2009). A key argument is that every major development in the EU, with the exception of the euro, has been accompanied by some policy provision designed to manage core–periphery relations and alleviate divergence. Throughout the history of integration, there were two key drivers of EU policy on convergence. First, EU enlargement was a significant driver, because the expanding Union added a substantial number of poor states following the first enlargement in 1973. The EU was never a club of only the rich and most advanced states in Europe. Second, the deepening of economic interdependence as a result of the intensification of market integration, especially the

---

[1] The European Union (EU) is used throughout this chapter even when referring to its antecedents: the European Economic Communities and the European Community.

creation of the single market and the single currency, firmly placed the challenge of core–periphery dynamics on the EU agenda. The economic consequences of integration for core and periphery are widely discussed and disputed in the literature (Majone et al. 2016). Cuaresma et al. (2011) find that long-term growth has stimulated convergence as a result of EU membership. Tsoukalis in his 2006 Journal of Common Market Studies Annual Lecture also concluded that the EU had in 'many ways worked as a kind of convergence machine for the less developed countries of the European continent' and that this had 'helped to reduce the geographical as well as political and cultural distance between the centre and the periphery in Europe' (Tsoukalis 2006: 2). The history of integration is not, however, characterized by a one-way trajectory from divergence to convergence. Convergence generally occurred when the growth rates of peripheral countries and regions outperformed those of the core, but this was not always the case. Moreover, globalization and market integration had distributional effects for different social groups, not just regions and states (Tang 2000). Tsoukalis (2006: 2) reminded us of the challenge of winners and losers arising from these distributional effects. The EU may be a convergence machine for peripheral states, but this may disguise rising inequality within states. Moreover, particular EU regimes such as the single currency may increase nominal convergence, but not real convergence (Eichengreen 2019).

The argument is developed in three sections. The first concerns enlargement. This section traces the impact of the first enlargement on EU regional policy, which involved a tentative development of tools to address core–periphery relations. This was followed by a step change when the Iberian enlargement coincided with the Single Market Programme. Treaty change and an ambitious market liberalization strategy drew attention to economic divergence and uneven development. The EU responded with a doubling of financial flows for cohesion to the poorer member states, the cohesion club. Enlargement into central and eastern Europe in the 2000s greatly exacerbated economic and social divergence within the EU. The second section analyses the creation of the euro and the tension between the nominal convergence of interest rates and the divergence of current-account balances that culminated in a crisis that almost broke the Eurozone apart. The third section addresses the Covid-19 pandemic and the breaking of member state taboos on public finance and integration, which may have a lasting effect on the EU and budgetary politics.

The Enlargement Dynamic

The first enlargement of the Union in 1973, which included the United Kingdom, Denmark and Ireland, altered the politics of core and periphery relations within the EU. Ireland joined the EU with a per capita GDP of 64.4 per cent the EU average, and the United Kingdom was characterized by internal peripheries, notably in Scotland, Wales, and Northern Ireland. UK membership led directly to the establishment of a policy instrument designed to address regional problems, the European Regional Development Fund (ERDF). During the negotiations on UK accession, it became clear that the UK would become a major contributor to the EU budget once the transition period ended, given the profile of its economy and the impact of agricultural expenditure on the EU budget. It was agreed as part of the negotiations that the Union would develop a new policy instrument that the UK would benefit from. In tandem with the first enlargement, the EU started to address the possibility of establishing Economic and Monetary Union (EMU) following the 1969 Hague Summit. A high-level committee submitted its report on EMU, known as the Werner Report after its chair, Pierre Werner, the then prime minister and finance minister of Luxembourg, in October 1970. Apart from sketching a three-phased approach to the establishment of EMU, it argued that there would have to be a high level of coordination of national economic policies and the establishment of 'common industrial and regional policies' in a monetary union (EU 1970: 23). In the light of EU enlargement and the commitment to EMU, the 1972 Paris Summit concluded that priority should be given to correcting 'structural and regional imbalances' and invited the European institutions to create a Regional Development Fund (EU 1972). There were two impulses behind the prioritization of regional imbalances at this juncture, one relating to UK membership and the need to mitigate its expected budgetary contributions and the second relating to the goal of a single currency. Market integration per se did not play a role.

The first European Regional Development Fund (ERDF) was established in 1975. The regulation referred to the purpose of the fund, which was to 'correct the principal regional imbalances within the Community resulting in particular from agricultural preponderance, industrial change and structural under-employment' (EU 1975). The ERDF had limited financial resources and represented approximately 5 per cent of the budget of the time. A salient feature of the agreement was that all member states were eligible to benefit from the fund, although it was recognized that some countries had greater needs than others. Italy and the UK between them were allocated 68 per cent of the financial resources while Ireland, with just over 3 million people, was assigned 6 per cent, just below Germany at 6.4 per cent (EU 1975: 73/2). The distribution of ERDF money across the member states pointed to a continuing dilemma in this policy field: namely, the challenge of directing resources to the areas of greatest need. All states had to get something if they were to garner support for the establishment of this new instrument. This upholds the argument that regional policy in the Union was a side payment designed to facilitate agreement—in this case, to address the UK budgetary problem—and was not at the heart of the paradigm of integration. In its early years, the fund was an 'interstate transfer mechanism' (Hooghe and Keating

1994), but it provided institutional resources and policy space for the Commission to develop a range of instruments and an approach to governance in this field that was distinctly supranational. The Commission and the EU's poorer states and regions never accepted this limited and instrumental interpretation of European cohesion policy.

The 1985 Second Periodic Report on developments in the EU's regions brought the continuing regional disparities in the Union sharply into focus. It concluded that there had been no improvement during the 1970s in productivity and employment, and that these problems would acquire greater prominence during the 1980s, particularly labour market problems. The report also identified the likely impact of the Iberian enlargement in the following terms: 'Regional dispar-ities will be greater in the Community of Twelve' and 'with a doubling of the population in less-developed regions, the problem of the Community's regions will appear in an even harsher light' (EU 1985: 5). The Single European Act (SEA) which coincided with the Iberian enlargement represented a new EU 'grand bargain' with major implications for core–periphery relations.

The EU embarked on a step change in integration by agreeing to the 1992 programme for the completion of the internal market. In June 1985, the Commission issued a White Paper on the Completion of the Internal Market for the Milan European Council. Hidden behind the technocratic language was a transformative programme designed to create a unified market of 320 million people by abolishing physical, technical, and fiscal barriers to economic exchange. This drive to complete the single market became the key strategic goal of the first Delors Commission in 1985. It represented, according to Young, 'the critical turning point between stagnation and dynamism, between the "old" politics of European integration and the "new" politics of European regulation' (Young 2015: 116). There were, however, concerns that the single market would exacerbate agglomeration tendencies in capital- and skills-intensive industries in the core EU. Tommaso Padoa-Schioppa, in an analysis of the Union's economic system, argued that market liberalization might aggravate regional imbalances and thus supported measures to speed up adjustment in Europe's economically weak regions and countries (Padoa-Schioppa 1987). Fears that the benefits of the internal market would flow disproportionately to Europe's richer regions pro-vided support for a major review of European regional policy in 1988.

The SEA strengthened the Union's constitutional commitment to addressing the challenge of Europe's poorer regions. For the first time EU primary law established a direct link between market integration and regional imbalances. This was a step change from the 'inter-state' transfer mechanism that character-ized the ERDF at the outset. Addressing core–periphery dynamics became central to the deepening of market integration, the core of the Single Market Programme. It could be argued that this was a shift from dependence to interdependence, albeit a form of asymmetrical interdependence. The SEA contained an entirely new chapter, Title Five, on 'Economic and Social Cohesion'. The use of the word 'cohesion' rather than convergence was deliberate. Cohesion is a more ambiguous concept than convergence; the former implies cohesiveness whereas the latter can be measured. The EU's richer states were wary of inserting into the treaty a strong commitment to convergence but accepted the fuzzier language of cohesion. The SEA contained provisions that were 'market correcting' as a complement to the market making of the internal market programme. The Commission president, Jacques Delors, armed with the SEA and the commitment to the 1992 programme, was determined to complement the market with a larger EU budget and a reform of the structural funds. Agreement in February 1988 on what became the known as the Delors-1 package represented a major change in EU budgetary politics. It signalled the arrival of multi-annual financial frameworks that would allocate financial resources across different fields. Each framework would be accompanied by a reform of the main spending programmes. Thus from 1988 onwards, cohesion policy was reformed in tandem with each new financial agreement. A combination of improved macroeconomic policy, product and labour market liberalization, and the injection of EU structural funding led to a resumption of convergence in the four states in the cohesion club (Spain, Ireland, Greece, and Portugal) from the mid-1980s onwards following a period of divergence during the two oil crises (Barry 2003). The cohesion club was about to lose its status with the membership of 13 states from the eastern half of the continent.

The Big Bang Enlargement

The accession of ten countries from central and eastern Europe in the 'big bang' enlargement of 2004 was followed quickly by the accession of Romania and Bulgaria (2007) and Croatia (July 2013). The 2004 enlargement added 20 per cent to the Union's population but only 5 per cent to its GDP (EU 2015). In its report on progress towards economic and social cohesion in 2002, the Commission concluded that 'Enlargement will be accompanied by a major fall in average per capita GDP and a widening of regional disparities on a scale without precedent in any previous enlargement. The fall in GDP in an EU of 25 will be 13 per cent' (EU 2002). Once more, enlargement altered the politics of cohesion policy. Given both the extent of this enlargement and its impact on relative per capita incomes in the Union, it was a major challenge to arrive at agreement given the addition of new and more divergent preferences. The first challenge was to get the beneficiary countries within the EU15 existing member states to agree to a reduction in their receipts given the greater needs of the new member states. The second was to ensure that the new member states had the institutional capacity to absorb cohesion transfers. The Sapir Group, which met intensively in 2002 and 2003, was convened by Commission president Romano

Prodi to analyse the key economic issues facing the Union as it enlarged east-wards. Its report argued strongly for a focus on low-income countries in the Union and a move to direct budget transfers rather than complex programming (Sapir et al. 2004: 7). DG Regio and the then commissioner, Michel Barnier, successfully opposed the Sapir recommendations on programming. The existing cohesion states and regions from among the EU15 acknowledged that funds would have to flow east, but secured transition funding to ease the change.

Following the 2004 enlargement the Union agreed two further financial pack-ages, the Multiannual Financial Frameworks (MFFs) for, respectively, 2007–13 and 2014–20. The countries of central and eastern Europe were full participants in these negotiations and brought with them strong preferences concerning cohesion policy. They displayed strong growth potential and began to converge economic-ally with the western half of the continent, which had been consolidated by EU membership (Andor 2019: 22). However, economic convergence disguised under-lying imbalances as capital flowed east and people flowed west. The eastern enlargement doubled intra-EU labour mobility as young people travelled west for jobs and better economic prospects. This generated a debate in Europe's richer states about 'welfare tourism' and the mythical 'Polish plumber', and certainly contributed to the outcome of the 2016 Brexit referendum. Because the workers from east-central Europe were young and well qualified, they contributed signifi-cantly to the economies of the old member states but there was an enormous loss of human capital in their home states. Although remittances were sizeable and welcome, the outflow led to demographic decline and a brain drain in many countries (Andor 2019: 22). The fruits of economic convergence were not evenly distributed as investment flowed into the large urban areas. The absence of social convergence fed into a politics of backsliding with the arrival of an authoritarian turn in Hungary and Poland. This then led to demands from other member states for stronger conditionality to be attached to the structural funds. Andor, a former social affairs commissioner, argued in 2019 that 'The EU has to pay attention to the East–West imbalances and consider new strategies for cohesion and conver-gence' (Andor 2019: 23). The arrival of authoritarians in power in a number of countries, particularly Hungary and Poland, led to calls for enhanced 'rule of law' conditionality in EU budgetary flows to the east. Imbalances between east and west were overtaken during the financial crisis by the urgency of acute imbalances within the Eurozone.

EMU

While the aim of a single currency goes back to the early years of the EU, and the 1970 Werner Plan provided the first outline of how it might be achieved, it was not until the late 1980s that the creation of a single currency became a serious prospect. Consensus on the single market project together with treaty change opened up a window of opportunity to place EMU on the agenda. The argument 'One Market: One Money' proved compelling, and the creation of a Committee on EMU, chaired by Jacques Delors, provided a blueprint. The Delors Report was clear that in order to prepare for a single currency: 'Greater convergence of economic performance is needed' (EU 1989: 11). The report pointed to divergences of budgetary positions and external imbalances that would need to converge. It argued that: 'A particular role would have to be assigned to common policies aimed at developing a more balanced economic structure throughout the Community. This would help to prevent the emergence or aggravation of regional and sectoral imbalances which could threaten the viability of an economic and monetary union' (EU 1989: 12). In its analysis of the policies that would be needed for the 'E' in EMU, the report identified the need for 'common policies aimed at structural change and regional development' (EU 1989: 16). Prophetically, the report suggested that 'If sufficient consideration were not given to regional imbalances, the economic union would be faced with grave economic and political risks' (EU 1989: 18). In the policy and academic debate leading up to the (Maastricht) Treaty on European Union (TEU), and in the period before the actual launch of the single currency, considerable attention was given to issues such as 'optimal currency areas' and the prospect of asymmetric shocks in the new currency zone. During the preparatory stage leading up to the single currency, there was considerable debate and disagreement among economists about the Maastricht EMU design. It was argued that the Maastricht design did not include instruments to deal with asymmetric shocks and that the absence of such instruments left the single currency vulnerable (Belke and Gros 1998). The prospect of asymmetric shocks was somewhat dependent on the degree of heterogeneity within the currency area. In other words, much depended on the actual membership of the Eurozone. The importance of nominal convergence was established in the TEU, which made provision for a set of criteria that EU states had to meet before joining the single currency. This was intended to limit the number of countries eligible to join.

During its first decade, the euro appeared to consolidate as a currency and the ECB maintained a low inflation regime. However, vulnerabilities built up that would prove particularly challenging for this young currency without a state. Current-account imbalances emerged and in the absence of exchange-rate risk there was an acceleration of borrowing and lending in the periphery driven by low interest rates. 'The current account imbalances have been accompanied by persistent changes in real exchange rates between member countries of the euro area' (Mackowiak, Mongelli, Noblet, and Smets 2008: 7). Ten years after its establishment, the Eurozone experienced the beginnings of a crisis that would shake it to its foundations and threaten its survival (Feldstein 2008; Bergsten 2012). The Eurozone crisis began in Greece when, following an election in autumn 2009, the new government announced that it had found a major and unsustainable fiscal gap; it acknowledged that the deficit was 12.7 per cent and not 6.7 per cent as previously calculated. The Eurozone lacked the policy instruments and the political will to address the Greek crisis until May 2010, when contagion to other member states emerged as a real threat. Financial markets identified in turn a number of troubled Eurozone countries. Following a bailout of Greece in May 2010, three other countries—Ireland (November 2010), Portugal (2011), and Cyprus (2012)—became 'programme' countries: that is, subject to bailout and Troika governance. Spain avoided a full bailout but needed financial assistance for its financial system. Italy, a country that was identified as too big to bail and too big to fail, was under sustained market pressure but never lost market access. The vulnerable countries, known by various acronyms, notably the GIIPS (Greece, Ireland/Italy, Portugal, and Spain), were either peripheral or semi-peripheral states. There was a pronounced creditor–debtor cleavage in the Eurozone which translated into a north–south divide. Divergence rather than convergence was to the fore during the crisis.

The Eurozone responded to the crisis by muddling through, rescuing the vulnerable, imposing strict conditionality, and establishing new rules of fiscal governance. The solutions were driven by the creditor states, particularly the most powerful Eurozone country, Germany. The economic, social, and political costs of adjustment were borne by the debtor states. As the Eurozone struggled to bring the crisis under control, a debate opened up concerning the future architecture of the Eurozone. There was recognition that the currency was not stable and would require further integration in the medium term. The challenge of divergence was back on the agenda. An agenda-setting process was launched at the EU level by the European Council when it requested the supranational presidents, chaired by President Juncker of the European Commission, to draw up a roadmap for *Completing Europe's Economic and Monetary Union*. The report, known as the Five Presidents' Report because it involved the presidents (Juncker, Tusk, Dijsselbloem, Draghi, and Schulz) of the Union's supranational institutions, was published in June 2015. The report was an exercise in policy framing and establishing a road map for the Eurozone. Both the leaders of the supranational institutions and the European Council were aware that the Eurozone as then constructed was an unstable hybrid and would need further policy development. They were deeply divided on what needed to be done and who should bear the public finance costs.

The stronger-performing states, notably Germany and the other creditor countries, were unwilling to engage in positive solidarity, understood here as transfers before the countries have addressed their structural problems. The report acknowledged the challenge of divergence in the following terms: 'There is now significant divergence across the euro area. Today's divergence creates fragility for the whole Union. We must correct this divergence and embark on a new convergence process' (EU 2015c: 4). Moreover, it defined convergence as 'convergence between member states towards the highest levels of prosperity and convergence within European societies, to nurture our unique European model' (EU 2015c: 7). The challenge, of course, is not to commit to convergence but to create policies that foster and deliver it. The report crucially distinguished between the short and medium term. The prescription for the short term was to embed a convergence process within the European Semester, the process of economic governance designed to track, monitor, and facilitate budgetary and economic reform within the member states. Resilient economic structures were to be built around competitiveness authorities, the Macroeconomic Imbalance Procedure (IMP), a focus on employment and social performance, and a stronger coordination of economic policy (EU 2015c: 7). Put simply, the focus continued to centre on convergence through rules-based economic governance. These processes were designed to trigger structural reform within the member states; this is a convergence of policy but may not lead to convergence in performance. The arrival of Covid-19 in spring 2020, less than 10 years after the global financial crisis, forced the EU to contemplate a step change in its policy toolkit.

Covid-19

In early 2020, Covid-19 arrived in Europe as a global pandemic. First Italy and then Spain were at the epicentre of the crisis before it spread to other countries, and both suffered significant economic and social disruption when their economies were frozen. As this was a public health crisis, primary responsibility rested with the member states, but the EU collectively addressed the crisis with a series of ad hoc responses. During the trauma of Covid-19, Italian society perceived a lack of European solidarity. In early March 2020, when Italy asked for assistance from the other member states, they failed to respond as they were preoccupied with the demands of their own health systems. This had a devastating impact on attitudes towards the EU in Italy with a collapse in support for membership. It became clear that Covid-19 would affect some parts of Europe more than others, and that those states particularly in southern Europe would be less able to offset the costs or support their businesses. As the continent struggled to respond, key leaders responded urgently and began to address the crisis with a speed that was not evident in the early years of the Eurozone crisis. In April, the Eurogroup agreed a €540 billion response for workers, businesses, and the most seriously affected member states, but more was needed. Nine heads of state and government wrote to their counterparts supporting the creation of Coronabonds, a joint European response. Germany continued to oppose this policy instrument strongly, but together with France supported the creation of a recovery fund. A European Council meeting on 23 April represented a significant breakthrough.

The Commission was asked to produce a proposal for a recovery instrument based on the Multiannual Financial Framework 2021–7 (MFF), the EU's budgetary framework. The outcome of the European Council was striking. It marked a decisive Franco-German input in EU policy making for the first time for many years and a pronounced shift in German policy. The member states did not opt for a Eurozone-only response but relied on the EU27's budgetary framework and entrusted the Commission to come up with the scoping proposal.

By 27 May, the Commission was ready with its package; boldly named *Next Generation EU*, it consisted of a new instrument to support Europe's recovery from Covid-19 and a revamped MFF (European Commission 2020). The proposal represented the most significant step change in EU budgetary politics since the mid-1980s, when President Delors unveiled the first Multiannual Financial Framework, pledging a doubling of funds for the poorer regions. It broke a number of taboos by proposing the lifting of the 'own resources' ceiling to 2 per cent of gross national income on a temporary basis, and using this to enable the Commission to borrow on the financial markets and to channel additional resources to the worst-hit member states and sectors. The European Council had the first opportunity to discuss the Commission proposals at a video meeting on 19 June, with a further meeting in mid-July. The negotiations were marked by both momentum and urgency, given the economic and social fallout of Covid-19. That said, there was much that divided the member states, notably the size of the recovery fund, its distribution across member states and sectors, and the balance between grants and loans. A group of states known as the 'frugal four' (the Netherlands, Austria, Sweden, and Denmark) accepted that the EU had to have a collective response to Covid-19 but remained unconvinced by the proposed size and design of the response. At a lengthy European Council in July 2020, agreement was reached on an ambitious recovery effort that enabled the Commission to borrow on behalf of the Union on the capital markets (European Council 2020). Just over ten years since the beginning of the Eurozone crisis, the EU appeared to have learned some of the lessons of that crisis and was prepared to respond to Covid-19 with greater speed and breaking some taboos.

Conclusions

Core–periphery dynamics have mattered enormously in the evolution of the European Union, which in a halting but defining manner has created policy instruments designed to address economic divergence. The underlying political bargain is that EU cohesion policy is designed to foster place prosperity and is committed to assisting peripheral countries and regions to catch up. The accession of poorer states has been a major driver in this development. In turn, the Union's northern, southern, and eastern peripheries have exerted pressure for redistribution in the Union. The big bang enlargement in the 2000s exposed a tension between economic and social convergence. The eastern half of the continent began to converge economically but lost a significant proportion of its most educated workers to richer Europe. In the evolution of EU cohesion policy, enlargement had to be linked to a step change in market integration and treaty change. The single market in the mid-1980s was a major breakthrough for cohesion policy for two reasons. First, it was convincingly argued that the EU's periphery might not benefit sufficiently from market integration and needed assistance. Second, the Single European Act contained a new cohesion chapter which facilitated the Delors Commission's efforts to increase budgetary flows to the periphery. By the mid-1980s the link between market integration and core–periphery dynamics was established in the EU's budget and primary law. Moreover, every major treaty change, apart from EMU, has involved a redistributive bargain, a feature of the Union from the outset.

The relationship between the single currency and core–periphery relations has been somewhat different. From the outset, there was a heated debate concerning the prospect of economic divergence within the Eurozone. No policy instruments were established to help countries deal with asymmetric shocks or poor economic performance. Unlike market integration, which has been a component of EU membership since accession, membership of the single currency was intended to be more limited and achievable only when countries were strong or flexible enough to cope with the loss of the Exchange Rate Mechanism. It was not intended that the Eurozone would have to address core–periphery dynamics as they have emerged. The convergence criteria, the no-bailout clause, and the Growth and Stability Pact were designed to avoid the moral hazard of weak domestic management but failed or were breached under pressure. In hindsight, some countries joined the single currency without careful consideration of the vulnerabilities it would create. The first decade of the single currency was characterized by convergence but this disguised the serious build-up of current-account imbalances. These led to severe problems for euro states in the south and for Ireland when the financial crisis morphed into a Eurozone crisis. Public and private debt in these countries had built up due to the availability of cheap money and low interest rates. The debt became unsustainable when the markets responded and there was a sudden stop in lending from the core to the periphery, thereby forcing the ECB to step in to meet the liquidity crisis and forcing the troubled countries into programmes.

The depth of divergence poses long-term challenges to the governance of the euro. To date the emphasis has been on achieving convergence by structural reform and putting pressure on the poorly performing economies. The creation of a fiscal capacity for the Eurozone has been mooted but does not yet appear to have sufficient political traction. The urgency of Covid-19 and its potential to exacerbate divergence in the Eurozone and the wider EU has created an impetus that was lacking in the financial crisis. Germany has agreed to enabling the Commission to borrow on the financial markets to assist the worst-hit countries. This breaks a deeply rooted taboo while not representing an acceptance of a Transfer Union. Although the Covid-19 Recovery Instrument is time-bound, its legacy for EU budgetary politics may outlive the pandemic. Tensions arising from core–periphery dynamics in the EU will nevertheless persist for decades to come.

References

Andor, László (2019). 'Fifteen Years of Convergence: East–West Imbalance and What the EU Should Do about It.' *Intereconomics* 54, Forum Article: 18–23.

Barry F. (2003). 'Economic Integration and Convergence Processes in the EU Cohesion Countries', *Journal of Common Market Studies*, 41(5): 897–921.

Belke, Ansgar and Daniel Gros (1998). 'Asymmetric Shocks and EMU: Is There a Need for a Stability Fund?' *Intereconomics* 33(6): 274–88.

Bergsten, C. Fred (2012). 'Why the Euro Will Survive: Completing the Continent Half-Built House.' *Foreign Affairs* 91(5): 16–22.

Bulmer, Simon (2009). 'Politics in Time Meets the Politics of Time: Historical Institutionalism and the EU Timescape.' *Journal of European Public Policy* 16(2): 307–24.

Cuaresma, Jesus Crespo, Doris Ritzberger-Grunwald, and A. M. Silgoner (2011). 'Growth, Convergence and EU Membership.' *Applied Economics* 40(5): 643–56.

Deutsch, Karl Wolfgang (1957). *Political Community and the North Atlantic Area.* Princeton, NJ: Princeton University Press.

Eichengreen, Barry (2019). 'Convergence and Divergence in the EU: Lessons from Italy.' *Intereconomics* 54(1): 31–4.

European Commission (2020). 'Next Generation EU: EU Long-term Budget 2021–2027.' https://ec.europa.eu/info/strategy/eu-budget/eu-long-term-budget/2021–2027_en.

European Council (2020). 'European Council Conclusions', 17–21 July. https://www.consilium.europa.eu/media/45109/210720-euco-final-conclusions-en.pdf.

European Union (1970). *Werner Report on Economic and Monetary Union.* Brussels. http://aei.pitt.edu/1002/1/monetary_werner_final.pdf.

European Union (1972). 'Statement from the European Summit', Paris, 19–21 October. http://www.cvce.eu/content/publication/1999/1/1/b1dd3d57–5f31–4796–85c3-cfd2210d6901/publishable_en.pdf.

European Union (1975). 'Regulation (EEC) No. 724/75 of the Council of 18 March 1975 establishing a European Regional Development Fund', OJ L 73, 21.3.1975, pp. 1–7. Brussels. http://eur-lex.europa.eu/legal-content/EN/TXT/?uri=CELEX:31975R0724.

European Union (1985). *The Regions of Europe: Second Periodic Report on the Social and Economic Situation of the Regions of the Community.* Brussels.

European Union (1989). *Report on Economic and Monetary Union in the European Community* (Delors Report), presented 17 April. Brussels. http://aei.pitt.edu/1007/1/monetary_delors.pdf.

European Union (2002). *First Progress Report on Economic and Social Cohesion, COM (2002) 46 Final*. Brussels. http://eur-lex.europa.eu/legal-content/EN/TXT/?uri=URISERV:g24004.

European Union (2015). *Completing Europe's Economic and Monetary Union*. Brussels. https://wayback.archiveit.org/12090/20191231140925/https://ec.europa.eu/commission/sites/beta-political/files/5-presidents-report_en.pdf.

Feldstein, Martin (2008). 'Will the Euro Survive the Current Crisis?' *Project Syndicate* 24, November. https://www.project-syndicate.org/commentary/will-the-euro-survive-the-current-crisis?barrier=accesspaylog.

Hooghe, Liesbet, and Michael Keating (1994). 'The Politics of European Union Regional Policy.' *Journal of European Public Policy* 1(3): 367–93.

Jones E. (2003). *The European Miracle*. 3rd edition. Cambridge: Cambridge University Press.

Lipset, Seymour Martin, and Stein Rokkan (1967). *Party Systems and Voter Alignments: Cross-national Perspectives*. Toronto: The Free Press.

Mackowiak, Bartosz, Francesco Paolo Mongelli, Gilles Noblet, and Frank Smets (2008). 'Introduction'. In Bartosz Mackowiak, Francesco Paolo Mongelli, Gilles Noblet, and Frank Smets (eds.), *The Euro at Ten: Lessons and Challenges*. Frankfurt: European Central Bank: 6–13.

Majone, José M., Brigid Laffan, and Christian Schweiger (eds.) (2016). *Core–Periphery Relations in the European Union: Power and Conflict in a Dualist Political Economy*. London: Routledge.

Padoa-Schioppa, Tommaso (1987). *Efficiency, Stability and Equity: A Strategy for the Evolution of the Economic System of the European Community*. Oxford: Oxford University Press.

Pierson, Paul (1996). 'The Path to European Integration: A Historical Institutionalist Analysis.' *Comparative Political Studies* 29(2): 123–63.

Pounds, N. J. G., and S. Simons Ball (1964). 'Core-Areas and the Development of the European States System.' *Annals of the Association of American Geographers* 54(1): 24–40.

Rokkan, Stein, and Derek W. Urwin (1983). *Economy, Territory, Identity: Politics of West European Peripheries*. London: Sage.

Sapir, André, Philippe Aghion, Giuseppe Bertola, Martin Hellwig, Jean Pisani-Ferry, Dariusz Rosato, Jose Viñals, Helen Wallace, Marco Buti, Mario Nava, and Peter Smith (2004). *An Agenda for a Growing Europe* (Sapir Report). Oxford: Oxford University Press.

Tang, Kwong-Leung (2000). *Social Welfare Development in East Asia*, New York, NY: Palgrave.

Thelen, Kathleen (1999). 'Historical Institutionalism in Comparative Politics.' *Annual Review of Political Science* 2(1): 369–404.

Tsoukalis, Loukas (2006). 'The JCMS Lecture: Managing Diversity and Change in the European Union', *Journal of Common Market Studies* 44(1): 1–15.

Tsoukalis, Loukas (2016). *In Defence of Europe*. Oxford: Oxford University Press.

Young, Alasdair R. (2015). 'The Single Market: From Stagnation to Renewal?' In Helen Wallace, Mark A. Pollack and Alasdair R. Young (eds.). *Policy-Making in the European Union*. Oxford: Oxford University Press: 115–140.

Wallace, William (ed.) (1990). *The Dynamics of European Integration*. New York: Pinter.

10

Integrating through Crises

Revisiting the Eurozone's Reform Conundrum

George Pagoulatos

Introduction

There are at least two things that attract a reader to the writings of Loukas Tsoukalis, from the uninitiated student to the scholar who has had the good fortune of knowing the man, being inspired by his mentorship and honoured by his long-standing friendship, as several of us contributors to this volume have.

The first is the crisp, elegant, captivating prose combined with the sharp pragmatism of his writings. Tsoukalis is not in the business of spewing out theories for the sake of it, then devoting the rest of his work to trying to show why they are true. Instead, his writings are driven by his ambition to *understand* the real-life phenomenon which is the European Union (EU) in all its fascinating complexity, rather than pretending to explain it schematically, let alone pontificating about its future.

The second feature is exactly his trained capacity to raise the big issues and ask the important questions about European integration, from the standpoint of someone who can see the whole elephant and the surrounding jungle, rather than simply being an expert on the trunk or the legs or the tusks, to resort to Puchala's (1971) famous parable.

In his long and distinguished scholarly career Tsoukalis has opened wide explanatory avenues. He has fleshed out with great insight the new European economy built around the single market, without losing track of the national political economies underlying it (Tsoukalis 1991/1993; 1997). He has approached the European Union as a novel multilevel governance and political system (Tsoukalis 2003; Pagoulatos and Tsoukalis 2012). He has not shied away from raising the big normative questions of trade-offs, grand bargains, packages, winners and losers—for example, pointing out the interconnectedness of the single market with structural funds, or seeking to draft the next grand bargain that could drive the EU out of its poly-crisis mess (Tsoukalis 2016).

This chapter discusses the European Economic and Monetary Union (EMU) in light of the Eurozone's recent crises, focusing on lessons learned and the way

George Pagoulatos, *Integrating through Crises: Revisiting the Eurozone's Reform Conundrum* In: *Europe's Transformations: Essays in Honour of Loukas Tsoukalis.* Edited by: Helen Wallace, Nikos Koutsiaras, and George Pagoulatos, Oxford University Press. © OUP 2021. DOI: 10.1093/oso/9780192895820.003.0010

forward. True to Tsoukalis' intellectual tradition, we take a broader, 'holistic' political-economy view: we approach economic policy decisions and outcomes as embedded in institutional and political contexts, and (by the same token) political decisions as being subject to institutional constraints and economic dynamics at the national, EU, and global level.

EMU, Imperfect by Construction

From its inception, monetary integration served a concatenation of objectives. Monetary integration was about defending monetary stability in the face of currency destabilization in a post-Bretton Woods world; shielding Europe from aggressive US administrations weaponizing the dollar, exploiting the 'exorbitant privilege' afforded by a global reserve currency to extricate the USA from large deficits or external indebtedness at the expense of its European trade partners; protecting the common market and the Common Agricultural Policy (CAP) from beggar-thy-neighbour currency depreciation; establishing a framework of macro-economic stability to leverage and maximize the benefits of the single market by eradicating the (intra-euro) exchange-rate risk and transaction costs associated with multiple currencies within a single market; and delivering lower interest rates and borrowing costs, as a pan-European social dividend from monetary stability and anticipated (German) monetary credibility. Crucially, monetary integration was also about orchestrating the big leap towards a political union. But one did not need to have been a federalist to appreciate the functional advantages of monetary integration. From a company that no longer had to change currency when moving goods across borders to a European citizen who could visit all 12 member states of what was then the European Community without losing 40 per cent of their money's value in transaction charges alone, there were visible, tangible advantages for everyone to reap.

Thus, the euro remained shielded behind a mix of technocratic abstruseness and universal for-all-to-see benefits during its first fair-weather decade, up to the crisis. Besides, hardly any political debate about EMU took place at either the pan-European or member state level.

The combined result of powerful imperatives for launching a monetary union and a lack of political will to develop monetary into real economic union was a highly incomplete architecture surrounding the single currency; 'a post-modern construction defying the laws of gravity', as Tsoukalis (2003: 150) would pithily put it. The Eurozone was inherently prone to disequilibria, as a function of having too much integration in monetary and exchange-rate policy, where member states had surrendered crucial instruments, but simultaneously insufficient economic, fiscal, financial, and political integration to compensate for the loss of these instruments.

All that said, EMU had the potential to operate as a positive-sum arrangement for all, if it was followed up by appropriate national policies and Eurozone-wide coordination. For the more advanced, export-oriented economies, the single currency enhanced the advantages of the single market, opening new markets up for their products and services to expand into. But for the southern economies, too, suffering from a tradition of weak economic governance, depreciating currencies, inflation, higher deficits, and higher borrowing costs, EMU offered a welcome disciplining effect. Monetary austerity and the nominal convergence criteria for EMU up to 1999 generated a benign framework of externally induced discipline, which allowed EMU candidates to eradicate high rates of inflation and deficits for the prize of joining the single currency. Inside the euro, lower borrowing costs facilitated fiscal consolidation, but also encouraged borrowing by both the public and private sectors. The euro offered opportunities to cheaply finance extensive productive investment in infrastructure and human capital, and to benefit from the benign environment of macroeconomic stability and growth to implement productivity-enhancing structural reforms. As we know, it did not work out quite like that. The abundance of low-cost finance generated complacency, and inflowing capital in the periphery (debt rather than equity) financed mainly consumption and real estate rather than productive investment, creating financial sector bubbles (as in Ireland, Spain, and Portugal), or government over-borrowing (as in Greece and Portugal). The responsibility lay mainly with national policy makers, but the EU institutions must bear some of the blame for not sounding the requisite alarms.

Thus during the first decade of the single currency, a semblance of convergence (lower deficits, inflation and interest rates; catch-up economic growth in the periphery) concealed the building up of divergences: macroeconomic imbalances, positive inflation differentials (which also resulted from inflationary credit expansion), and declining competitiveness for the peripheral economies. The latter's economic growth was debt-financed, driven by the expansion of consumption and non-tradable sectors in the main: real estate and construction, banking, media, and an array of related services—all of which contributed to the growth of imports.

The growing external indebtedness of the periphery (public or private sector or both) was demonstrated in growing current-account deficits—the inverse of the growing external surpluses of the export-growing core economies—financed through seemingly endless capital inflows. The foreign debt bubble in the Eurozone periphery could not be sustained indefinitely; and it was not. When the 2008 crisis shocked global markets, the risk premium for the peripherals surged, soon rendering the refinancing of their debt impossible to sustain. The crash was a 'sudden stop'. When private-sector creditors in 2010 demanded exorbitant yields to refinance the over-indebted economies of the periphery, a series of official bailouts had to be engineered to avert disorderly sovereign defaults. Being the first to fail, Greece did the EMU and itself a disservice in allowing a false narrative to be constructed. The false narrative maintained that the Eurozone crisis was a function of budgetary recklessness (true in the Greek case), obfuscating the real driver of the crisis: external imbalances, cross-border financial flows, current-account deficits, and the build-up of net foreign debt, rather than strictly public debt (Baldwin and Giavazzi 2015).

A Union Divided

Under the conditionality programmes attached to the official loans extended to the bailout countries, a wide array of austerity measures and structural reforms were imposed. They sought to generate fiscal surpluses, to restore external competitiveness through internal devaluation, and to raise potential growth via productivity-enhancing structural reforms. It did not escape critics that bailouts *cum* conditionality were the alternative to private-sector lenders accepting heavy losses on their peripheral sovereign debt holdings and governments being forced to directly recapitalize their banks. Still, wide-ranging adjustment was largely necessary, and aimed to steer the convergence of the crisis-hit economies with the rest of the Eurozone. However, the steep recession that inevitably ensued amplified divergence instead. The peripherals were left with higher unemployment, a large investment gap, financially fragile sovereign and banking systems, and a legacy of brain drain undercutting their potential to grow. Eurozone fragmentation and a north–south divide emerged during the adjustment period, generating its own toxic politics to match.

Central-eastern European economies (CEEEs) were also affected by the crisis, though they eschewed the north–south political polarization. These economies had implemented their market transition in the early 1990s, at the height of both neoclassical economic orthodoxy and optimism about Europe's transformative power. Ardent market-liberals instinctively averse to state interventionism, which they likened to socialism, and fiscal conservatives with low-tax, low-spending, relatively low-debt liabilities matching their minimalistic welfare state institutions, the CEEEs were natural allies of the German economic stance, given their dependence on German foreign direct investment (FDI) and supply chains. Trade integration, capital inflows, and reliance on externally financed domestic demand also made CEEEs more vulnerable to external shocks; some were hit hard by the 2008–9 financial crisis (Buti and Székely 2019). The Baltic states, in particular, implemented harsh internal devaluation that relied on unprecedented fiscal and nominal wage adjustment to defend their exchange rate to the euro (Purfield and Rosenberg 2010). This adjustment came at a heavy cost in terms of recession, unemployment, and brain drain, but they demonstrated remarkable social resilience in the face of economic hardship. The Eurozone crisis was not as divisive when it came to the CEEEs: those that were part of the Eurozone remained committed to the single currency and politically anchored to the Berlin-led 'creditors' coalition. Hungary's 2008 IMF bailout, whose harsh terms eased nationalist Orbán's rise to power, served as a reminder of conventional conditionality, relying as it did on currency depreciation (as opposed to internal devaluation) for an EU country that remained outside the euro.

The 2010 outbreak of the Eurozone debt crisis made it more difficult to maintain the neutral technocratic cloak of the earlier period of complacency. In the eyes of many, this was no longer a win-win project; no longer about distributing gains, but losses. In the division of labour that emerged, as Tsoukalis (2016: 103ff.) would gloomily observe, borrowers undertook the heavy socioeconomic cost of adjustment and creditors carried the credit risk.

While the official EU rhetoric emphasized the national causes of the Eurozone debt crisis, the crisis itself operated both as the headlamp revealing EMU construction defects and policy errors, and as a potent accelerator of corrective initiatives to address these deficiencies. Yet in the initial two years of the crisis (2010–12), a moralizing 'you break it, you own it' approach produced heavily front-loaded, excessively recessionary, and occasionally unrealistic adjustment programmes. These were justified on the normative premise of national responsibility and the analytical pretext of moral hazard, made possible by the gaping power asymmetry around the Council table between creditor and borrower countries. This was especially true if the latter also happened to be running large primary budget and trade deficits, rendering them even more dependent on external financing for their economic survival.

It was only after the national adjustment programmes were under way, and fiscal consolidation was progressing in tandem with steep recession and mutual negative stereotyping between member states, that the EU began to shift more decisively towards treating the crisis in systemic Eurozone terms, rather than simply as the sum of national failures. A crucial turning point was the 'whatever it takes' moment of European Central Bank (ECB) president Mario Draghi in July 2012—a phrase the European Council or Eurogroup never quite uttered with regard to the prolonged spectre of Grexit without attaching qualifying conditions and footnotes.

Successive waves of policy and institutional innovations sought to improve the functioning, cohesion, and governance of a persistently incomplete economic and monetary union. These included new legislation, such as the two-pack and six-pack; new institutions, such as the European Financial Stability Facility (EFSF) and the European Stability Mechanism (ESM); a new treaty establishing the Fiscal Compact; the launch of a banking union; and the steady deployment of 'unconventional' instruments and schemes by a progressively bolder ECB. The EU institutions sought to provide the direction and momentum for a shift towards a more genuine EMU through successive reports authored by the presidents of EU institutions or by the European Commission; reports that were typically met with a mix of unenthusiastic praise and a preference for inaction by the European Council.

Asymmetries to the Fore

Thus it was that the structural asymmetries of EMU came to the fore during the prolonged crisis that erupted in 2010: a centralized monetary union flanked by a weak, decentralized, incomplete cross-national system of economic coordination; a 'currency without a state'; a monetary regime kept together by imperfect rules and lacking a real hegemon, Berlin being highly reluctant to assume such a role, with the German economy too big and competitive to be like 'the rest', but not large enough to be the obvious hegemon. Keeping the EMU both governed and moving relies heavily on close Franco-German partnership and leadership, a relationship both parties have aspired to for diametrically opposed reasons: Germany to conceal its strength and France to disguise its weakness. Yet this mutually desired symbiosis, too, presupposes a convergence of preferences—and that has not always been the case.

EMU asymmetries had very real implications. When the ECB sought to apply a monetary policy appropriate for the Eurozone, that policy ended up being too lax for the periphery (up until the debt crisis), then not lax enough despite loosening (during the crisis), given a broken monetary transmission mechanism (Brunnermeier et al. 2016). Eventually, following the post-2015 asset purchase programmes and zero-to-negative interest rates, the policy was just right for the periphery but the cause of grievances and a political backlash in Germany, an economy of savers whose real returns became negative. Clearly, divergent fiscal and incomes policies coupled with non-synchronized business cycles—the lack of either cyclical or real economic convergence—underlay this key problem. Could nominal convergence under a shared currency generate cyclical or real economic convergence? Certainly not under the uncoordinated policy regime of the first complacent euro decade, when current-account deficits and external imbalances were officially viewed as immaterial. The probability would certainly have grown following the reforms of the 2010s, had it not been undermined by the procyclical policy mix in the crisis economies, the highly deficient application of the macroeconomic imbalances procedure by surplus economies not spending enough, and the still missing instruments to address asymmetric shocks.

This is not a theoretical difference. As the ECB is prohibited from directly facilitating the financing of sovereign debt, the credit risk for euro member states becomes higher compared to states controlling their own currency, as if the debt is denominated in a foreign currency (De Grauwe 2011). This is one more institutional feature that is appropriate for fair-weather conditions, but which crucially undermines the Eurozone's capacity to react effectively to crises.

Indeed, the Eurozone was glaringly ill-equipped to address the procyclicality[1] that resulted from its asymmetries during the first decade, and it only made small and insufficient steps in that direction during the crisis. Up until the crisis, higher inflation rates in the peripheral economies also meant a lower real interest rate, encouraging a further expansion of credit demand, more inflation, and an appreciation of the real effective exchange rate eroding competitiveness. The opposite effects took place in the export-led creditor economies of the Eurozone core, widening intra-EMU divergences (higher real interest rates, more saving, lower inflation, competitiveness-boosting real exchange-rate depreciation). Post-2010 reforms (including the European Semester)[2] introduced stronger instruments of economic policy coordination; the ECB, especially after 2012, has also tried to facilitate convergence, within the limits of its mandate. However, and even though the fiscal stability framework has become more flexible, EMU continues to lack sufficient countercyclical instruments. This is even more true when it comes to addressing asymmetric shocks. A true fiscal stabilization function and fiscal capacity (EU Five Presidents 2015; European Commission 2017; Buti and Carno 2018), by way of a European Investment Stabilization Function (European Commission 2018) or a European Unemployment (Re)Insurance Scheme (European Commission 2017), would be a vital addition to the Eurozone policy infrastructure. However, despite valiant efforts by the Commission and advocacy by a wide range of experts and policy makers, we are not yet there.

What we learned from the tumultuous Eurozone experience after 2010 was that a crisis brings EMU asymmetries and deficiencies to the fore, accelerating hitherto politically intractable reforms, but also raising their socio-economic cost. Vulnerability in the face of a debt crisis translates into a rise not just in default risk, but in euro-exit risk—in euro-plumbing jargon, 'currency redenomination risk', an obvious challenge to the 'constitutionally' assumed irrevocability of the single currency. This leads to financial fragmentation (or the breakdown of monetary transmission) cancelling the ECB's effort to lift the boats in the periphery by opening the monetary floodgates. It raises the cost of capital for public and private sectors in the periphery, locking them into a recessionary cycle of seeking to make up for the rising cost of capital by repressing wages more and more (Pagoulatos 2020). It drives away savers, investors, and high-skilled mobile human capital. It further undermines national banking systems, subjecting them to liquidity drain. It exacerbates the bank–sovereign doom loop, spreading financial contagion from sovereign to banks and back to the sovereign.

---

[1] 'Procyclicality' refers to economic policies that magnify the impact of the business cycle, i.e. they further deepen a recession or overheat an economy that is already in an upswing. In contrast, countercyclical policies cool the economy down when it is in an upswing and stimulate the economy when it is in a downturn.

[2] The European Semester is a cycle of economic and fiscal policy coordination within the European Union, as part of the EU's economic governance framework.

Moreover, the Eurozone crisis also demonstrated that the markets are not to be relied upon for stability, but rather quite the opposite. Before the 2008 global financial crash, the markets were oblivious to underlying macroeconomic vulnerabilities and treated all Eurozone economies as a single area; the spread between the Greek 10-year bond and the German bund rarely exceeded 10–20 basis points. From 2010, true to their procyclical behaviour, markets generated the typical self-fulfilling prophecy of a default, locking the crisis economies into self-feeding vicious cycles of perpetuated vulnerability, demonstrating that even the healthiest enterprises cannot escape the risk-rating of their sovereign. In other words, capital flew from core to peripheral economies during the boom, fuelling inflation, and back to safety after the sudden stop of 2010, amplifying deflation and recession.

Crisis Legacies and the Need for Risk Sharing

All this demonstrated the need for a Eurozone countercyclical instrument, but the gap remained unfilled. It also corroborated the wisdom of establishing the European Stability Mechanism as an institutional lender of last resort for the sovereign and source of recapitalization for the banks when market access is impossible, providing long-maturity, low-cost lending and spreading risk cross-temporally into the future to buy time for fiscal consolidation and national reforms. An open issue in this case is the specifics of debt restructuring or reprofiling as a precondition for ESM intervention (as was agreed in December 2018), so that private-sector creditors participate in the bailout cost. On the one hand, collective action clauses should facilitate restructuring. On the other hand, easier restructuring would raise the default risk premium and consequently market financing costs for highly indebted sovereigns. No wonder Italy has resisted the introduction of a regulatory cap on bank holdings of sovereign debt, an otherwise desirable policy of promoting Eurozone-wide financial risk sharing and the reduction of sovereign–bank contagion.

The Eurozone debt crisis demonstrated that prolonged downturns can lead to persisting fragility, as hysteresis effects take over. Unemployment of well over 20 per cent in Spain and Greece led a large part of their labour force to leave the country or face declining living standards and the erosion of human capital which prolonged unemployment brings. The austerity programmes in the 2010s left productive firms struggling with higher taxes, higher capital costs, declining investment, and a shrinking pool of qualified employees. All these factors jointly suppressed potential economic growth.

If labour mobility becomes the main unemployment adjustment mechanism in the Eurozone, this implies the movement of the higher-skilled part of the labour force from the poorer peripheral to wealthier core economies, depriving the former of precious human capital vital for their future economic growth. This regressive redistribution of resources is compounded by capital movements following the same direction, from south to north.

Mobilizing risk-sharing mechanisms at the EU level can prevent the south from sliding into a new round of growing divergence (Pisani-Ferry 2013; Bénassy-Quéré et al. 2018). There are three main channels through which this can be done. The first is the monetary channel. The European Central Bank is prohibited from entering the primary market of public debt, but purchased large quantities of sovereign debt, under the PSPP and (later) PEPP,[3] slightly diverging from the capital key, and justifying this on the basis of the proper transmission of its monetary policy. The ECB could even accept to roll over maturing debt. However, the ECB initiatives have made it vulnerable to constant legal challenges and conservative political recriminations, with President Draghi a favourite villain for German right-wing tabloids. The German Federal Constitutional Court, in May 2020, put a lid on further ECB initiatives.[4]

The second risk-sharing channel is the financial. Completing the third pillar of the banking union, with a European joint deposit insurance scheme, would ease the concerns of depositors in the periphery, thus reversing a tendency to flee to safety. Reducing the exposures of banks to their sovereigns would also undercut the vicious sovereign–bank doom loop. However, transition to a truly single capital market also takes time and cannot deal with the urgent challenges of the Covid-19 legacies (more on which anon).

What is left is the fiscal channel. Common debt issuance to finance a fiscal investment stimulus provided by way of grants (not loans) to the economies in need is an important demonstration of risk sharing through the fiscal channel. This was the joint Merkel–Macron proposal of May 2020, at the outbreak of the pandemic crisis, which opened the way to the European Commission's 'Next Generation EU' proposal and the European Council's historical decision of July 2020, as outlined below.

The Pandemic as Reform Accelerator: Getting It (Almost) Right the Second Time Round

Many of the pathologies of the Eurozone debt crisis were also present in the Covid-19 crisis, necessitating a response more rapid and far bolder in firepower and scope.

---

[3] PSPP: Public Sector Purchase Programme; PEPP: Pandemic Emergency Purchase Programme.
[4] The German court ordered the Bundesbank to no longer participate in purchases under the PSPP, and to wind down all purchases made in the past in an orderly way, insofar as the ECB had not demonstrated the proportionality of the PSPP.

The Covid-19 crisis revived the north–south divide, this time putting France solidly on the side of the Mediterranean bloc. During the 2010s, southern economies made an arduous effort to catch up. They turned budget shortfalls into surpluses and eradicated current-account deficits by increasing exports, applying recessionary internal devaluation, and implementing reforms. Italy eschewed a bailout and externally imposed reforms, but delivered sustained primary budget surpluses, struggling with a legacy debt/GDP ratio which had grown not because of fiscal recklessness, but due to a two-decade stagnation. Southern adjustment was not made easier by the constantly growing current-account surpluses of the 'north'. During the 2010s, the current-account surpluses of Germany and the Netherlands in a three-year average consistently exceeded the threshold of 6 per cent of GDP set in the Macroeconomic Imbalance Procedure (MIP) (8 per cent and 9.9 per cent respectively in 2020) (European Parliament 2020). In other words, during the previous decade, the Eurozone south struggled to converge with a north that was further diverging.

Enter Covid-19. Italy, Spain, Portugal, and Greece, weakened after prolonged economic adjustment, found themselves with very limited fiscal space, unable to pump enough money into their economies as their north European partners could. Southern European governments were faced with a painful predicament. They needed to stimulate their economies out of the deepest global recession since the 1930s and invest in necessary human, health, digital, and green infrastructure. However, any additional fiscal stimulus (seeking to rescue crisis-hit companies and jobs) threatened to leave the Mediterranean economies with a public debt overhang the markets would deem unsustainable, threatening them with the familiar vicious cycle of higher borrowing costs, fiscal austerity, stagnation, fiscal slippage, further debt deterioration, and so on. Very low average Eurozone inflation (in the vicinity of 1 per cent) meant that southern economies continued to be pressured to restore competitiveness through wage deflation, while also being subject to debt deflation, with their debt burden—public and private—growing as a proportion of GDP.

Southern European economies were bound to emerge from Covid-19 with even higher unemployment and even weaker banks, as a new generation of non-performing exposures (NPE) were added to the already high NPE stock. Their businesses could not be sufficiently supported by their sovereigns, whereas northern companies could resort to their own governments' deeper pockets. By the summer of 2020, about half the total state aid approved by the European Commission was granted to German companies—twice the country's share in the EU economy. This, too, was further widening the north–south gap and undermining that most fundamental EU project, the single market.

Such considerations necessitated the historically unprecedented fiscal response provided by the European Council on 21 July 2020 in its remarkable shift to accepting the European Union jointly borrowing funds of up to €750 billion over six years, on top of the €1.074 billion MFF (Multiannual Financial Framework: the EU's seven-year budget, 2021–7). For the first time, the European Commission, on behalf of the EU, would be issuing debt of such magnitude, mainly to finance grants (€390bn) as well as loans directed primarily at member states in the greatest need in terms of unemployment, investment gap, and recession. The EU raised the own-resources ceiling by a buffer of 0.6 per cent of gross national income to repay the borrowed money, envisaging new EU taxes on *inter alia* plastics, carbon emissions, and digital companies.

A combination of factors underlay this consequential EU demonstration of fiscal readiness and European solidarity: a symmetric 'human catastrophe' carrying an asymmetric impact on EU member states, auguring an even harder day-after for those in a state of greater weakness, rendering moral hazard reservations far less convincing; lessons learned from the previous debt crisis, when the EU did too little too late, its popularity collapsing in the Eurozone south; the spectre of nationalist-populist forces on the rise again in Italy, after an initial failure on the part of the EU to demonstrate sufficient solidarity with its large southern founding member when it was savaged by the pandemic.

Thus, significant reputational damage lay ahead for the Merkel government and Germany if, for a second time since 2010, it were to be perceived as leaving the Eurozone south behind. The damage had already begun following the May 2020 ruling of the German Federal Constitutional Court which appeared to undermine the ECB, the only institution standing between the pandemic and a new full-scale Eurozone financial crisis. After Karlsruhe, Berlin could no longer rely on Frankfurt alone to do the job.

An important factor was Germany's belated graduation to a geopolitical mind-set: assuming a newly found burden of responsibility for defending the EU's position and credibility in the world, deciding not to allow Europe to slide into irrelevance and failure in the new, zero-sum Hobbesian world order created by Trump's bullying and China's over-expansion. In that, the evolution of German policy followed (or preceded, depending on the preferred standpoint) the evolution of the European Commission, from Barroso's technocratic/bureaucratic approach through Juncker's 'political' Commission, to the potentially 'geopolitical' Commission under Ursula von der Leyen.

Domestic conditions were favourable, too. Chancellor Merkel's legacy considerations, and her ever stronger political capital following an efficient handling of the pandemic, allowed her to co-sign the bold Franco-German initiative that opened the way for the Commission to propose the recovery fund. This was a remarkable policy shift from the first crisis to the second, as the German government changed both its mind and its bedfellows, siding this time with the southern economies and against the 'frugal four' (or five). Led by a Rutte government in the Netherlands punching well above its country's weight, the 'frugals' had rallied against increasing the EU budget; they were what remained of the previous neo-

Hanseatic League, comprising a group of countries that made no secret of their intention to block the bold Eurozone reform initiatives promoted by President Macron. Much of the credit for the German shift goes to the French president, who had engaged his German counterpart early on with an ambitious agenda of EMU deepening. Merkel's shift was reluctant in the beginning, the jointly drafted Meseberg declaration of 2018 falling short of the original ambition. Franco-German proposals were further watered down in the European Council of December 2018, which established something resembling a Eurozone budget (Budgetary Instrument for Convergence and Competitiveness: BICC) but took care to deprive it of any substantial resources as well as of any claim to a stabilization function, as Macron (and the European Commission) had originally recommended.

So while very little was happening on the EMU reform front, Covid-19 restored the importance of fiscal policy and a joint European fiscal response in the face of a recessionary shock. Eurozone-wide fiscal policies during the post-2010 crisis had been heavily procyclical in the periphery and mildly procyclical in the core economies, which (at least until the mid-2010s) eschewed more expansionary fiscal and incomes policies, even though their external surpluses were growing and they had ample fiscal space. In the 2020 pandemic, it was not just that national fiscal policies assumed the appropriate countercyclical stance; the escape clause of the Stability and Growth Pact was also activated, and the consensus quickly converged on accepting that a joint EU-wide fiscal stimulus was necessary, especially in support of those economies with insufficient fiscal space. The ECB was prompt to react to the Covid-19 economic shock with a massive expansion of its balance sheet and bond-buying programme; but this time round it was not left alone.

With the momentous European Council decision of July 2020 to authorize the European Commission to borrow funds in the capital markets on behalf of the EU, the European Union realized another important aspiration, that of launching a euro 'safe asset', thus bolstering the euro's global position as a parallel reserve currency. This is what European monetary unification had sought to achieve *inter alia* back in the 1970s: a strengthening of Europe's global monetary and financial standing that would allow it to defend its interests in the world financial system, rely on a larger, deeper, and more liquid euro-denominated money and capital market to finance European investment and other priorities, widen the pool of euro-denominated AAA[5] 'safe assets' for European lenders and institutional investors to hold in their portfolios, and shield itself from the weaponization of the dollar by aggressive US presidents like Trump.

---

[5] AAA: the highest possible credit rating.

Conclusion: Deepening through Crises

From its inception, the Economic and Monetary Union has been the brainchild of contrasting parental personalities. Integrationist European ambition joined disparate national pursuits to create an imperfect EMU architecture, though this has proved amenable to substantial correction, primarily through crises. In the euro's first complacent decade, under the beguiling semblance of macroeconomic convergence, EMU asymmetries and flawed policies (national and European) generated divergence. When the global financial shock hit a Eurozone periphery that was more exposed to external indebtedness, national adjustment was steep and recessionary, supported by significant but insufficient Eurozone-level reforms. These were adopted by an EU that was consistently behind the curve, opting for incremental crisis management, doing less than needed, and paying a higher price in terms of fragmentation. The political technology of European reforms relied extensively on brinkmanship, present and imminent danger providing both the momentum and the legitimizing discourse national leaders needed to overcome the resistance of national parliaments and public opinion and concede to the formerly inconceivable in order to prevent the otherwise inevitable. The Eurozone crisis bequeathed a contradictory legacy of both raising the visibility of the need to reform and raising the bar of political difficulty in bringing it about, having poisoned the common pool of mutual trust between (heartless) 'creditor' and (reckless) 'borrower' countries.

'Next Generation EU' was still not the Hamiltonian moment for Europe that many rushed to celebrate: there was no mutualization of existing debt, and it was not strictly speaking a Eurobond. It represented a one-off non-permanent arrangement, though consequential nonetheless, even if at the time of writing the precise sources of the EU tax revenue through which EU bondholders are to be repaid remain unclear. Intra-EU divisions persist, especially in the Eurozone. The implementation of the recovery package over the post-Covid-19 period carries the risk of pitting recipient countries against the scrutiny of 'net contributors'. Some of these 'frugals' are becoming increasingly inimical to further integration and what they see (with fear, not hope) as signs of creeping 'federalization'. In that respect, the aspirations of those who seek to turn the crisis into an accelerator for closer EMU integration are simultaneously the worst dystopia of those who are keen to repatriate national competences, as is the case with taxation, rather than surrender more of them.

That said, the joint fiscal reaction to the Covid-19 crisis demonstrated that, even in this crisis-responsive mode of reform, the European Union maintains an indomitable survival instinct, drawing on the formidable political capital invested in its creation and preservation. It is also fair to note that the July 2020 decision would have been far less likely if the UK had still been sitting at the European

Council table, proving that even the worst historical accidents can come with a silver lining.

The Eurozone's reform conundrum has been of the type famously described by Jean-Claude Juncker, when still a Eurogroup president (2007): 'We all know what to do, but we don't know how to get re-elected once we have done it.' The 'Juncker curse' summarizes the difficulty national governments and heads of state face in agreeing with hard EU-level decisions and reforms that promote the greater collective good of the European Union but are unpopular at home. But this is not just a problem of executive leaders reluctant to face their parliaments and public opinion at home—that would make it relatively easy. It is about the disjunction between EU-level policies being European, while European politics are (before anything else) national—a distinction that has not gone unnoticed by Tsoukalis. And it becomes an intractable challenge if the domestic unpopularity of European-level reform is a matter not just of reluctant reformers, but of 'object-ively' divergent national preferences and national interests. National leadership by Chancellor Merkel was able to convince German public opinion that time-limited solidarity with the weaker economies during the worst global pandemic so far of the twenty-first century was both the right thing to do and in Germany's best interests. But would that be the case if larger-scale semi-permanent Eurozone-wide transfers were to become necessary? One seriously doubts it.

Add the above to the construction defects and asymmetries, and the surround-ing context has almost been reversed. The EMU architecture was designed to respond to the legacy of 1970s stagflation and the lessons drawn over the 1980s. The evils to be avoided were budget deficits, public debt, and inflation. The goals were budgetary discipline, monetary credibility, and an exclusive central bank commitment to price stability. Draconian fiscal rules and rigid guarantees of central bank independence were enshrined in the EMU's constitution. But how wise is that institutional apparatus in the light of a Eurozone debt crisis that was largely the result of private-sector liabilities and imbalances?

How relevant is this institutional apparatus in a world of high-tech globalized finance, where money creation by the private sector eschews the control of public authorities? How opportune is the 'below but close to 2 per cent' inflation benchmark for the ECB in a global environment of secular stagnation and a post-crisis Eurozone economy where deflation or 'lowflation' seems to have become the new normal? How helpful is the ECB's institutional straitjacket in the post-crisis world, when a public debt overhang (inevitable following consecu-tive recessions and necessitated by the imperative of investing in the future) requires more far-reaching and prolonged monetary accommodation than the strict orthodox separation of monetary from fiscal policy would allow?

There are some ways out of the EMU straitjacket. One is formally deferring the rules, as in the formal suspension of the Stability and Growth Pact during the 2020 pandemic. Another is saying things without doing them: empty rhetoric and decisions that are never implemented (sanctions for exceeding national budgetary limits) or even (foolishly) instituted rules that are left unapplied (the Fiscal Compact). Another strategy is doing things without saying them, which is what many ECB initiatives during the Eurozone's crises have been about. That should also include the historic 'whatever it takes' utterance, a threat so credible that it amounted to action, what philosophical jargon would identify as a 'speech act' or (per J. L. Austin) an 'illocutionary act'. Will the ECB be delegated to the role of permanent saviour of the euro, putting in extra shifts for EMU member states that fail to concede to more fiscal or financial integration and risk sharing? This would not be a wise (let alone courageous) political strategy, and it would only feed into the anti-elite populist backlash.

Progress notwithstanding, the agenda of EMU deepening remains wide open. A fiscal capacity or an actual EU Treasury are still not part of the Eurozone infrastructure; a European Deposit Insurance Scheme remains semi-frozen under permanent formulation; the Eurozone is not ready to see banks disentangle from their sovereigns given the implications on the ability to refinance public debt; a 'safe asset' for the European Union has been introduced in practice, but the EU continues to punch well below its weight in the global monetary system and financial markets; and national economic policies remain insufficiently coordinated. And that is to name just a few of the outstanding headline items on the unfinished Eurozone reform shopping list.

The EMU remains incomplete, even though confidence in its ability to survive has been greatly boosted by its resilience in the face of two severe and consecutive crises; those who rushed to forecast its dissolution have been forced to munch on humble pie. It may be that an imperfect project 'defying the laws of gravity' may in fact be sustained indefinitely, for as long as it possesses the elemental wisdom to constantly adjust and correct. It may also be that the next 'make it or break it' moment is lying in wait for the Eurozone in the form of yet another crisis—one that will once again pit European prudence and sticking together against the national instinct to go it alone. If Europe has learned something over the last decade of two crises, Trump, Brexit, and a global pandemic, it is probably that predictions are a sensible activity apart from when they concern the future.

The optimistic understanding of the European project as the pursuit of 'enlightened self-interest'[6] (Tsoukalis has often subscribed to Mario Monti's aphorism) hangs on a fragile conditional; all that Europe needs to revert to nationalisms is for the lights of enlightened reason to switch off. The writings of Tsoukalis have supplied the optimism, a reason for, and a passionate commitment to defending our common European home; and for that we can only be grateful.

---

[6] 'We should use less the term solidarity, more enlightened self-interest' (Mario Monti, 18 October 2011, quoted in http://pr.euractiv.com/pr/bonino-monti-tajani-italy-s-role-key-exit-eu-crisis-91548).

References

Baldwin, Richard and Francesco Giavazzi (2015). *The Eurozone Crisis: A Consensus View of the Causes and a Few Possible Remedies*. A VoxEU.org eBook. London: CEPR Press.

Bénassy-Quéré, A., M. Brunnermeier, H. Enderlein, E. Farhi, M. Fratzscher, C. Fuest, P.-O. Gourinchas, P. Martin, J. Pisani-Ferry, H. Rey, I. Schnabel, N. Veron, B. Weder di Mauro, and J. Zettelmeyer (2018). 'Reconciling Risk Sharing with Market Discipline: A Constructive Approach to Euro Area Reform.' CEPR Policy Insight, No. 91.

Brunnermeier, Marcus, Harold James, and Jean-Pierre Landau (2016). *The Euro and the Battle of Ideas*. Princeton, NJ: Princeton University Press.

Buti, Marco and Nicolas Carno (2018). 'The Case for a Central Fiscal Capacity in EMU', December. https://voxeu.org/article/case-central-fiscal-capacity-emu.

Buti, Marco and István Székely (2019). 'Trade Shocks, Growth, and Resilience: Eastern Europe's Adjustment Tale', 28 June. https://voxeu.org/article/eastern-europe-s-adjustment-tale.

De Grauwe, Paul (2011). 'The Governance of a Fragile Eurozone.' CEPS Working Document, No. 346, May.

EU Five Presidents Report (2015) (J. C. Juncker, D. Tusk, J. Dijsselbloem, M. Draghi, M. Schulz). *Completing Europe's Economic and Monetary Union*. Brussels: European Commission.

European Commission (2017). *Reflection Paper on the Deepening of the Economic and Monetary Union*. Brussels: European Commission.

European Commission (2018). 'Proposal for a Regulation of the European Parliament and of the Council on the Establishment of a European Investment Stabilization Function', COM (2018) 387.

European Parliament (2020). 'Implementation of the Macroeconomic Imbalance Procedure: State of Play, August 2020.' https://www.europarl.europa.eu/RegData/etudes/IDAN/2016/497739/IPOL_IDA(2016)497739_EN.pdf.

Pagoulatos, George (2020). 'EMU and the Greek Crisis: Testing the Extreme Limits of an Asymmetric Union.' *Journal of European Integration* 42(3): 363–79.

Pagoulatos, George and Loukas Tsoukalis (2012). 'Multilevel Governance.' In Erik Jones, Anand Menon, and Stephen Weatherill (eds.), *The Oxford Handbook of the European Union*. Oxford: Oxford University Press.

Pisani-Ferry, Jean (2013). *The Euro Crisis and Its Aftermath*. Oxford: Oxford University Press.

Puchala, Donald (1971). 'Of Blind Men, *Elephants* and International Integration.' *Journal of Common Market Studies* 10(3): 267–84.

Purfield, Catriona and Christoph Rosenberg (2010). 'Adjustment under a Currency Peg: Estonia, Latvia and Lithuania during the Global Financial Crisis 2008–09.' IMF Working Paper, 10/213, September.

Tsoukalis, Loukas (1991/1993). *The New European Economy: The Politics and Economics of Integration*. Oxford: Oxford University Press.

Tsoukalis, Loukas (1997). *The New European Economy Revisited*. Oxford: Oxford University Press.

Tsoukalis, Loukas (2003). *What Kind of Europe?* Oxford and New York: Oxford University Press.

Tsoukalis, Loukas (2016). *In Defence of Europe: Can the European Project be Saved?* Oxford: Oxford University Press.

11

Implications of Brexit for the UK and the EU

The Knowns and the Unknowns

Matthew Bevington and Anand Menon

At 4.39 a.m. on 24 June 2016, David Dimbleby appeared on British television screens to announce that the people of the UK have voted to leave the European Union (EU). For the next three and a half years, politicians argued about how—and indeed whether—to implement that decision. Finally, some 1,300 days after the referendum, at 11 p.m. local time on 31 January 2020, the UK left the EU.

Of all the European transformations that Loukas Tsoukalis wrote about, Brexit was perhaps the least expected. Whether it turns out to be among the most momentous remains to be seen. Certainly, the vote to leave and the subsequent process of implementing that decision have transformed the UK. Politically and economically, the country will emerge from the process in a far different state from that in which it embarked on the journey. As for any impact it might have on the EU, this may be far less marked, but it will be many decades before we can fully appreciate how losing a member state—particularly such a large and active one—has affected the Union. Nevertheless, there are lessons to be learned by the UK's erstwhile European partners; lessons that the Union has been slow to consider.

The Referendum

Speaking in Cambridge in 2013, Loukas Tsoukalis argued that a referendum in the UK might in fact be desirable. His logic? A popular vote might provide a long overdue opportunity for a serious debate on Europe in the UK. Yet he must have been taken aback by the nature of the referendum that followed, and probably regrets his assessment that the chance of demagogues hijacking the referendum were slim, given that 'the choice facing citizens will be quite clear'.

The campaign did not provide an opportunity for 'proper debate, with facts and arguments'. Indeed, such was the paucity of substantive debate—on both sides—that the referendum instead laid the groundwork for the subsequent years of bad faith and unresolvable political divisions. What were differences of opinion and agreements to disagree prior to the referendum became entrenched, opposed identities for which political careers were sacrificed.

Matthew Bevington and Anand Menon, *Implications of Brexit for the UK and the EU: The Knowns and the Unknowns*
In: *Europe's Transformations: Essays in Honour of Loukas Tsoukalis*. Edited by: Helen Wallace, Nikos Koutsiaras, and George Pagoulatos, Oxford University Press. © OUP 2021. DOI: 10.1093/oso/9780192895820.003.0011

Scepticism about grand theorizing and an interest in the contingent as much as the structural have characterized Loukas's work. And any electoral event in which a swing of two percentage points in the other direction would have produced a different result (Electoral Commission 2019) is clearly shaped by contingent factors. Consider the way in which the Eurozone crisis allowed Conservative Eurosceptics to argue that the UK was 'shackled to a corpse'. Or how the migration crisis that followed ensured a steady supply of images of migrants arriving on EU shores. Thus, by the time the referendum arrived, the EU appeared not as the stabilizing safe haven of 1975 but as crippled by instability and a risk in itself.

The latter was perhaps particularly important, given that immigration was a key theme in the referendum. And in May 2016, just a month before the vote, the Office for National Statistics (2016) announced that in 2015 net migration to the UK had been 333,000—the second highest annual total on record—with half the migrants coming from the EU.

Yet such contingencies merely reinforced the impact of longer-term factors. At a political level, the UK's membership was characterized by deep-seated divisions that hamstrung any attempts to make a positive case for British membership of the EU. As Stephen Bush (2016) put it, 'anti-European arguments provided the background hum of political discourse at Westminster and in the country'. The EU, like an embarrassing family member, was something it was thought best not to draw attention to. Recall Gordon Brown's initial reluctance to attend the signing of the Lisbon Treaty in December 2007 (Woodward 2007). And this was an ostensibly pro-European British prime minister, one who would go on to make as strong a case[1] as any to remain during the referendum campaign.

Even attempts to revisit the terms of UK membership via David Cameron's renegotiation (European Council 2016b) proved insufficient to convince the British public. He did not come away empty handed from the crucial summit of 18–19 February 2016. The prime minister sought (Cameron 2016), and got, an explicit opt-out from ever closer union with a pledge that a British exemption would be written into the treaties at a later date. On the single currency, Cameron secured a guarantee that non-euro states would not have to fund euro bailouts, and would be reimbursed for any central EU funds used to prop up the currency. There was also an undertaking that non-euro states could refer concerns about discrimination against them to the European Council. A new 'red card' procedure meant that legislative proposals by the Commission could be blocked by 55 per cent of the EU's national parliaments. Even in the area of free movement, where many observers had expressed doubts that any real progress was possible, Cameron secured the ability to restrict payments of in-work benefits, and to

---

[1] https://www.bbc.com/news/uk-politics-eu-referendum-36513921.

index link child support payments to the conditions of the member state in which the child lived.

Yet these achievements proved too little, too late. The renegotiation did not achieve enough to convince many within the prime minister's own parliamentary party, let alone shift public opinion. In fact, by the Monday after the crucial summit, it was clear that a decision had been taken by the Remain camp that the renegotiation should not be mentioned during the campaign.

Turning to that campaign itself, several things are worthy of note. First is the effectiveness with which the Leave campaign exploited 'blue on blue' attacks. The government, by contrast, was more focused on the need to bring the Conservative Party back together after the referendum and was hence guilty, as one Downing Street source (Behr 2016) put it, of 'bringing knives to a gun battle'. Moreover, as Lord Cooper stated, the Leave campaign had 'the best tunes', with slogans such as 'I want my country back' and 'Take back control'.

Second, domestic issues were every bit as important as the relationship with the European Union. The Leave campaign mobilized grievances extending far beyond those with the EU. Take Iain Duncan Smith's resignation[2] from a government that had prided itself on driving through austerity, on the grounds that the budget unduly benefited higher-rate taxpayers. Consider also the infamous red bus (its colour was not coincidental) with 'NHS' emblazoned along its side, which was as much a protest against austerity as against Brussels.

Finally, while the evidence suggests that few people actually changed their minds as a result of the campaign (Brexit revealed a values division in the electorate, and values change slowly), it nevertheless played a crucial role in shaping turnout. Across the country, people who do not usually bother to turn out for general elections—why would they, for instance, in safe Labour seats, where their votes hardly matter?—made a point of voting for Brexit. In the northeast of England, Gateshead saw Leave winning with almost 59 per cent of the vote on the basis of a 71 per cent turnout (compared to 59 per cent in the previous general election). In nearby Hartlepool, Leave managed to gain 70 per cent of the vote on a 73 per cent turnout (as compared to 61 per cent in 2015). Areas where people had fewer educational qualifications, experiencing lower pay and higher unemployment, as well as those that had suffered disproportionately from austerity measures and experienced higher levels of migration from newer EU member states, were associated with higher support for leaving the EU.

In the tumultuous days that followed the vote, it appeared that the leaders of the Leave campaign were every bit as stunned by the outcome as their opponents and the numerous commentators who had predicted a relatively comfortable Remain victory. So much so, in fact, that they failed to capitalize by taking control of

---

[2] https://www.bbc.com/news/uk-politics-35848891.

government at their moment of triumph. As a result, it was the (*sotto voce*) Remain backer Theresa May who replaced David Cameron as prime minister.

One can only speculate as to what might have happened had a leading figure from the Leave campaign acceded to the top job. As it was, May's compromised Brexit position would shape how her government approached the Brexit issue, with May herself spending much of her first year in office seeking to prove her Brexit credentials to the Leave supporters in her parliamentary party. This led her to proclaim[3] what would become irreconcilable red lines at the Conservative Party Conference in October 2016: 'We are not leaving the European Union only to give up control of immigration all over again. And we are not leaving only to return to the jurisdiction of the European Court of Justice.' This demonstrated naivety at best; however, most of all, it laid bare from the start the tension that May would be unable to resolve: achieving the least damaging economic outcome while regaining full control over 'money, laws and borders'. May herself had much to learn about the European Union but also about the UK economy and the reality of her red lines for businesses on the ground.

In terms of what followed, there are perhaps three things worthy of note. First, any doubts that leaving the EU would be an extremely complicated and time-consuming endeavour proved unfounded. Some issues that were expected to create huge problems—negotiating the financial settlement, for instance—were settled rather quickly and amicably. Yet the complexity of the task also meant that the resources committed to it were enormous. The National Audit Office claimed that by March 2020 there were roughly 30,000 civil servants working on Brexit (National Audit Office 2019). If it had been a government department, it would have been the fourth biggest.

That even the British civil service, long feted as one of the most effective administrations inside the EU, should have struggled with the task is telling. Observers pointed to the way that, in fact, the civil service 'lacked a deep understanding of the extent to which the UK was intertwined with the EU and how this interacted with devolution and the delicate balance in Northern Ireland' (Rutter 2019). The government also had to go through a process of relearning how the EU worked as it tried to extricate itself from it. This was the result of an historical hollowing out of EU expertise across Whitehall, but also of an ideological aversion on the part of the government to utilizing what EU expertise was available. While EU expertise ought to have been considered an invaluable resource, in many cases it was actually seen as compromising the individuals in whom it was invested. The Brexit process led to highly personal attacks (ibid.) on individual civil servants by politicians as well as calling into question the civil

---

[3] https://www.bbc.com/news/av/uk-politics-37563510.

service's reputation for impartiality. The civil service that Loukas Tsoukalis so long admired has emerged from the process far from unscathed.

Second, few could have predicted—and little attention was paid to those who did—the degree to which Northern Ireland would dominate the Brexit process. Even the Democratic Unionist Party (DUP) made no demands about Northern Ireland and Brexit when it negotiated its deal to support Theresa May following the 2017 election. It was not just the European Union that the government had to learn about, it was the British Union as well. Brexit came at a time when political unionism appeared increasingly vulnerable, with the loss of the unionist majority at the Stormont elections in 2017; this weakness was reaffirmed in the 2019 general election. The re-establishment of government in Northern Ireland in early January 2020 was a positive sign, but Brexit will soon—potentially interminably—return to the agenda in Northern Ireland. Brexit will reappear on the agenda when consent for existing arrangements is sought four years after the end of the transition period, and possibly every four years beyond that. The reality of how the Northern Ireland backstop functions is sure to have profound implications, both economically and politically.

The political impact of Brexit on Scotland might turn out to be even more marked. Scottish Parliament elections in 2021 were the first post-Brexit electoral test of opinion anywhere in the UK, albeit filtered through the issue of Scottish independence. The result will trigger moves towards a formal request to the UK government to hold a second independence referendum. This will only reinforce the lethal embrace that the Conservatives (in England at least) and the SNP now find themselves in: the greater the SNP threat north of the border, the better it is for the Conservatives south of it, while the Conservatives being in power in London provides the perfect foil for the SNP.

Finally, and perhaps most strikingly of all, politics has consistently triumphed over all other considerations. Even before he became prime minister, David Cameron took the Conservatives out of the centre-right grouping—the European People's Party (EPP)—in the European Parliament, damaging relationships that he would later need with key European counterparts such as Nicolas Sarkozy and Angela Merkel, and voluntarily removing himself from an important EU network. And it was party politics that drove the march towards the referendum. In October 2011, 81 Conservative MPs rebelled to support the idea of a referendum. In January 2014, 95 Tory backbenchers signed a letter calling for Parliament to repeal the European Communities Act so as to be able to block and repeal EU law. In May 2014, the victory of the United Kingdom Independence Party (UKIP) in the European Parliament elections marked the first time in modern history that neither the Conservatives nor Labour had won a nationwide election. That autumn, two Conservative MPs defected to UKIP, a trickle that for a time looked as though it might become a flood. We could go on. This shows the sheer urgency of the EU issue, from the perspective of Conservative Party survival, at least—which, after all, is a reasonable preoccupation for a Conservative prime minister.

For all that Brexit helped to blur party loyalties and superimpose a new values divide over the pre-existing left–right cleavage that had for so long characterized British politics, tribal party politics was still a defining feature of what transpired. It was the reason why the idea that Theresa May—and especially Theresa May, who had spent a lifetime in the Conservative Party—might reach out to the Labour benches post-election was never as feasible as critics (Bercow 2020) made it sound. It also accounted for the ultimate reluctance of even those Labour MPs who thought the referendum should be honoured, but that Brexit should be as soft as possible, to cross the aisle and support Mrs May's deal.

And of course it was politics that ultimately defeated Mrs May and ushered in her successor. Boris Johnson moved quickly to support a significantly harder Brexit than even his predecessor had been willing to contemplate. The combination of the dire results for the Conservatives in the European elections of May 2019 and the purging of 21 MPs from the parliamentary party meant that Boris Johnson achieved what Mrs May had failed to: initial approval for his deal in the House of Commons, even without the DUP, which had been alienated by Johnson's acceptance of a Northern Ireland-only backstop following a general election victory.

Johnson's accession to the post of prime minister reinforced a trend that had been in evidence since before the 2016 referendum. The primacy of politics over economic considerations had been mitigated somewhat under Theresa May, not least because of her determination to find an all-UK solution to the Northern Irish question, which had in turn necessitated a closer economic relationship with the EU than many in her party were comfortable with. Freed from the need to depend on the DUP—to a degree before the 2019 election and completely so thereafter—Johnson was able to pursue his political objectives as a priority. This became apparent during the general election campaign, when simply 'getting Brexit done' became the overriding campaigning slogan and political priority, with any discussion of the relative impacts of different kinds of Brexit being largely relegated to the margins. Indeed, the Conservative manifesto referred to Brexit solely as a task to be completed, rather than attempting to elucidate any benefits that it would provide.

Once elected, Mr Johnson acted in a manner consistent with his stated objectives. Some observers seemed unable to take seriously his claim that he would do what was needed not only to get Brexit done, but to get it done in a way that was consistent with the UK 'taking back control' of its money, laws, and borders. The implications of this for the future of UK–EU relations were made clear in a speech delivered—curiously, it must be said, given his formal status as a special adviser to the prime minister—by David Frost in Brussels in February 2020 (Frost 2020).

Certainly, Frost made some passing references to the economic gains to be had from leaving the European Union. He took issue with those, such as Michel Barnier, who assumed that 'Brexit is going to do economic harm'. He caricatured the economic models on which such assumptions have been based, saying: 'Speculative predictions about the economy in fifteen years' time have become in many minds an unarguable depiction of inevitable reality next year.' Frost argued that the impact of non-tariff barriers had been exaggerated in official forecasts, while contesting the notion that an 'unproven decline in trade' would impact negatively on productivity. Finally, and in passing, he mentioned 'upsides': expanded trade with the rest of the world and (unspecified) regulatory change.

However, the main thrust of his argument was still political. Brexit, as he put it, 'was surely above all a revolt against a system'. And its purpose was to reclaim 'the ability to get our own rules right in a way that suits our own conditions'. Given the insistence on the UK being able to set its own laws, the notion of EU supervision over compliance with level-playing-field conditions—that 'complex armoury of rules and regulations negotiated with fellow Europeans', as Loukas Tsoukalis (2015) put it, without which genuinely free trade is impossible—was simply inconceivable. 'That', as Frost pointed out, 'isn't simply a negotiating position which might move under pressure—it is the point of the whole project'.

And the new government, unlike the old, has explicitly been willing to recognize the trade-offs that this implies. Frost himself pointed out that they 'understand the trade-offs involved' in that 'there is going to be friction there is [sic] going to be barriers. We know that and have factored this in'. Indeed, the prime minister reiterated this point in early September 2020 when he said that, even without a deal with the EU, 'that would be a good outcome for the UK'.

And the EU?

What, then, of the impact of Brexit on the EU itself? The loss of one of its larger member states will inevitably have a significant impact on the Union. This will be felt in terms not only of the absence of the British contribution to the EU budget, but also in terms of the balance of power between member states and the EU's relations with its neighbours.

To understand this impact, we should first recall the role the UK played as a member state. It is wrong to imagine that London was continually isolated, one against 27, tempting though it may be to read the dynamics of the Brexit negotiations across to the UK's membership. The UK was one among 28. Although it was perhaps more troublesome at times than other members, it was by no means alone; indeed, the UK was at the heart of some of the most successful European initiatives, including eastern enlargement and the single market.

However, under David Cameron, the UK did find itself increasingly on the losing[4] side in policy terms, even if this was largely self-inflicted. The futile resistance[5] to the EU Fiscal Compact in 2011, which was agreed by all member states except the UK and went ahead without it, is a case in point. Though Cameron acted on the pretext of protecting the single market, he was accused by his colleagues of doing precisely the opposite. This formed part of a pattern of behaviour whereby the British prime minister would seek to stir up a political fight over the EU prior to summits so that he could be seen at home to be taking a hard line.

Whether the Cameron approach would have become the new normal for British membership without a referendum is hard to tell. Because he had set the Brexit train in motion so early with his 2013 Bloomberg speech, in which he mooted the idea of an in–out referendum following a renegotiation of terms, he effectively ruled out any continuation of the status quo. The UK would either stay in on adjusted terms or it would leave. Yet had the result been just a few percentage points different and gone the other way, it is conceivable—likely even—that Cameron would have reacted as he did to the Scottish independence referendum in 2014 and seen the issue as 'settled for a generation' (Cameron 2014).

Brexit has already begun to influence the European Union, not least in the EU's financial response to the Covid-19 outbreak. As a member state, limiting EU spending was the UK's first priority. As the UK's former ambassador to the EU, Sir Ivan Rogers, has pointed out, the UK would likely have vetoed the plan, agreed in July 2020, to collectively borrow up to €750 billion and redistribute a substantial portion to member states as grants. Its exit has already rebalanced political alliances on budgetary issues in particular. The UK's former EU budget allies, the so-called 'frugal four' countries—Austria, Denmark, the Netherlands, and Sweden—now have significantly less weight in favour of their arguments. While they managed to negotiate a more even balance of loans and grants in the EU recovery fund, its overall size remained unchanged from the Commission pro-posal and grants made up a majority of the fund, despite the frugals' stated aim only to have such funds distributed to member states as loans.

By any measure, the UK is a big piece to remove from the puzzle, with inevitable consequences for the dynamics among member states. The third largest by population, sceptical of political integration, economically liberal and Atlanticist in outlook, the UK has taken a substantial portion of the political weight in favour of these arguments with it. Should we, then, expect the European Union to deprioritize these issues in the future?

---

[4] https://ukandeu.ac.uk/does-the-uk-win-or-lose-in-the-council-of-ministers/.
[5] https://www.bbc.com/news/world-europe-16115373.

It seems almost certain that these ideas will be more difficult to pursue without the UK. As Loukas Tsoukalis pointed out (2011), when it comes to the development of European integration, the 'French usually provided the driver, the Commission the map, the Germans paid for the petrol and the British oiled the brakes'. Others may now provide the oil in their place, but there will be substantially less of it. The UK's traditional allies will find blocking minorities harder to assemble. The changing political strategies of these member states will be fascinating to observe as, given their relatively small size, they will not be able—nor necessarily want—to replicate the British approach.

But it is not simply in terms of political and voting weight that the UK's absence will be felt. London's overall approach to EU policy was one of the most comprehensive in the EU, taking as it did considered (and often combative) positions on all EU issues. Without a UK voice attempting to set the agenda, other highly engaged member states, notably France, may gain greater influence, especially if they act in concert with a re-engaged Germany, as the recovery fund process hints may be the case in the years to come. Other member states, perhaps used to being able to hide behind British opposition to ideas they themselves did not support, will now have to make their voices heard more loudly. Will the Swedes become more vociferous defenders of the rights of euro outs? Will The Hague replace London as the voice of scepticism in Council meetings? Will a reinvigorated Franco-German tandem come to the fore?

Of course, we should not take this idea too far. The UK was just one member state, albeit an important one. Much remains the same. There remains no single EU view on most policy issues—after all, if there were, there would be no need for the EU as a set of mediating institutions. Coalitions will continue to form and break apart according to the issue at hand, and a desire to seek consensus will remain, especially on the biggest issues. We should not expect the UK's absence to transform the workings and output of EU institutions. Rather, it will most likely be at the margins that changes take place.

Moreover, change is happening anyway, irrespective of any UK influence. Much of the new Commission's agenda is couched in 'protective' terms, whether it relates to migration, trade or, controversially, 'European culture'. Put simply, we should be wary of loosely attributing changes at the EU level to the UK's absence; such mechanical effects do not sit comfortably with reality, especially given that, practically speaking, the UK was on the way out for many years prior to its actual exit, and that the institutions had long adapted to the lack of a substantive UK presence.

Nonetheless, it is conceivable that Brexit might—at long last—prompt the EU to reconsider the ways in which it deals with its neighbours. The defining feature of the EU's response to Brexit has been rigidity. Consider the supposed legal constraints: the UK, so the EU argument goes, has to choose either a Norway-style deal inside the single market or a free trade agreement, with no options in between. Michel Barnier, the EU negotiator, suggested (implausibly) that allowing selective UK access would mean 'the end of the single market and the European project'. Yet, as Professor Stephen Weatherill (2017) points out, 'The indivisibility of the freedoms is a political construct: the legal reality is already more messy.' Level-playing-field issues, too, are not mere technocratic demands but political calculations. The change in the EU's position on state aid demonstrates this clearly. The EU initially demanded that the UK retain EU rules but then moved to a softer position. To give Michel Barnier credit, he recognized early that the initial position was unrealistic. There is scope, therefore, for a compromise that recognizes the uniqueness of the UK–EU relationship, assuming the UK plays ball. The trouble is that there is, at the time of writing, no guarantee that the UK will.

The arrangements that the EU has come to with other non-member states show that greater flexibility is possible. The European Economic Area (EEA) provides some leeway with barriers on cross-border trade and excludes significant swaths of economic activity, including fisheries and agriculture. With Switzerland, the EU took a piecemeal approach. Granted, this began many decades ago and developed on the assumption that it was part of the country's path to membership. Yet the EU single market is not dysfunctional as a result of Switzerland's cherry-picked arrangements. On the contrary, the single market has been touted throughout the Brexit process—and with much justification—as one of the main prizes of EU membership. Rarely, if ever, has it been suggested that Switzerland is the Achilles heel of the single market. Of course, it is for the EU to define its own interests and priorities. If it does not wish to replicate the Swiss arrangements with the UK, it is entirely within its rights not to do so. But we ought to be clear that this is about neither legal constraints nor potentially causing fatal damage to the single market. It is a political choice, albeit one made for understandable reasons.

Partly, this has been explicable in terms of a lack of member-state engagement and an egregious failure (with the exception of Ireland) to think about the longer-term relationship. The UK was not alone in setting out on this journey with little idea of the final destination. The EU, too, and national leaders especially, have failed in their responsibility to strategically guide the Union in respect of its relationship with the UK. Perhaps because some see Brexit as essentially the accession process in reverse, they see no need to think in detail about an 'end point'. We would argue they are wrong not to do so. 'EU unity', precisely because it is in short supply on other substantive questions, has been paraded as an end in itself, eclipsing the substance. Yet the UK is an important partner—arguably the most important in the immediate EU neighbourhood—and deep collaboration is in the interest of both sides. It may be that, once the Brexit process itself is over (with the caveat that discussions will last well beyond the period of formal negotiations), both sides might approach the issue of future cooperation in a more pragmatic way than either has managed to date.

Finally, and perhaps most profoundly, the institutions have yet to begin serious self-reflection on the deeper significance of Brexit. The September 2016 Bratislava roadmap (European Council 2016a) was the most meaningful attempt to date. It is notable for highlighting—somewhat ironically, given the Leave campaign's slogan—'a perceived lack of control' on the part of citizens, and a 'need to be clear about what the EU can do, and what is for the member states to do, to make sure we can deliver on our promises'. Yet this remained a relatively shallow exercise, aimed as much at bolstering the unity of the 27 as at thinking deeply about how to build a sustainable Union for the future. The loss of a member state is, though you would be hard pushed to hear it admitted in Brussels, a failure of the EU and must be analysed as such.

Such a lack of frankness is understandable given the incompatible views of member states on many profound issues concerning the EU's future. It might be relatively easy to agree imprecise, abstract goals for the Union, but turning these into concrete policies is another matter. The Conference on the Future of Europe (see Chapter 17 in the volume) could provide a context in which such deep thinking can take place and practical solutions can be reached, but the notable lack of enthusiasm on the part of heads of government is a worrying sign.

Such self-reflection must start from a solid base. The UK was frequently described, and even presented itself on occasions, as an outlier among member states. Yet this is misleading. It was often argued that the UK was alone in having a problem with free movement of persons within the EU, and that other member states were solely concerned with migration from without. Yet Eurobarometer data show that this is simply untrue. When asked in November 2019 whether migration from other member states evoked a positive or negative feeling, a fifth of EU citizens overall (19 per cent) chose negative, with figures as high as 48 per cent in the Czech Republic, 43 per cent in Slovakia, and 40 per cent in Greece. In the UK, the figures were 69 per cent positive and just 21 per cent negative, which were more favourable than in either France or Italy (European Commission 2019). The uncomfortable truth is that the free movement of persons—contrary to what many might like to believe—is not seen by all citizens as an unquestioned benefit of EU membership. To assume otherwise would mean being guilty of profound complacency.

Other data signal similar trends. Asked in November 2019 whether the EU was heading in the wrong or right direction, almost half (49 per cent) said the wrong direction, far outweighing positive responses (31 per cent) (European Commission 2019). That said, positive responses were up from just 17 per cent in May 2016 (European Commission 2016). UK citizens were less negative than the average and far from the most negative. In Belgium, Greece, and France, 60 per cent or more thought the EU was heading in the wrong direction; in Italy, Sweden, Germany, Spain, Finland, and the Netherlands, it was 50 per cent or more (European Commission 2019).

Finally, the UK was hardly the first member state to host a sizeable and active Eurosceptic movement, although its Eurosceptics have clearly enjoyed by far the most success to date. Almost every member state has some sort of Eurosceptic presence (indeed, Hungary and Poland have Eurosceptic governments), and such movements are particularly sizeable in the larger member states, notably France, Italy, and Germany. Where the UK differs is in the way this Eurosceptic influence filtered its way into the political system: unlike Italy, for instance, or Finland, where such parties have been in government, this did not happen in the UK owing to the dominance of a two-party system and the rarity of governing coalitions. Instead, this influence came via the Conservative Party, which, as we have noted, came increasingly to occupy Eurosceptic policy positions, notably on immigration, when the electoral challenge from UKIP threatened its ability to win a parliamentary majority.

This is in no way an argument that Brexit might be emulated elsewhere (see Chapter 6 in this volume). Note the way that populist leaders in France and Italy in particular have backtracked from earlier demands for an exit from the euro or indeed the EU itself. If nothing else, the problems experienced by the UK have served as a salutary warning to others. Yet, more than anything, the lesson the EU must draw from Brexit is that there is a lesson to be drawn. Attributing the loss of a member state entirely to the peculiarity of the British is complacent. The UK may have been unique in its mixture of opt-outs and rebates, and it may have a particularly Eurosceptic press (though, we must add, some of the best Brussels-based journalists, too) that has fomented a neurotic debate about the EU. But in many respects the UK was not unique and reflected many trends—rising Euroscepticism, concerns over immigration, and resistance to multilateralism—that are also extant in other member states. Nothing could send a worse signal to EU citizens than trying to make these problems specifically British problems that have apparently disappeared along with the UK itself.

References

Begg, Iain (2020). 'The Franco-German Proposal for a €500 Billion Recovery Fund.' *The UK in a Changing Europe*, 20 May. https://ukandeu.ac.uk/the-franco-german-proposal-for-a-e500-billion-recovery-fund/.

Behr, Rafael (2016). 'How Remain Failed: The Inside Story of a Doomed Campaign.' *The Guardian*, 5 July. https://www.theguardian.com/politics/2016/jul/05/how-remain-failed-inside-story-doomed-campaign.

Bercow, John (2020). 'Parliament and Brexit: Keynote by John Bercow.' *The UK in a Changing Europe*, 12 March. https://ukandeu.ac.uk/multimedia/parliament-and-brexit-keynote-by-john-bercow/#.

Bush, Stephen (2016). 'Westminster Has Yet to Come to Terms with the Consequences of Brexit.' *New Statesman*, 2 July. https://www.newstatesman.com/politics/uk/2016/07/westminster-has-yet-come-terms-consequences-brexit.

Cameron, David (2013). 'EU speech at Bloomberg.' https://www.gov.uk/government/speeches/eu-speech-at-bloomberg.

Cameron, David (2014). 'David Cameron's Statement on the Scottish Result.' *Financial Times*, 19 September. https://www.ft.com/content/68686a20–3fc5–11e4-a381–00144feabdc0.

Cameron, David (2016). 'Prime Minister's Statement on EU Renegotiation: 3 February 2016.' https://www.gov.uk/government/speeches/prime-ministers-statement-on-eu-renegotiation-3-february-2016.

Electoral Commission (2019). 'Results and Turnout at the EU Referendum.' https://www.electoralcommission.org.uk/who-we-are-and-what-we-do/elections-and-referendums/past-elections-and-referendums/eu-referendum/results-and-turnout-eu-referendum.

European Commission (2016). *Standard Eurobarometer 85*. https://ec.europa.eu/commfrontoffice/publicopinion/index.cfm/ResultDoc/download/DocumentKy/75905.

European Commission (2019). *Standard Eurobarometer 91*. https://ec.europa.eu/commfrontoffice/publicopinion/index.cfm/ResultDoc/download/DocumentKy/88420.

European Commission (2020). 'Europe's Moment: Repair and Prepare for the Next Generation.' 27 May. https://ec.europa.eu/commission/presscorner/detail/en/ip_20_940.

European Council (2016a). 'The Bratislava Declaration.' 16 September. https://www.consilium.europa.eu/media/21250/160916-bratislava-declaration-and-roadmapen16.pdf.

European Council (2016b). 'Letter by President Donald Tusk to the Members of the European Council on his Proposal for a New Settlement for the United Kingdom within the European Union.' https://www.consilium.europa.eu/en/press/press-releases/2016/02/02/letter-tusk-proposal-new-settlement-uk/.

Frost, David (2020). 'Reflections on the Revolutions in Europe.' *No. 10 Media Blog*, 17 February. https://no10media.blog.gov.uk/2020/02/17/david-frost-lecture-reflections-on-the-revolutions-in-europe/.

National Audit Office (2019). *The UK Border: Preparedness for EU Exit*. Report by the Comptroller and Auditor General, October. https://www.nao.org.uk/wp-content/uploads/2019/10/The-UK-border-preparedness-for-EU-exit-October-2019.pdf.

Office for National Statistics (2016). *Migration Statistics Quarterly Report*. May. https://www.ons.gov.uk/peoplepopulationandcommunity/populationandmigration/internationalmigration/bulletins/migrationstatisticsquarterlyreport/may2016.

Rutter, Jill (2019). 'How Brexit Has Battered Britain's Reputation for Good Government.' *The Guardian*, 27 December. https://www.theguardian.com/commentisfree/2019/dec/27/brexit-britain-reputation-government-civil-service.

Tsoukalis, Loukas (2011). 'The JCMS Annual Review Lecture: The Shattering of Illusions—And What Next?' *Journal of Common Market Studies* 49(s1): 19–44. https://onlinelibrary.wiley.com/doi/abs/10.1111/j.1468–5965.2011.02185.x.

Tsoukalis, Loukas (2015). 'Alcuin Lecture 2013: Is There a Future for the European Union—and with Britain in It?' *Cambridge Review of International Affairs* 28(4): 589–98. https://www.tandfonline.com/doi/full/10.1080/09557571.2014.886554.

Weatherill, Stephen (2017). 'The Several Internal Markets.' *University of Oxford Legal Research Paper Series.* https://papers.ssrn.com/sol3/papers.cfm?abstract_id=3032513#.

Woodward, Will (2007). 'Brown Will Now Go to Lisbon and Sign EU Treaty—but by Himself.' *The Guardian*, 12 December. https://www.theguardian.com/politics/2007/dec/12/uk.eu.

PART III

WHAT KIND OF POWER IN WHAT KIND OF GLOBAL SYSTEM?

12

The End of Multilateralism?

Ngaire Woods

> Our world cannot afford a future where the two largest economies split the globe in a Great Fracture—each with its own trade and financial rules and internet and artificial intelligence capacities. A technological and economic divide risks inevitably turning into a geostrategic and military divide. We must avoid this at all costs.
>
> Secretary-General Antonio Guterres speaking in September 2020 at the opening of the United Nations General Assembly

The international system is rapidly being reshaped by the strategic rivalry between the USA and China. For all other countries and regions in the world, this rivalry has profound consequences. At stake are the rules of the game, which will affect markets, technologies, and the ways disputes are resolved.

Different forms of multilateralism have long shaped the international rules of the game. The term 'multilateralism' describes the arrangements created and agreed by states which facilitate cooperation by enshrining commitments to diffuse reciprocity and peaceful dispute settlement (Keohane 1990; Ruggie 1992). It can include formal treaties, informal arrangements, and international institutions involving a number of countries.

Over the last two centuries, the world has seen several forms of multilateralism. A *Concert of Great Powers*—Austria, Great Britain, Prussia, Russia, and France in the early nineteenth century—convened extensive multilateral consultations through which they settled rivalries and agreed, for example, on the neutrality of Belgium and Greece. This system gave way to *rival alliances* as Prussia expanded, beating Austria-Hungary in 1866 and France in 1871. The Triple Alliance comprising a Prussia-led Germany, Austria-Hungary, and Italy confronted the Triple Entente of France, Russia, and the United Kingdom in the First World War.

International institutions began to play more of a role after the First World War with the development of the League of Nations and then, after the Second World War, the United Nations and its raft of agencies. That said, these emergent universal-membership multipurpose agencies were soon forced to coexist with USA–USSR Cold War rivalry. This created a *balance of power* system and a debate

Ngaire Woods, *The End of Multilateralism?* In: *Europe's Transformations: Essays in Honour of Loukas Tsoukalis.* Edited by: Helen Wallace, Nikos Koutsiaras, and George Pagoulatos, Oxford University Press. © OUP 2021. DOI: 10.1093/oso/9780192895820.003.0012

among scholars of international relations as to whether sheer power politics determined outcomes, or whether institutions played (at least) an intervening role.

Multilateralism during the Cold War was used by the USA and the Soviet Union to advance arrangements within their respective blocs, as well as to regulate the rivalry between them. At times, multilateralism served to moderate excesses in superpower competition and its impact on other countries. At other times, their rivalry sidelined formal multilateral institutions because of a stalemate between the rivals.

The new strategic rivalry between China and the USA raises questions about what role international institutions are likely to play as China and the USA vie for control of the rules and of the institutions which help implement, interpret, and adjudicate those rules.

A Changing Context: The USA–China Strategic Rivalry

The rise of China and the ebbing of US primacy in global institutions sped up after the global financial crisis of 2008. The resulting strategic rivalry is driven by three classical elements of great power competition, which form the backdrop to the evolving role and nature of international institutions.

Competition to control resources and access to resources and markets is the first element of their strategic rivalry. For the USA, much has changed. After the Second World War, the USA mostly managed its markets through a combination of foreign direct investments, bilateral and regional free trade agreements, and the creation and upholding of multilateral rules, such as those enshrined in the World Trade Organization (WTO), into which China was inducted in 2001. But two forces have changed the US position.

China is now a competitor for markets. We saw this play out in the Pacific when the USA proposed a Trans-Pacific Partnership in 2010 which would encompass 12 countries in the Pacific (and from which they would withdraw).[1] Within two years, China had proposed its own alternative, the Regional Comprehensive Economic Partnership (RCEP) encompassing the ten members of the Association of South-East Asian Nations (ASEAN)[2] plus Australia, Japan, New Zealand, and South Korea.

More broadly, China has developed its Belt and Road Initiative (BRI), which was launched in 2013 by President Xi Jinping to create an infrastructure linking partners to the west of China (the former Soviet republics), to the south (India,

---

[1] Australia, Brunei, Canada, Chile, Japan, Malaysia, Mexico, New Zealand, Peru, Singapore, Vietnam, and China.

[2] Brunei, Cambodia, Indonesia, Laos, Malaysia, Myanmar, the Philippines, Singapore, Thailand, and Vietnam.

Pakistan, south-east Asia) and elsewhere (see Chapter 13 in this volume). Huge investments have poured into railways, energy pipelines, highways, efficient border crossings, special economic zones, and other strategic investments. The BRI is buttressed by new multilateral organizations which China has created (about which, more below).

In Europe, Chinese investments have increased rapidly. Where in 2008 annual Chinese outbound foreign direct investment into the 28 EU economies was €700 million, by 2016 it had grown to €35 billion.[3] The Eurozone crisis accelerated China's investments in infrastructure—in the ports of Piraeus, Zebrugge, and Valencia, for instance—and in the gas and electricity grid of Portugal. In 2019 Italy became a formal partner in China's BRI.

Meanwhile, the USA has also changed its strategy of engagement with the rest of the world. In the Pacific, the USA opted to withdraw its signature from the Trans-Pacific Partnership (TPP) in early 2017 and sought to negotiate new terms for its existing free trade agreements, such as the North American Free Trade Agreement (NAFTA). In fact, the TPP partners went ahead without the USA, signing the Comprehensive and Progressive Agreement for Trans-Pacific Partnership, which entered into force on 30 December 2018.

In Europe, President Trump began his presidency by setting an aggressive tone, criticizing European allies over the North Atlantic Treaty Organization (NATO), announcing that the USA would withdraw from the Paris Climate Accord, withdrawing from the Iran nuclear deal, and castigating European countries for permitting Huawei to provide 5G equipment. In January 2020, President Trump announced his intention to take further action on the trade front, renewing his threat to increase the US tariff on European cars.[4]

In a global competition for resources and access to resources, China is expanding its investments and treaties with countries, while the USA (although loud about its discontent with the current system) has not yet clarified its new strategy for securing resources and markets abroad in the face of that competition.

The second element of their strategic rivalry is *competition for dominance in new technologies* and the data that enable their full exploitation. This includes artificial intelligence (AI) and data science, advanced battery storage, advanced semi-conductor technologies, genomics and synthetic biology, 5G cellular networks, quantum information systems, and robotics.

In the aftermath of the Second World War, the USA enjoyed a dominant position in technology through a powerful set of policies. Government-driven investments in basic research and development resulted in radical discoveries that served as well-springs for later-stage development activities in private industry

---

[3] https://merics.org/en/report/eu-china-fdi-working-towards-more-reciprocity-investment-relations.
[4] https://www.cnbc.com/2020/01/22/trump-claims-the-eu-has-no-choice-but-to-agree-a-new-trade-deal.html.

and government. These were translated into military capabilities at unrivalled speed. Outstanding training in science, technology, engineering, and mathematics (STEM) attracted the best and brightest from across the world. Commitments to open trade won new markets abroad, further fuelling domestic innovation.

US leadership in technology is now less clear. Federal support for research and development has stagnated. Insecure supply chains, a deteriorating manufacturing capability, and reliance on competitor nations has hampered the military uptake of new technologies. The Trump administration's trade and immigration policies are likely to have exacerbated the blunting of America's competitive edge, alienating the allies, students, and researchers who help to keep the USA competitive. A recent report also notes that 'a persistent cultural divide between the technology and policymaking communities threatens national security by making it more difficult for the Defense Department and intelligence community to acquire and adopt advanced technologies from the private sector and to draw on technical talent'.[5]

China meanwhile has been investing hugely. Its 2015 'Made in China 2025' plan aims rapidly to expand China's high-tech and advanced manufacturing base, especially in AI, advanced robotics, next-generation information technology and telecommunications, and electric cars and new energy vehicles.[6] The plan explicitly seeks greater global self-sufficiency in high-tech industries (70 per cent by 2025) and a dominant position in global markets. It has been estimated that by 2030 China will be the world's largest investor in research and development.[7]

Today, the technology competition between the USA and China has become fierce as a raft of recent US trade and commerce restrictions have driven a wedge between US and Chinese companies, breaking the global production chains which linked them. In the short term, this has imposed great costs on Chinese companies, most obviously in the case of Huawei. But US policies are also accelerating the development of China's technological self-sufficiency. The strategic rivalry over technology could move rapidly from competition within a system which binds China and the USA together to the emergence of ever more separate spheres of influence.

Controlling the rules which govern interactions among countries is a third element of the strategic rivalry. After 1945, parallel patterns of cooperation emerged between East and West, as well as within each bloc. Within the US sphere of influence, NATO and the Organization for Economic Co-operation and Development (OECD), the International Monetary Fund (IMF), the World Bank, and General Agreement on Tariffs and Trade (GATT) emerged. In the East, the

---

[5] https://www.cfr.org/report/keeping-our-edge/.
[6] Other major sectors include agricultural technology, aerospace engineering, new synthetic materials, advanced electrical equipment, emerging bio-medicine, high-end rail infrastructure, and high-tech maritime engineering. https://www.cfr.org/backgrounder/made-china-2025-threat-global-trade.
[7] https://www.cfr.org/report/keeping-our-edge/.

USSR developed the Warsaw Treaty Organization and the Council for Mutual Economic Aid (COMECON). Bringing the two blocs together was the United Nations (UN), a raft of long-standing institutions of technical cooperation (such as the Universal Postal Union, the World Meteorological Organization and the International Atomic Energy Agency), and specific summits, agreements, and treaties.

At the end of the Cold War in 1990, the Soviet institutions collapsed and what had previously been Western international organizations became universal, with Russia and the countries that had formerly been in its sphere of influence joining the IMF, the World Bank and the GATT/WTO. Initially, these organizations remained dominated by the USA. But over the past two decades, the US dominance of organizations has begun to wane. The 2003 war in Iraq split the US-led Western alliance. The 2008 global financial crisis accelerated the rise of China and the BRICs (Woods 2010). President Trump's administration, by withdrawing engagement and support from international organizations, accelerated the diminishing of US influence.[8]

Meanwhile, China has greatly increased its engagement with existing multilateral institutions (more on this below), while building new multilateral arrangements at the same time. These include: the Shanghai Co-operation Organization, an eight-member group that includes Russia and central Asian countries as well as India and Pakistan; the Asian Infrastructure Investment Bank, a multilateral organization with 102 members based in Beijing which helps to finance infrastructure; and the New Development Bank, formed by emerging economies and based in Shanghai.

What Role for Multilateral Organizations in the China–USA Rivalry?

As the USA and China seek new forms of control over markets, compete for dominance in technology, and vie for greater influence over the rules of the game, history highlights some trade-offs. Effective international institutions rely on the 'buy-in' of powerful members who don't have to buy in. They can refuse to participate, as the USA and USSR did in the 1920s with the League of Nations. They can participate nominally, but mostly circumvent the multilateral process or institution, as the USA and USSR did in respect of the UN Security Council during much of the Cold War. Or powerful states can make their participation

---

[8] This withdrawal includes late payments and arrears in its UN contributions, threatening to further reduce its contributions (e.g. to the WHO), refusing to fund the UN Relief and Works Agency and the UN Population Fund, and withdrawing from the UN Human Rights Council and UN Economic and Social Council.

conditional on a high degree of control, which creates ongoing tension between what the majority of member states in an institution wish it to do and what its most powerful members will agree to it doing.

In the aftermath of the Second World War, these choices played out in the new institutions created to rebuild the global economy. The IMF and the World Bank were designed in 1944 as mechanisms for cooperation among countries, regardless of their political ideology. The idea was to provide a forum for agreeing common rules and pooling financial provisions which would help to buffer the effects of monetary shocks and financial crises while also providing financing for post-war reconstruction.

The rivalry between the USA and the Soviet Union soon trumped the multilateral processes. The Soviet Union joined neither the IMF, the World Bank, nor the new trade arrangements set out in the GATT. And for its part, the USA quickly opted for more direct and politically conditional ways of lending with a view to shaping reconstruction in Asia and Europe: in Europe through the Marshall Plan and in Japan through the Supreme Command of Allied Powers (SCAP).

The USA also sought, through informal means, to expand its influence and control over the IMF and World Bank. As the Cold War developed and the IMF and World Bank grew their operations, their lending patterns and conditionality came closely to reflect US geostrategic interests (Woods 2006). Likewise, the GATT became a 'club' for members with similarly political views (Davis and Wilf 2011). Meanwhile, the United Nations Security Council and General Assembly soon became fora for set-piece debates and votes which entrenched the East–West divide and rivalry.

That said, international cooperation also played an important role in limiting aspects of the USSR–USA strategic rivalry. Treaties helped in specific instances to contain the impact of superpower competition on other countries. For example, the Soviet Union and the Western occupying powers (the USA, France, the UK) agreed on the Austrian Independence Treaty and that country's neutrality in 1955. In 1962, the Soviet Union and the USA signed the International Agreement on the Neutrality of Laos.

Later in the Cold War (signalling what would be called détente), the superpowers agreed treaties which included arms restraints, including the Anti-Ballistic Missile Treaty (ABM) in force 1972–2002; the Strategic Arms Limitation Agreement signed in 1972; the Accidents at Sea Agreement of 1972; and the Berlin Quadripartite Agreement of 1971. Less effective were efforts to engineer broad-based agreements, such as Nixon and Brezhnev's Basic Principles Agreement of 1972.

Informal negotiations and summits also opened up important avenues for problem solving. For example, the July 1955 summit which brought the heads of government of the Soviet Union, USA, UK, and France together in Geneva to discuss European security, disarmament, and East–West relations did not result in any formal agreement, but did lead to what was described as a 'Geneva spirit' of willingness to engage in a limited way. The resolution of the Cuban Missile Crisis and the 1977–8 USA–USSR agreement that the USSR would limit its engagement in Somalia offer further examples of structured informal talks.

The Cold War period also highlighted that international organizations can acquire a more independent role, not least because they can insert themselves into the setting of agendas, the gathering of information, and the resolving of states' collective action problems (Abbott and Snidal 1998). Crucial to shifting this from theory to practice is the leadership of the international organization. Powerful heads of organizations can increase the scope for multilateral action by adeptly forging coalitions in support of their mandate and finances, and by managing their organizations staff, ethos, and performance effectively (Hall and Woods 2018). Two examples illustrate this.

Dag Hammarskjöld, as secretary-general of the United Nations, seized the opportunity presented by the 1956 Suez Canal crisis, which did not directly involve the superpowers (Israel, France, and Britain were using force to respond to Egypt's President Nasser nationalizing the canal), to create a peacekeeping mandate under the control of the secretary-general rather than the great powers on the Security Council.

Another example is provided by Robert McNamara, who as president of the World Bank from 1968 to 1981 transformed the organization. Its membership grew and he personally undertook to ensure negotiations brought China into the bank in 1980. He increased the bank's resources severalfold, including an increase in the bank's concessional lending arm (the IDA) from $400 million to $4 billion per year. In short, he massively increased the organization's financial and technical power.

So multilateral organizations can play an important role, even amidst a great power rivalry. This will necessarily involve achieving a fine balance between the wishes of their most powerful members and the legitimacy and effectiveness of their mandate. The leadership of any organization can make a difference to whom it serves and how. This may be why China has been seeking greater influence over the leadership of existing multilateral organizations.

The Rise of China within Existing Institutions

Unlike the Cold War rivalry between the Soviet Union and the USA, the new strategic rivalry has China seeking to compete with the USA mostly within the rules, institutions, and precedents created by the USA.

China has greatly enhanced its position and role in key organizations. In the United Nations, China is now the second largest contributor to the general budget as well as the peacekeeping budget. Chinese officials now head up four of the

15 UN specialized agencies: the International Civil Aviation Organization, the International Telecommunication Union, the Food and Agriculture Organization, and the UN Industrial Development Organization.

China has used its engagement with UN agencies to craft programmes which complement and reinforce its Belt and Road Initiative; these agencies include the United Nations International Children's Emergency Fund (UNICEF)[9] and the United Nations High Commissioner for Refugees (UNHCR)[10]. In 2016, China pledged $200 million to create a new United Nations Peace and Development Trust Fund (UNPDTF),[11] which is administered by a steering committee of five, four of whom are senior Chinese officials. In 2019, the UNPDTF's projects were heavily focused on 'enhancing the complementarities and synergies between the Agenda and the Belt and Road Initiative' and 'strengthening capacities of developing countries participating in the Belt and Road Initiative'.[12] That said, other countries have begun to push back against China's influence.[13]

In the IMF, China is now the third most powerful member state with 6.08 per cent of the voting power (Japan has 6.15 per cent, Germany has 5.32 per cent, the USA has 16.51 per cent); it is also one of the few states with its own seat on the executive board.[14] Since 2011 a succession of senior Chinese officials have held the position of deputy managing director of the organization. Similarly in the World Bank, China is now the third largest vote-holder, and a senior Chinese official is the managing director and World Bank group chief administrative officer.

The World Trade Organization does not have weighted voting power. The agency exists to facilitate trade negotiations, to monitor compliance with existing rules, and to provide a dispute settlement mechanism. Powerful countries use the dispute mechanism, which requires costly and time-consuming preparation, technical knowledge, and information.[15] China has become the third most active country in the dispute settlement process (having mostly been a third party in disputes until 2006). By the end of 2019, China had been involved in 65 disputes, and had generally agreed to abide by WTO rulings on disputes, albeit more slowly and with less effect than complainants would like.[16]

[9] https://www.unicef.org/press-releases/henrietta-fore-unicef-executive-director-high-level-symposium-belt-road-initiative.

[10] https://www.unhcr.org/news/latest/2019/3/5c9df95b4/un-refugee-chief-connects-chinese-companies-boao-forum.html.

[11] https://www.un.org/en/unpdf/index.shtml.

[12] https://www.un.org/en/unpdf/2030asd.shtml.

[13] https://thewire.in/diplomacy/china-obor-belt-road-un-pushback.

[14] https://www.imf.org/external/np/sec/memdir/members.aspx.

[15] The five most active users are five of the largest economies in the world: the USA, EU, China, Canada and India.

[16] https://chinapower.csis.org/china-world-trade-organization-wto/.

The US Response to China's Engagement in Multilateral Organizations

The US response to China's engagement in multilateral organizations has changed over time. At first, the USA urged China to 'take responsibility' and to engage more with multilateral organizations. But since 2016, the USA has itself sought to take a step back from multilateral engagements and to weaken institutions (including NATO, the TPP, the Paris Climate Agreement, and the Iran deal), even as it now seeks to counter China's influence within them.

On 14 April 2020, President Trump announced that he would cut funding to the World Health Organization (WHO),[17] on account of its defence and praise of China's response to the coronavirus; this despite the fact that he had himself effusively praised China at first (on Twitter) for its handling of Covid-19. Subsequently, in early July 2020, the US president gave notice to the US Congress and the United Nations that the USA was formally withdrawing from the WHO (effective as of 6 July 2021).[18] This will exclude the USA from mechanisms of reporting and information sharing which enable America's own agencies to be more effective. Equally, without US participation, global efforts will be less effective. Meanwhile, at the WHO's annual meeting in May 2020, China pledged $2 billion over two years to help fight the pandemic.

Since December 2019, the USA has continued to block any appointments of new judges to the appellate body of the World Trade Organization. The effect has been to render the body inoperative since 11 December 2019, since it does not have the requisite minimum of three judges to hear a case. China's response has been to circulate a reform proposal underscoring the importance of global trade rules and criticizing those blocking appointments to the appellate body.[19]

Earlier in 2019, against a backdrop of rising concerns about China's growing influence in Latin America, the Trump administration began to assert its control over the InterAmerican Development Bank. The regional bank's board had decided to hold its annual meeting in Chengdu, China. It was an important meeting, with the 48 members of the regional development bank (which include the USA, which holds 30 per cent of votes, and China with 0.004 per cent of the votes) celebrating the bank's sixtieth anniversary. On 22 March 2019, six days

---

[17] https://www.whitehouse.gov/briefings-statements/remarks-president-trump-press-briefing/.
[18] Gostin has questioned the legality of the withdrawal on the grounds that a) the USA must first fulfil all its financial obligations to the organization, and b) that withdrawal could need congressional approval, since US President Truman had specifically referencing a joint resolution of both houses of Congress in 1948 when joining the WHO. In the words of the Supreme Court: 'When the President takes measures incompatible with the expressed or implied will of Congress, his power is at its lowest ebb.' Gostin at https://www.thelancet.com/pdfs/journals/lancet/PIIS0140-6736(20)31527-0.pdf.
[19] https://docs.wto.org/dol2fe/Pages/FE_Search/FE_S_S009-DP.aspx?language=E&CatalogueIdList=254127&CurrentCatalogueIdIndex=0&FullTextHash=371857150&HasEnglishRecord=True&HasFrenchRecord=False&HasSpanishRecord=False.

before the event, the bank announced that the annual meeting would not be held in Chengdu, but would be relocated to another venue.[20] Journalists reported that this was due to a disagreement over whether a representative of Venezuela's opposition party should be permitted to attend.[21] The meeting was held later in Guayaquil, Ecuador.[22] Further to this, in 2020, the US administration pressed for its nominee—a former aide to President Trump—to be appointed to the presidency of the bank, in the first ever imposition by the USA of an American rather than a Latin American president. In all, 16 of the Bank's 48 governors abstained from the vote.[23]

In November 2019, when the World Bank tabled its latest five-year lending plan for China,[24] US officials objected loudly (as well as formally).[25] The chairman of the Senate Finance Committee opined that the 'World Bank, using American tax dollars, should not be lending to wealthy countries that violate the human rights of their citizens and attempt to dominate weaker countries either militarily or economically', and Representative Anthony Gonzalez (Rep., Ohio) who has introduced legislation to curb World Bank funding to China, added: 'For me, even a dollar is too much for our taxpayers to be contributing to China.'[26]

In fact, the World Bank does not use US taxpayers' money to lend to China. The World Bank earns money by lending to China, money which is then used to pay for its operations (based in Washington DC) and which contributes to the bank's concessional lending to poorer countries. China is in a category of borrowers that pay up to 1.9 per cent over the London Inter-Bank Offer Rate (LIBOR),[27] and in 2019 the bank reported an increase in its income, due in part to an increase in loan spread revenue.[28] Furthermore, China's borrowing from the World Bank permits other countries to share practices with China (as well as to learn from China). It is noteworthy that the bank's lending aims in China include advancing market and fiscal reforms to encourage private-sector development; promoting greener growth by reducing pollution and reducing carbon emissions;

[20] https://www.iadb.org/en/news/idb-changes-location-annual-meeting.

[21] https://www.reuters.com/article/us-venezuela-politics-china-iadb-exclusi/exclusive-iadb-cancels-china-meeting-after-beijing-bars-venezuela-representative-idUSKCN1R32NU.

[22] https://www.idbinvest.org/en/news-media/guayaquil-ecuador-host-2019-annual-meeting-idb-and-idb-invest.

[23] https://www.devex.com/news/mauricio-claver-carone-overcomes-regional-opposition-to-become-first-american-idb-president-98080.

[24] http://documents1.worldbank.org/curated/en/902781575573489712/pdf/China-Country-Partnership-Framework-for-the-Period-FY2020-2025.pdf.

[25] 'US Objects to World Bank's Lending Plans for China.'
https://www.nytimes.com/2019/12/05/business/us-china-world-bank.html?referringSource=articleShare.

[26] https://www.aljazeera.com/ajimpact/world-bank-china-billions-loans-objections-191206010906821.html.

[27] https://treasury.worldbank.org/en/about/unit/treasury/ibrd-financial-products/lending-rates-and-fees.

[28] http://pubdocs.worldbank.org/en/625641565356285634/IBRD-Financial-Statements-June-2019.pdf.

and increasing Chinese citizens' access to health and social services. It is not clear to which of these the USA objects.

Simply put, if the World Bank lends less to China and other countries that can afford to pay its full lending charges, then the bank will have to shrink or have members such as the USA make greater contributions to it. If the Washington DC-based World Bank shrinks, it will be other lending institutions, such as the Beijing-based Asian Infrastructure Investment Bank, that will step in.

In other multilateral organizations, the USA has sought to ensure that China-backed candidates do not head international organizations. In 2019 the agency at stake was the Food and Agriculture Organization (FAO), an organization conceived and born in the USA (its first headquarters were in Washington DC). The USA is one of the largest contributors to its budget and a key resource partner.[29] In 2019 all member countries participated in the election of a new head. The USA was determined to beat the Chinese candidate. However, the Trump administration miscalculated in its refusal to support the EU-backed French candidate, splitting the vote, and leaving the way clear for the Chinese vice-minister Qu Dongyu to be elected.[30] The USA did better in early 2020 when China campaigned for a Chinese candidate to be appointed head of the World Intellectual Property Organization (WIPO).[31] The USA threw its support behind a candidate from Singapore, who beat off the challenge from China.

The US strategy towards multilateral organizations (many of which it created) is not yet clear. In some cases, it is engaging with other countries to uphold multilateral rules and processes for changing the organizations, thereby shaping multilateralism and counter-balancing China's new influence, as it did in the WIPO leadership election. In other cases, such as the WHO and WTO, it has adopted a more aggressive, unilateralist approach which risks estranging potential allies, weakening the multilateral processes, and pushing the world towards 'rival alliances'.

Writing in September 2020, the race is now on to see who is appointed director-general of the World Trade Organization. The US Trade Representative has already declared that a successful candidate must understand the need for 'fundamental' reform of the WTO, recognize that China cannot currently be dealt with in the WTO, and not have so much as a 'whiff' of anti-Americanism in their background.[32] Meanwhile, China's ambassador to the WTO has said that a key criterion for selecting the next director-general will be whether he or she has a

[29] https://usunrome.usmission.gov/wp-content/uploads/sites/54/Brochure.pdf.
[30] https://foreignpolicy.com/2020/01/22/us-state-department-appoints-envoy-counter-chinese-influence-un-trump/.
[31] https://www.scmp.com/news/china/diplomacy/article/3048799/horse-trading-and-arm-twisting-us-battles-china-over.
[32] https://www.bloomberg.com/news/articles/2020-07-28/the-next-wto-chief-treads-a-fine-line-between-the-u-s-and-china.

'firm belief in the multilateral trading system with strong determination and adequate ability to bring WTO members together', and whether they are 'someone who can shoulder pressure from the non-believers and march on'.

This and other leadership races may themselves shape future multilateralism[33] by cementing rival coalitions around candidates, and/or advancing candidates who have (or who do not have, by design) the independence and capabilities to affect how the multilateral organization advances international cooperation.

Conclusions and the Implications for Europe

Multilateralism is evolving as the strategic rivalry between the USA and China plays out across three domains: markets (and access to markets), technology, and influence over the rules of the game. To date the European Union has been part competitor (for markets), part referee (on technology), and often 'punching below its weight' in setting the rules of the game. As multilateralism evolves, European powers will need to evolve their own strategies.

This chapter has laid our three types of multilateralism which are likely to persist. Multilateralism within alliances—formalized in international institutions—is one. China and the USA will each use institutions they dominate to cement relations with their own allies, while they simultaneously develop other arrangements such as the BRI mentioned above: for example, the USA in the InterAmerican Development Bank (where it has 30 per cent of the voting power and China only 0.004 per cent), and China in the Asia Infrastructure Investment Bank (where it has 29 per cent of voting power and the USA is not a member). European powers will now have to decide whether to continue mostly to look inwards, strengthening arrangements within the European Union, or to use their shared institutions (from the European Central Bank and the European Investment Bank, to the EU's aid programme and trade policy) to cement alliances outside of the EU.

For the rest of the world, this is not a wholly bad thing. Classical realists would say that balance-of-power politics—the competition for dominance between superpowers—necessarily sacrifices the sovereignty of small states. But within an alliance, these formal institutions can give smaller states some influence over the rules. One example is the IMF in the 1980s, when the Soviet Union was not a member and the USA had a dominant voice and role. The IMF's lending practices and policies were tightly aligned with US national security priorities. But the formal and informal agenda setting and decision making within the IMF in the 1980s offered opportunities for European and other states to influence the rules.

---

[33] Other leadership selections taking place during this period include those of the OECD, the European Bank for Reconstruction and Development, and the International Finance Corporation.

Today the strategic question for European powers is: what alliance do they wish to lead or join? The US-led alliance is changing fast. So too is European support for it. In a very recent poll of 11,000 citizens across nine European countries, reported in June 2020, a staggering percentage of people (up to 70 per cent) noted that their perceptions of the USA had worsened over the course of the virus. This led researchers to conclude that the Covid-19 crisis revealed 'a US divided in its response to the present crisis and haunted by its history' with the risk that Europeans will come 'to see the US as a broken hegemon that cannot be entrusted with the defence of the Western world'.[34]

A second form of multilateralism is that provided for by international institutions in which both superpowers are represented. Today the IMF is in the process of becoming a different institution. As mentioned above, China now has the third largest share of votes in the organization, as well as senior officials. While the USA is still dominant and continues to urge the organization to be 'tougher' on China over its exchange-rate regime (and President Trump accuses China of currency manipulation),[35] the institution reports that China's external positions are balanced.[36] China's influence has increased dramatically. And China, the USA, and other countries will have a shared interest in seeing the IMF act to preserve financial stability and to manage debt crises on every continent in the wake of Covid-19. Meanwhile, European members of the IMF still act separately, formulating their own policies, with Germany, the UK, and France enjoying their own executive directorships, while other European countries are represented in constituency groups. The result is that their influence is less than it could be. If Europeans wielded their voting power as one, they would enjoy a powerful immediate veto (as does the USA) over decisions requiring a special majority, a power which reverberates informally across the work of the management and staff of the organization. Similarly, in other organizations, European powers have begun, rather belatedly, to think about how better to join forces, such as in the UN Security Council.

The impact of international organizations on cooperation between the USA and China will be influenced by the leadership of the organizations themselves. Past examples underscore that an executive head who can mobilize a coalition of countries to counter a dominant member's view, and/or can maximally leverage the staff, information, technical knowledge, and resources of the organization, can have an impact. Dag Hammarskjöld did this as secretary-general of the United Nations when he created peacekeeping, and Robert McNamara did this as president of the World Bank when he greatly expanded the institution's membership

---

[34] https://www.ecfr.eu/page//europes_pandemic_politics_how_the_virus_has_changed_the_publics_worldview.pdf.
[35] https://www.cnbc.com/2019/08/05/trump-accuses-china-of-currency-manipulation-as-yuan-drops-to-new-low.html.
[36] https://www.imf.org/en/Publications/ESR/Issues/2019/07/03/2019-external-sector-report.

and activities. Without such leaders, international organizations are almost guaranteed to be stalemated by the vetoes of rival superpowers, sidelined by both, or turned into pawns of one rival or the other. It is vital for Europe to act both to ensure such leaders are selected, and subsequently to hold them to account.

Multilateralism is also likely to proceed outside of formal institutions. Multilateral consultations took place among Europe's five great powers in the early nineteenth century to resolve matters of mutual reciprocal interest. Today the leaders of the world's largest economies have many such issues. They meet as the G20, which is principally a committee for crisis management. At their summit in April 2020, they collectively committed to coordinate some of their own responses—on fiscal policy, for example, on resolving trade disputes, and in monetary policy. They also agreed to use existing international agreements and institutions including the International Health Regulations, the IMF, World Bank, International Labour Organization, and OECD. European powers will most powerfully shape such ad hoc and informal multilateralism by looking outwards and forging common strategies which advance European aspirations vis-à-vis markets, the development of technology, and global governance.

The strategic rivalry between China and the USA is a rivalry between nations which both depend on global markets, global finance, global innovation, and the co-option of other countries and regions of the world to sustain their own success. So too do European powers. For this reason, they will need to find more powerful ways to shape the emerging multilateralism.

References

Abbott, Kenneth W. and Duncan Snidal. 'Why States Act through Formal International Organizations.' *Journal of Conflict Resolution* 42(1): 3–32.

Davis, Christina and Meredith Wilf (2011). 'Joining the Club: Accession to the GATT/WTO.' Working Paper, Princeton University. https://www.journals.uchicago.edu/doi/abs/10.1086/691058?journalCode=jop.

Hall, Nina and Ngaire Woods (2018). 'Theorizing the Role of Executive Heads in International Organizations.' *European Journal of International Relations* 24(4): 865–86.

Keohane, Robert O. (1990). 'Multilateralism: An Agenda for Research.' *International Journal* 45(4): 731–64.

Ruggie, John Gerard (1992). 'Multilateralism: The Anatomy of an Institution.' *International Organization* 46(3): 561–98.

Woods, Ngaire (2006). *The Globalizers*. New York: Cornell University Press.

Woods, Ngaire (2010). 'Global Governance after the Financial Crisis: A New Multilateralism or the Last Gasp of the Great Powers?' *Global Policy* 1(1): 51–63.

13

The Return of Global Asymmetries

Jean Pisani-Ferry

Five decades ago, when the young Loukas Tsoukalis started thinking and writing about the global economy, the conventional wisdom was that despite the demise of colonialism, a handful of rich countries would continue to dominate the world.[1] It was widely assumed—certainly, but by no means exclusively, on the side of the political spectrum he belonged to—that they would keep on competing fiercely with each other and get richer along the way, while short of a major overhaul the poor countries would get poorer, at least in relative terms. The iron law seemed to be that the centre would concentrate power and amass riches, while the periphery would struggle and stumble.

Having studied the development of capitalism through the centuries, the historian Fernand Braudel spoke of successive dominance by 'world economies' and of repeated core–periphery patterns (Braudel 1977; 1992). Economists like Samir Amin in Egypt, Andre Gunder Frank in the USA, Gunnar Myrdal in Sweden, François Perroux in France, and Raul Prebisch in Argentina warned of economic dependency, the development of underdevelopment, and rising inequality. In the intellectual climate of the times, many regarded the web of international trade, investment, finance, and money as the conduit of unequal exchange and a system built to perpetuate the domination of the established powers.

Evidence for such views was found in the successive ascent of powerful city-states since the fourteenth century—from Venice to New York; in the 'Great Divergence' in income and wealth between, on the one hand, Europe and its offspring, and, on the other hand, the ancient powers, China and India (Pomeranz 2000); in the relative decline of commodity prices and the income of commodity producers; and in the perpetuation of neocolonial relations.

Few observers recalled Adam Smith's 1776 warning that if their 'superiority of force' enabled the Europeans to 'commit with impunity every sort of injustice', the natives of developing countries 'may grow stronger, or those of Europe may grow weaker' so that 'the inhabitants of all the different quarters of the world may arrive

[1] This chapter draws on research done at the European University Institute. I am grateful to Laurence Boone, Kemal Dervis, Manuel Lafont-Rapnouil, Elina Ribakova, and André Sapir for comments on an earlier draft, and to Loïc Baptiste Savatier for research assistance.

Jean Pisani-Ferry, *The Return of Global Asymmetries* In: *Europe's Transformations: Essays in Honour of Loukas Tsoukalis.* Edited by: Helen Wallace, Nikos Koutsiaras, and George Pagoulatos, Oxford University Press.
© OUP 2021. DOI: 10.1093/oso/9780192895820.003.0013

at an equality of courage and force'. Even fewer anticipated that this equality of force would result from a 'mutual communication of knowledge and of all sorts of improvements which an extensive commerce from all countries to all countries naturally, or rather necessarily, carries along with it'.[2]

Two beliefs structured the grim perspective of the 1970s. The first was that, barring a major geopolitical overhaul, strong asymmetry between the centre and the periphery would persist in international economic relations. The second was that such asymmetry would prevent the development of the periphery. 'The blunt truth', Myrdal said in his 1975 Nobel lecture, 'is that without rather radical changes in the consumption patterns in the rich countries, any pious talk about a new world economic order is humbug' (Myrdal 1975).

The second of these beliefs was proved wrong by the economic history of the last 50 years. In 1970 high-income countries accounted for 90 per cent of world manufacturing output, 80 per cent of world GDP, and 65 per cent of world exports.[3] By the late 2010s these proportions were down to 55 per cent, 65 per cent, and 50 per cent respectively. After having remained on a declining trend from the early nineteenth century to the 1970s, relative income per capita in the South bottomed out abruptly and has continuously increased for about five decades.[4] The single most important economic development of the last half-century has been the catch-up in output, income, and economic sophistication of a significant group of formerly poor countries.

The world, for sure, has not become equal. If anything, the income gap between countries at the top and countries at the bottom has continued to widen. Too many of the world's poor live in countries whose GDP per capita has remained stagnant for decades. But the characteristically bimodal global distribution of income among world citizens that still prevailed in the 1970s has vanished. Overall, income inequalities within countries have increased, while inequalities between countries have diminished. As a consequence, the global distribution of income has become less unequal. As Branko Milanovic puts it: if this trend continues, 'we might return to the situation that existed in the early nineteenth century, when most of global inequality was due to income differences between rich and poor Britons, rich and poor Russians, or rich and poor Chinese' (Milanovic 2016: 5).

There is no doubt, therefore, that the global economy has become less divergent. However, whether or not the first belief has also been proved wrong, because it has also become less asymmetric, is a distinct question. Of course, the proponents

---

[2] The quotes are from Chapter 7 ('Of Colonies') of Part 4 of *The Wealth of Nations*. They serve as an epigraph to Branco Milanovic's *Capitalism, Alone* (2019).

[3] Sources: Unido, Unctad, and CEPII.

[4] In *Capitalism, Alone* (2019: fig. 5.1), Branko Milanovic observes that the incomes per capita in China, Indonesia and India relative to those of their former colonial masters all followed the same V-shaped evolution.

of the dependency theory regarded asymmetry and the persistence of underdevelopment as two sides of the same coin. But as Loukas Tsoukalis knows well from having repeatedly travelled to and from between economics and political science, they are not.

The Making of a Less Divergent World

Two main factors account for the extraordinary change in fortunes witnessed since the 1970s: technology and policies. As Richard Baldwin explains in his illuminating book *The Great Convergence*, a major reason why Adam Smith's prediction finally materialized and a group of developing countries caught up with the advanced nations was *the dramatic fall in the cost of moving ideas*—what he calls the 'second unbundling' (of technology and production) (Baldwin 2016). Instead of perpetuating the divide between technology-rich and technology-poor countries, flows of knowledge and know-how embedded in foreign direct investment or involved in the contractual relationships developed between purchasers and suppliers have resulted in major productivity gains in formerly peripheral economies. This barely happened within the framework of the old trading relationship. Only the breakthrough brought by the telecommunication revolution could allow it to take place on a massive scale.

Good journalism has been famously defined as simplification followed by exaggeration, and this certainly applies to Tom Friedman's characterization of the resulting world. The playing field, the *New York Times* columnist claimed in 2005, has been levelled: *The World is Flat* (Friedman 2005). Wherever production takes place, he said, it benefits from the same access to knowledge, technology, and markets. This was obviously hyperbole: the economic world was never, and will never be, flat. Over recent decades poorly governed, remote, landlocked countries have struggled to gain access to technology and overcome obstacles to development. Too many nations are still failing to do so (Acemoglu and Robinson 2012). But for all his exaggerations, Friedman captured the essence of the economic transformation triggered by technology.

Policies implemented at national level were the second trigger. It was in the late 1970s that China under Deng Xiaoping changed course, opened up to foreign investment and started building its own variety of capitalism. China's return to the market clearly marks a bifurcation in the economic history of the world. But, as observed by Ronald Findlay and Kevin O'Rourke, the 1970s represented a turning point for many more countries: whereas the advanced world had already started reducing trade protection in the 1950s, in the rest of the world tariffs continued to rise during the early post-war period (Findlay and O'Rourke 2007). It was only in the 1980s that developing countries changed course *en masse* to implement reform and liberalization packages.

Economists trained in the tradition of Adam Smith and David Ricardo tend to regard the pattern of successful development that emerged in the late twentieth century as the result of this large-scale liberalization of trade and investment. It is certainly true that liberalization and an export orientation succeeded in eliciting the economic catch-up that import substitution had failed to deliver. But as Baldwin points out, the benefits of industrialization have been tightly concentrated: in a first phase, they went to a handful of east Asian NICs (Newly Industrialized Countries, a.k.a. the Four Asian Tigers), then starting in the 1990s they went to China and another small group of industrializing economies.[5] In both cases, government policies played a strong part in steering development through the allocation of resources and credit. Many other countries, especially in Latin America, experienced what Dani Rodrik has called premature deindustrialization instead (Rodrik 2015).

The story, therefore, is a complex one. First, the prediction of an inexorable divergence between central and peripheral countries was proved wrong, but convergence is by no means a generalized phenomenon. Second, neither technology alone, nor liberalization alone can account for the successful catch-up of a series of countries initially ranked as middle- or low-income. Rather, development was brought about by their interaction in the context of calculated development strategies.

The Asymmetry Question

Has this less divergent world also become flatter through a levelling of asymmetries? Answering this question is more challenging, for relative power is harder to measure than relative prosperity. Broadly speaking, though, it has—for the simple, materialistic reason that, in peacetime at least, economic weight is a major determinant of relative power. The establishment in 2008 of the Group of Twenty as the venue for global coordination at the leaders' level illustrates the point. But the question is not simply if the law of gravity applies; it is whether the international system, and the changes wrought to it, has intensified or diminished the asymmetry implied by mere economic weight.

Fifty years ago, the global economic system was highly asymmetric. Trade patterns had been transformed by the dissolution of colonial empires and the rise of intra-industry trade. As more and more transactions took place between advanced countries, poor countries that exported commodities and imported manufactured goods were becoming marginalized, as rich ones reaped the benefits of intra-industry specialization. Foreign direct investment flows were even more

---

[5] The Four Asian Tigers are Hong Kong, Korea, Taiwan, and Singapore; the Industrializing Six are China, Korea, India, Indonesia, Thailand, and Poland.

asymmetric, as the USA accounted for the bulk of them. Europe was actually a major recipient of US investment, and sometimes worried about the resulting dependence.[6]

Monetary relations were asymmetric by design. The still-prevailing Bretton Woods system gave the US currency a unique role and involved a deeply unequal distribution of obligations among participating countries. The US dollar enjoyed a special status, as no other currency could rival it in its roles of unit of account (because of the exchange-rate system), store of value (because of its gold equivalence and the resulting composition of foreign exchange reserves), and medium of exchange (because it served as the vehicle currency for international trade). Correlatively, countries participating in the fixed exchange-rate system needed to accumulate dollar liquidity in the form of reserves, thereby ensuring a near-automatic financing of the US current-account deficit. This built-in asymmetry—the (in)famous 'exorbitant privilege'—was a core feature of the system, and resulted in Robert Triffin's dilemma between preserving the global pre-eminence of the US dollar and ensuring the smooth functioning of the global system.

Moreover, a strong view, associated with Charles Kindelberger's account of the Great Depression, was that asymmetry is a necessary feature of a stable global system. Writing in 1973, Kindelberger explained that the international economic and monetary system needed a lender and a consumer of last resort that could act in a discretionary way to preserve overall stability in times of crisis. He also claimed that it needed leadership by 'a country which is prepared, consciously or unconsciously ... to set standards of conducts for other countries' (Kindelberger 1973).

A particular feature of the post-war international economic system was, however, that its rules were not designed to ensure sheer dominance or to maximize rent extraction, but rather, to quote from the famous United States NSC-68 strategic plan of 1950, to 'build a healthy international community' and 'a world environment in which the American system [could] survive and flourish'.[7] The ultimate aim was to contain Soviet expansion, and this required the establishing of a multifaceted and mutually beneficial alliance with like-minded countries in Europe and east Asia—what John Ikenberry (2015: 405) called 'the most intensive institution building the world has ever seen'.

In this world, even if the USA remained central both economically and politically, it regarded development among its partners—that is, ultimately, the attenuation of its relative economic power—as fundamentally favourable to its national interest. The more like-minded countries grew and the stronger they became in

[6] As illustrated by the French best-seller Le Défi Américain by Jean-Jacques Servan-Schreiber, a prominent journalist and news editor (Servan-Schreiber 1967).

[7] The NSC-68 report by the National Security Council (1950) set out military, political, and economic options for confronting rivalry with the Soviet Union.

comparison to the Soviet bloc, the better it was for Washington, DC. To foster growth and development, the USA was willing to place limits on the exercise of its own discretionary power. The liberal international order, to use the characterization of John Ikenberry, was both multilateral (in that all participants were subject to the same rules) and hegemonic (in that it had been built by and around the USA). Its core quid pro quo was that the hegemon would both benefit from its central position and accept being significantly (though not entirely) constrained by multilateral rules, for example international trade rules. In the words of Ikenberry (2018), the USA was supposed to behave as the 'first citizen' of that world.

The reference point of multilateralism is a world characterized by the equality of rights and obligations among participating countries, irrespective of their size or their might. This distant goal has never been approached in practice: in the absence of criminal justice, trade rules and a dispute settlement system (which did not exist yet) could only mitigate the balance of economic power. But as economic integration developed, emphasis was increasingly put on a system of rules and institutions that gave a voice to the least powerful players. They ended up making use of it, belatedly but spectacularly, in the multilateral trade negotiations conducted under the Doha Round, whose outcome could not be settled among the advanced countries. Their failure to agree with the developing countries resulted in the collapse of the talks.

The monetary system also underwent a significant overhaul with the introduction of floating exchange rates in the early 1970s. Proponents of exchange-rate flexibility such as Milton Friedman and Harry Johnson regarded it as another flattener that would give countries 'autonomy with respect to their use of monetary, fiscal, and other policy instruments' (Johnson 1969: 12). True, not every currency would float: according to Johnson, advantages would mostly accrue to the 'currencies of the major countries', which derive their usefulness 'from the great diversity of goods, services and assets available in the national economy'. But a floating-rate system would at least diminish the dollar's 'exorbitant privilege'. After financial account transactions began to be lifted in the 1980s, Triffin's dilemma made way in the policy makers' intellectual toolbox to Mundell's trilemma between exchange-rate stability, monetary policy autonomy, and free capital movements—a choice *all* countries were confronted with.

By 2000 it seemed likely that the international system would continue evolving towards a less asymmetric regime. There were no capitalist and socialist blocs any more, only a global economy. The reach of the US system extended the world over, and its very success was transformative. Successive waves of formerly developing countries had made major inroads into manufacturing and trade. As far as exchange rates were concerned, the prevailing view was that Harry Johnson had got it right and the monetary system had become more symmetric. Writing in 2002, Maurice Obstfeld and Kenneth Rogoff offered a remarkably benign view of its functioning: they found that 'as domestic monetary rules improve, and as international asset markets become more complete, there are plausible circumstances in which the outcome of a Nash monetary rule-setting game begins to approximate the outcome of a cooperative system' (Obstfeld and Rogoff 2002: 528). It was hoped that the global role of the US dollar, which was in any case not a major concern, would gradually diminish, making way for the emergence of other international currencies. And international institutions, now legitimized by their truly global character, served as equalizers.

Europe, obviously, was a major part of the push for a more symmetric international system. As well illustrated by Tsoukalis' own intellectual journey and his insightful contributions to the debate on the future of Europe, gradual integration within the EU cannot be separated from the broader transformation of the international regime that has taken place over recent decades. The (occasionally frustrated but ultimately successful) EU attempt to build a legally grounded, symmetric European policy system developed in parallel with the far more challenging, but fundamentally parallel, attempt to build a global rules-based international economic system.

When Asymmetries Strike Back

Things, however, have changed again. In recent years a series of factors have contributed to putting the emphasis back on asymmetries. In part this is because they have actually grown stronger under the influence of changes in the pattern of economic interdependence. The functioning of international economic relations has also been reassessed in the light of evidence and/or acute stress conditions, while existing systemic asymmetries are also being exploited more than before as a vehicle for asserting power. In one way or another, centrality is being restored as a pivotal feature of the global system. Several factors enter into play: industrial concentration and market power have strengthened; technology has given a new prominence to network-type structures; global finance does not equalize countries, it singles out the chosen ones; the dominant role of the US financial system and the US dollar are being revaluated; global institutions have weakened; and great power rivalry has become a central feature of international relations. Symmetry is bound to be the victim of each of these transformations.

The first factor is *industrial concentration*. In a more economically balanced world it could have been expected to diminish mechanically, at least at global level. But this is not what recent data on corporate profits suggest. According to the McKinsey Global Institute, 10 per cent of the largest 6,000 firms worldwide account for 80 per cent of economic profit, a larger proportion than 20 years ago, and the top 1 per cent (58 'superstar firms') account for 36 per cent of it (Manyika et al. 2018). Despite the rise of emerging corporate giants, US firms alone still represent 60 per cent of the global profits of these superstar firms— exactly the same proportion as 20 years ago, despite the rise of emerging countries.

US firms therefore retain a dominant role as far as market power is concerned. This trend is magnified in an increasingly digitalized economy, where a growing proportion of services are provided at zero marginal cost, where value creation and value appropriation are increasingly concentrated in the centres of innovation, and where intangible investments are made, leaving less for the production facilities where tangible goods are made.

Other data for the USA and, to a lesser degree, Europe (see Chapter 3 in this volume) also point to an increase in the share of sales and, especially, profits accruing to the top firms.[8] Innovation rents and their role in the organization of global value chains help them capture a large part of the value added. Productivity data also suggest that an increasing share of macroeconomic growth is attributable to 'frontier firms' (another name for the superstars), whose performance and profitability are far above average (Andrews, Criscuolo, and Gal 2015). This rise is particularly apparent in technology-driven sectors where high fixed costs and low marginal costs favour massive concentration, but it is by no means limited to the tech industry.

The second, related but distinct, factor is the *rise and transformation of networks*. Networks are ubiquitous in data-driven industries but also in finance and manufacturing. From macroeconomics to trade and finance, a growing realization that they matter is transforming the way we look at interdependence (Carvalho and Tahbaz-Salehi 2019).

By itself, a network structure does not necessarily entail hierarchy. Point-to-point networks are fundamentally symmetric, and because they diminish the impact of remoteness and improve access they were once regarded as major flatteners. But a network structure involves and causes asymmetry if it is organized along a hub-and-spokes model. Wherever the fixed cost of building links between two nodes is meaningful, but the marginal cost of using them is low, hub-and-spokes patterns have emerged from the natural search for cost minimization as economically efficient structures.

Such a hub-and-spoke pattern can be found in many fields. Digital services are an extreme example, but a similar pattern can be found in finance. Global value chains (GVCs), which account for about half of total world trade, also exhibit hub-and-spoke structures, in which a few countries and firms play a central role. In manufacturing, for example, Germany, the USA and increasingly China are home to globally central hubs (Criscuolo and Timmins 2018). According to the World Bank, the expansion of GVCs since 1990 has been driven by the fragmentation of

---

[8] See Furman (2018) and Autor et al. (2019). For a discussion of industrial concentration in the USA, see Philippon (2019).

production processes in major advanced countries—of which Germany, the USA and Japan are the top three—and by a few large trading firms that engage in both imports and exports. The 2020 World Development Report speaks of 'a novel, relational conceptualization of GVCs that shifts the focus away from the mere allocation of value added across countries through anonymous spot exchanges of goods and services' and considers that within GVCs, 'relationships are more likely to exhibit persistence' (World Bank 2020: 32. True, GVCs are the channels through which ideas and technologies move seamlessly. But they also embody a persistent asymmetry between hubs and second- or third-tier nodes.

Financial liberalization was once thought of as an equalizer. Liberalization would allow all countries to tap into the global capital market to finance their development or offset temporary shocks to their income. In 1997, the International Monetary Fund (IMF) even considered being officially given a mandate to promote the liberalization of the financial account.[9] But in fact, network structure can be found in the international financial system, which is structured around a handful of global centres that are home to major markets, provide services, and serve as hubs for the rest of the world. Liberalization has proved disruptive for the weaker countries. Experience has revealed a pattern of recurrent capital flows reversals, mostly driven by 'push' factors rather than by policy failures in the recipient countries (Eichengreen and Gupta 2018). As a consequence, financial-account liberalization has stalled in emerging countries. The Asian crisis of the late 1990s was a watershed.

Asymmetries remain strong as regards currencies of denomination for international debt. The divide between countries that are able to borrow in their own currencies and those—emerging and developing ones—that are forced to borrow in a foreign currency (what Barry Eichengreen, Ricardo Hausmann, and Ugo Panizza (2005) called their 'original sin') is only slowly receding. Furthermore, the USA remains unique among advanced countries: whereas bonds denominated in other currencies can also serve as safe assets for the rest of the world, US Treasury bonds offer unrivalled depth and liquidity, and only the US dollar regularly appreciates in times of global financial stress (Caballero, Farhi, and Gourinchas 2008).

Finally, the global financial crisis highlighted the centrality of Wall Street. It revealed how defaults in a remote corner of the US credit market could contaminate the entire European banking system, highlighted the international banks' addiction to the dollar and the degree to which they had grown dependent on access to dollar liquidity for the financing of their global operations, and transformed the US Treasury and the Federal Reserve into vital providers of international liquidity. Whereas the system looked symmetric in good times, dollar

---

[9] The mandate of the IMF was (and since the decision was not adopted, still is) limited to promoting current-account liberalization.

liquidity shortage made asymmetry brutally apparent. The swap lines extended by the Federal Reserve to selected partner central banks to help them cope with the corresponding demand for dollars vividly illustrated the hierarchical nature of the international system (Tooze 2018 and Obstfeld 2013).

This brings us to the third factor: *monetary asymmetry*. Scholars have begun reassessing international economics in the light of the stronger-than-expected persistence of asymmetries. Hélène Rey (2013) of the London Business School has debunked the prevailing view that floating exchange rates provide insulation from the consequences of the US monetary cycle. She claims that the global financial cycle still originates in the USA and that countries can protect themselves from destabilizing capital inflows and outflows only by monitoring credit very closely or resorting to capital controls. Rather than facing a trilemma, most countries are therefore confronted with a dilemma. In a similar vein, Gita Gopinath, now the IMF's chief economist, has emphasized how dependent most countries are on the US dollar, and how much fluctuations in its exchange rate affect their foreign trade. Whereas the standard approach would make, say, the won–real rate a prime determinant of trade between South Korea and Brazil, the reality is that because this trade is largely invoiced in dollars, the dollar exchange rate of the two countries' currencies matters more than their bilateral exchange rate. Her dominant currency paradigm has profound implications for trade, macroeconomic policy autonomy, and international spillovers. Again, this result highlights the centrality of US monetary policy for all countries, big and small, and sheds light on Rey's finding. Gopinath also finds evidence that monetary policy shocks in the dominant currency country have 'strong spillovers to the rest of the world, while the converse is not true' (Gopinath et al. 2020). Far from having nurtured the emergence of a more symmetric world, financial opening and the move towards exchange-rate flexibility may have strengthened the asymmetry of the system.

The fourth major reason for the un-flattening of the world is *institutional*: multilateralism was meant to give all countries a stake in the governance of the global system. For sure, rules had been set by a few major powers and served their interests, but amending them and negotiating the outcome became increasingly participative processes. By the 2000s, however, hopes that globalization would be governed by a web of rules-based specialized institutions had been dashed: multilateral trade talks were unable to deliver agreement on a new round of liberalization, and hopes that the international community would agree on establishing new multilateral frameworks for investment, competition, climate or the internet had faded away. The weakening of global governance was already visible at the turn of the millennium. It would weaken further in the 2010s, after a short revival in international cooperation in the immediate aftermath of the global financial crisis, and even more in the wake of the populist wave of the 2010s.

Rules are still in force and institutions are still alive, but the momentum has been lost and fragmentation risks are very visible.[10]

Finally, *geopolitical rivalry* between the USA and China is fast restructuring international relations and the relationship between major powers and international organizations (see Chapter 12 in this volume). For all its vagaries and aggressive posturing, the Trump presidency introduced a fundamental and perhaps lasting paradigm shift in the US approach to international economic relations. Trump was peculiar in his attempt to leverage the unique trade and financial standing of his country in order to extract pecuniary rents from partners, to force them to abide by US unilateral sanctions, and to undermine global governance. But he was perhaps less peculiar in his change of perspective. In the words of Nadia Shadlow (2020: 43), a former senior National Security Council official, his trademark was to recognize that 'rivalry is an unalterable feature of the international system' and it would be a 'grave mistake to return to the premises of a bygone era'.

President Xi Jinping has launched the 'Belt and Road' initiative in the meantime, which aims to organize a China-centric web of bilateral agreements. While paying lip service to multilateralism, China does not in fact endorse the concept of a rules-based order, especially as the rules were written by others. Rather, it is actively building a network of essentially bilateral relations with countries that depend on its financial, technical or security support (Horn, Reinhart, and Trebesch 2019). Its perspective on international economic relations is fundamentally an asymmetric one. Instead of a single Western-dominated multilateral system, the world is therefore witnessing the gradual emergence of competing networks of trade, investment, credit, and—increasingly—currency arrangements. Instead of multilateralism, we may already be en route to a multipolar system.

But as political scientists, Henry Farrell and Abraham Newman (2019) have pointed out, a network structure provides considerable leverage to whoever controls its nodes. Networks are economically efficient, but network-based interdependence can be 'weaponized' and turned into an instrument of power to the benefit of whoever controls the key hubs. Whereas the intensification of multilateral trade acts as an incentive to cooperation, the rise of network-based economic relations in which hubs concentrate power and rents leads to battles for the control of their key nodes. The notion of 'weaponized interdependence' captures the mutation of efficient economic structures into power-enhancing ones. It also brings us back to the old models of international relations that underpinned the grim views of the Braudelian school.

---

[10] I developed these points and discussed the causes of the decline of global governance in my Wincott Lecture (Pisani-Ferry 2019b). See also Pisani-Ferry (2019a).

Conclusions

After a decades-long eclipse, asymmetry, a concept that underpinned analyses of international economic relations when Loukas Tsoukalis began his intellectual journey, is taking centre stage once more. The question is this: what should economists, scholars of international relations, and, especially, policy makers conclude from this observation?

Asymmetry is admittedly a complex and somewhat elusive concept. It is naturally involved in trade, along with comparative advantages or intertemporal exchange through the export of excess savings. In a way, most international transactions (excepting pure intra-industry trade or asset purchases motivated by the search for yield and portfolio diversification) entail a degree of asymmetry. It cannot be regarded in itself as a symptom of dysfunctionality.

What we are witnessing is not, however, merely the expression of the fact that international transactions involve countries that are different from each other. It is a revival of systemic asymmetries that confer power on a few countries, while making other ones dependent or vulnerable. These asymmetries do not primarily result from politics or policies—though these do play a role. Rather, they are rooted in the web of interdependence through trade, technology, finance, and money. There is nothing to indicate that they will be fading away any time soon. On the contrary, economic, systemic, and geopolitical factors all suggest they may prove persistent. We have to learn to live with them.

History provides many examples of prosperity without power, or power without prosperity. Fifty years ago, the perception that the international system was unfair fuelled deep grievances against it. Ultimately, however, asymmetries between the 'centre' and the 'periphery' did not prevent the transfer of knowledge from north to south, and they were used to a limited extent only as a vehicle for extracting rent and concentrating wealth. Neither did they prevent the newcomers to the global game from gradually gaining influence, grabbing power on the margins, and ultimately gaining seats at the G20 high table.

The difference today is that two implicit assumptions, both commonplace until recently in the analysis of international economic relations, have been called into question. The first is that, for all the existing asymmetries and the desire by established powers to retain their privileges, time would even out the ridges and the system would gradually become more symmetric; as long as this assumption held, the direction of travel seemed clear. The second is that any remaining asymmetries would not serve as vehicles for undue rent extraction; the rules of the game were that the 'exorbitant privilege' of the hegemon (and by extension of the other dominant countries) would remain matched by proportionate duties; for sure, the implicit contract was not exactly balanced, but there was some degree of fairness to it.

Recent experience has shed a harsh light on the naivety of these assumptions. Asymmetries within the global system are not only more entrenched than was believed until recently, they are also resurgent. The momentum is not towards a multilateral order within which all countries big and small will play by the same rules. Rather, a combination of technological, systemic, and geopolitical factors are driving a transformation towards concentration and multipolarity. Moreover, the willingness of the USA to play the role of 'first citizen' of the system is increasingly in doubt, while its Chinese rival does not display any intention to play by rules conceived by others. In this context, the fast escalation of USA–China rivalry is driving both rivals away from cooperative behaviour and threatening to lead to a fragmentation of the multilateral system.

This new context calls first for an analytical reassessment. It is only recently that research has cast a spotlight on economic, financial or monetary asymmetries and begun to uncover their determinants. Researchers have now developed analytical and empirical tools that make it possible to gather systematic evidence and to document the impact of asymmetries on the distribution of the gains from economic opening. We are on our way to knowing more about the policy implications of participating in an increasingly asymmetric global system.

Second, the relations between economics and geopolitics must be looked at in a more systematic way. For many years—even before the demise of the Soviet Union—international economic relations have been considered in isolation, at least by economists. They were looked at as if they were (mostly) immune from geopolitical tensions. This stance is not tenable any longer, at a time when great-power rivalry is reasserting itself as a key determinant of policy decisions. This calls for a new conversation between economists and international relations specialists.

Third, supporters of multilateralism need to wake up to the new context. They have too often championed a world made up of peaceful and balanced relations that bears less and less resemblance to reality. Power and asymmetry can only be forgotten at one's own risk. Neglecting them inevitably fuels mistrust of principles, rules, and institutions that are perceived as biased. The multilateral project must be rooted in reality.

This analytical and policy agenda brings us back to the research questions that underpinned Loukas Tsoukalis' doctoral dissertation on the economics and politics of monetary integration (see Chapter 2 in this volume). Now as then, both aspects of integration should be addressed jointly. Now as then, analysis should draw both on a precisely spelled-out economic framework and on an equally explicit political science framework.

Reassessment is especially needed in Europe. Because it has been assigned specific competences in a series of specific fields, the EU has traditionally approached international economic relations as a 'fragmented power', addressing sectoral policy challenges one by one and often failing to join up the dots (Sapir

2007). For a long time, the EU has had a regulatory, trade, competition, and monetary policy, but no foreign economic relations policy. And because it is itself a community of law, it has time and again approached sectoral challenges with an idealistic outlook. The EU must now adapt to a new geopolitical reality and rediscover the notion of sovereignty it strove for so long to expel from its *Weltanschauung*.

This reorientation will have practical implications in a series of fields, from technology to competition policy and the international role of the euro.[11] But, first and foremost perhaps, it has implications for Europe's strategic outlook and for its governance. In the immediate aftermath of the Second World War, the EU was created in a search for symmetry between former enemies on a continent that had repeatedly suffered from power rivalry. It was designed as one component within a wider global rules-based order. In this context, a rules-based, sectorally fragmented governance system ensured balance, protected the prerogatives of member states, and shielded against the temptation to abuse discretionary power. Moreover, this decision-making system was effective in a world where policy discussions were themselves fragmented along sectoral lines.

Such governance is no longer tenable. For all the might that the size of its market and the policy tools at its command may give it, a fragmented Europe that does not connect the dots across policy fields, that lacks a strategic perspective and does not tell its truth to the other powers, would not serve much purpose in the world that is emerging. No one knows that better than Loukas Tsoukalis.

References

Acemoglu, Daron and James Robinson (2012). *Why Nations Fail*. New York: Crown Books.

Andrews, Dan, Chiara Criscuolo, and Peter Gal (2015). 'Frontier Firms, Technology Diffusion and Public Policy: Micro Evidence from OECD Countries.' OECD Productivity Working Paper No. 2.

Autor, David et al. (2019). 'The Fall in the Labor Share and the Rise of Superstar Firms.' *Quarterly Journal of Economics*.

Braudel, Fernand (1992). *Civilization and Capitalism*, Vol. 3: *The Perspective of the World*. Berkeley, CA: University of California Press.

Braudel, Fernand (1997). *Afterthoughts on Material Civilization and Capitalism*. Baltimore, MD: Johns Hopkins University Press. French edition Armand Colin 1979.

---

[11] I have addressed them in detail in Pisani-Ferry, Leonard, Ribakova, Shapiro, and Wolff (2019).

Baldwin, Richard (2016). *The Great Convergence: Information Technology and the New Globalization*. Cambridge, MA: Harvard University Press.

Caballero, Ricardo, Emmanuel Farhi, and Pierre-Olivier Gourinchas (2008). 'An Equilibrium Model of "Global Imbalances" and Low Interest Rates.' *American Economic Review* 98 (1): 358–93.

Carvalho, Vasco and Alireza Tahbaz-Salehi (2019). 'Production Networks: A Primer.' *Annual Review of Economics* 11: 635–63.

Criscuolo, Chiara and Jonathan Timmins (2018). 'GVCs and Centrality.' OECD Productivity Working Paper, No. 12.

Eichengreen, Barry and Poonam Gupta (2018). 'Managing Sudden Stops,' Central Banking, Analysis, and Economic Policies Book Series, in: Enrique G. Mendoza, Ernesto Pastén & Diego Saravia (ed.), Monetary Policy and Global Spillovers: Mechanisms, Effects and Policy Measures, edition 1, volume 25, chapter 2, pages 009–047, Central Bank of Chile.

Eichengreen, Barry, Ricardo Hausmann, and Ugo Panizza (2005). 'The Mystery of Original Sin.' In Barry Eichengreen and Ricardo Hausmann (eds.), *Other People's Money: Debt Denomination and Financial Instability in Emerging-Market Economies*, Chicago: University of Chicago Press: 233–65.

Farrell, Henry and Abraham Newman (2019). 'Weaponized Interdependence: How Global Economic Networks Shape State Coercion.' *International Security* 44(1): 42–79.

Findlay, Ronald and Kevin O'Rourke (2007). *Power and Plenty*. Princeton, NJ: Princeton University Press.

Friedman, Thomas (2005). *The World Is Flat: A Brief History of the Twenty-First Century*. New York: Farrar, Strauss & Giroux.

Furman, Jason (2018). 'Market Concentration.' Hearing at the OECD, 7 June.

Gopinath, Gita et al. (2020). 'Dominant Currency Paradigm.' *American Economic Review* 100(3): 677–719.

Horn, Sebastian, Carmen Reinhart, and Christoph Trebesch (2019). 'China's Overseas Lending.' NBER Working Paper 26050, revised May 2020.

Ikenberry, John (2015). 'The Future of Multilateralism: Governing the World in a Post-Hegemonic Era.' *Japanese Journal of Political Science* 16(3): 399–413. https://scholar.princeton.edu/sites/default/files/gji3/files/the_future_of_multilateralism-august_2015_0.pdf.

Ikenberry, John (2018). 'The End of Liberal International Order?', *International Affairs* 94(1): 7–23.

Johnson, Harry (1969). 'The Case for Flexible Exchange Rates, 1969.' *Review*, Federal Reserve Bank of St. Louis: 12–24.

Kindelberger, Charles (1973). *The World in Depression 1929–1939*. Berkeley, CA: University of California Press.

Manyika, James et al. (2018). 'Superstars: The Dynamics of Firms, Sectors and Cities Leading the Global Economy.' MGI Discussion Paper.

Milanovic, Branco (2016). *Global Inequality: A New Approach for the Age of Globalization.* Cambridge, MA: Belknap Press.

Milanovic, Branco (2019). *Capitalism, Alone.* Cambridge, MA: Belknap/Harvard University Press.

Myrdal, Gunnar (1975). *The Equality Issue in World Development.* Nobel Lecture, 17 March.

National Security Council (1950). *United States Objectives and Programs for National Security* (NSC-68 report to the president). https://digitalarchive.wilsoncenter.org/document/116191.pdf?v=2699956db534c1821edefa61b8c13ffe.

Obstfeld, Maurice (2013). 'The International Monetary System: Living with Asymmetry.' In Robert Feenstra and Alan Taylor (eds.), *Globalization in an Age of Crisis: Multilateral Economic Cooperation in the Twenty-First Century.* Chicago, IL: University of Chicago Press.

Obstfeld, Maurice and Kenneth Rogoff (2002). 'Global Implications of Self-Oriented National Monetary Rules.' *Quarterly Journal of Economics* 117(2): 503–35.

Pastén, Ernesto and Diego Saravia (eds.), *Monetary Policy and Global Spillovers: Mechanisms, Effects and Policy Measures,* 1st edn. Vol. 25, chapter 2: 009-047. Santiago: Central Bank of Chile.

Philippon, Thomas (2019). *The Great Reversal: How America Gave Up on Free Markets.* Cambridge, MA: Belknap Press.

Pisani-Ferry, Jean (2019a). 'Collective Action in a Fragmented World.' Bruegel Policy Brief 2019/5, September. https://www.bruegel.org/2019/09/collective-action-in-a-fragmented-world/.

Pisani-Ferry, Jean (2019b). 'Wincott Lecture: Can Multilateralism Survive?' *Economic Affairs* 39(1): 3–24.

Pisani-Ferry, Jean, Mark Leonard, Elina Ribakova, Jeremy Shapiro, and Guntram Wolff (2019). 'Redefining Europe's Economic Sovereignty.' Bruegel Policy Contribution 9/2019. https://www.bruegel.org/2019/06/redefining-europes-economic-sovereignty/.

Pomeranz, Kenneth (2000). *The Great Divergence.* Princeton, NJ: Princeton University Press.

Rey, Hélène (2013). 'Dilemma not Trilemma: The Global Financial Cycle and Monetary Policy Independence'. Paper delivered to the Jackson Hall Conference, August.

Rodrik, Dani (2015). 'Premature Deindustrialisation.' NBER Working Paper, No. 20935. https://www.nber.org/papers/w20935.pdf.

Sapir, André (ed.) (2007). 'Fragmented Power: Europe and the Global Economy.' *Bruegel.* https://www.bruegel.org/2007/08/fragmented-power-europe-and-the-global-economy/.

Servan-Schreiber, Jean-Jacques (1967). *Le Défi Américain.* Paris: Denoël.

Shadlow, Nadia (2020). 'The End of American Illusion.' *Foreign Affairs,* September–October: 35–45.

Tooze, Adam (2018). *Crashed: How a Decade of Financial Crises Changed the World.* London: Penguin.

World Bank (2020). *World Development Report 2020: Trading for Development in the Age of Global Value Chains.* Washington, DC: World Bank.

14

The Quest for European Autonomy

Nathalie Tocci

Introduction

In his book *In Defence of Europe*, Loukas Tsoukalis (2016) posits that globalization and European integration are two sides of the same coin. Both are premised on the liberal understanding that openness and interdependence bring about peace and prosperity.

For decades, this view was unchallenged in mainstream European and, more broadly, Western thinking. True, as liberalism meshed into neoliberalism and eventually hyper-liberalism (Gray 2018), socio-economic inequalities in developed countries soared, while violent intra-state conflicts erupted, were exacerbated, and remained stubbornly unresolved, notably in eastern Europe and the Middle East (Tocci 2007). However, the absolute level of global prosperity rose constantly, fuelled foremost by the phenomenal catch-up of emerging economies, notably China, while in Europe the internal market generated economic gains for all member states. Moreover, the number of inter-state conflicts worldwide continued to fall, while EU citizens enjoyed the longest uninterrupted period of peace in Europe's troubled history. Summing up, the veracity of the assumption 'globalization + European integration = peace + prosperity' was broadly accepted in mainstream European thinking.

But the global financial crisis, coupled with the Eurozone crisis, the implosion—or explosion—of the regions surrounding the EU, and the political crisis caused by the ensuing migration into Europe, began to shatter these European convictions. This, as explained by Tsoukalis (2016), sowed the seeds of Eurosceptic nationalist populism, which has taken different shapes and forms across the Union.

But Europe is not alone in this respect.

A similar and in many ways more radical nationalist-populist wave has swept across Europe's staunchest ally, the USA. Whereas during the Cold War, the USA regarded economic integration into the free world as a good to be cherished, and then pursued this ideal globally after the fall of the Iron Curtain, under President Donald Trump, the belief that multilateralism and openness are inherently good was turned on its head. At most, interdependence was viewed as a condition to be exploited in order to extract as many national benefits as possible in an 'America

Nathalie Tocci, *The Quest for European Autonomy* In: *Europe's Transformations: Essays in Honour of Loukas Tsoukalis.*
Edited by: Helen Wallace, Nikos Koutsiaras, and George Pagoulatos, Oxford University Press. © OUP 2021.
DOI: 10.1093/oso/9780192895820.003.0014

first' vision of the world, even at the cost of harming allies or wrecking the multilateral rules-based system altogether. The USA has arguably entered a post-imperial mindset in which it is no longer able or willing to sustain an international order that it was instrumental in establishing and maintaining for 70 years. Under the Trump administration, this was clear for all to see. Be it by violating the Iran nuclear deal, withdrawing from the Paris Climate Agreement, obstructing the World Trade Organization, or disinvesting from the United Nations and its agencies, Trump was consistent in his frontal attack on the so-called international liberal order (Haas 2018). But it would be a mistake to assume that a different administration in Washington will simply turn back the clock to the 1990s, the heyday of US hegemony. Indeed the Biden administration has persisted in an 'America first' approach to its vaccination policy, and it remains sceptical of pursuing trade liberalization, intent as it is in ensuring it delivers a foreign policy for (its) middle class. The days of the so-called international liberal order premised on US hegemony have passed.

The rest of the world offers no solace to supporters of openness and integration. Other power poles are anything but committed to the liberal premises of the international order. Some, like Vladimir Putin's Russia, expressly champion illiberalism, not just within Russia but in the wider world (Barber, Foy, and Barber 2019), as well. Others, like Xi Jing Ping's China, pay lip service to openness and interdependence, but often act in a way that contrasts starkly with such norms. And relations between great powers, be it between the USA and Russia in Ukraine or Syria, or between the USA and China in global trade, technology, and most starkly in handling the Covid-19 pandemic, are certainly not governed by liberal rules of cooperative engagement (Allison 2017). Transactionalism, unilateralism or outright conflict increasingly prevail over rules, multilateralism, and cooperation in the international environment.

The European Union, for its part, has failed to manage adequately the root causes of European socio-economic discontent, not least because it is governed by the same (neo)liberal logic that underpins globalization itself, as Tsoukalis (2016) reminds us. Moreover, it is no longer able to disseminate its normative Pax Europea within and beyond the Union (Dûchene 1973; Manners 2002) because it is no longer shielded by the umbrella of a global Pax Americana, which secured peace in Europe along with a liberal rules-based international economic environment. In other words, the Union is increasingly unable to conduct both its internal and international policies while remaining insulated from geopolitical dynamics. Geopolitics made a rude comeback in eastern Europe when Russia annexed Crimea and destabilized eastern Ukraine (Youngs 2017) and when the Arab spring in North Africa and the Middle East inexorably spiralled into winter (Ehteshami and Mohammadi 2017). It is now raising its ugly head within the Union itself, as great power rivalry plays out within our borders, from the collapse of the Intermediate Nuclear Forces Treaty in Europe to the controversy over allowing access to Huawei's 5G technology within the Union or pursuing a Comprehensive Agreement on Investment with China, as well as the cynical great power beauty contest aimed at wooing over a disoriented European public opinion in the early days of the Covid-19 outbreak.

All of which poses an existential threat to the European project. Europeans are called upon both to learn the 'language of power' (Borrell 2019) and to resist the sirens of nationalism, closure, and transactionalism. Because it is not only true that globalization and European integration are two sides of the same coin. It is also true that the EU is the most radical form of rules-based multilateralism and interdependence worldwide, and as such it would not be able to thrive, and perhaps even to survive, in a world in which international cooperation, shared norms, and diffuse reciprocity are not defining features of international society (Tocci 2019, Dworkin and Gowan 2019). In fact, whereas nation-states might not flourish but would continue to exist in a Hobbesian world of great power rivalry, the EU, embedded in rules and norms as it is, would undoubtedly perish. Put more starkly, a fascist Europe is possible (albeit, thankfully, not probable); a fascist European Union, however, is a contradiction in terms.

Learning the language of power while remaining true to openness and multi-lateralism is no small feat. This is what has given rise to the debate on European sovereignty, or, as this chapter will argue, on European autonomy.

European Vulnerability

Henry Farrell and Abraham Newman (2019) challenge the proposition that globalization results in reciprocal dependence. Often translating into asymmetric interdependence instead, globalization generates the conditions for weaponized or weaponizable interdependence. Economic links, energy dependences, and digital connectivity are increasingly being weaponized to reap geopolitical advantages. This is not just happening between great powers with a penchant for competition and rivalry, but also between such powers and the EU. The Union, for the first time in its history, stands unprotected in this geopolitical game.

For the first time in the history of their Union, therefore, Europeans are coming to terms with the fact that interdependence, rather than always and necessarily being a force for good, can also be a source of vulnerability (Krastev and Leonard 2014). True, intra-European interdependence and integration has given the Union considerable market power (Damro 2015), which Europeans have used to negotiate a range of advantageous trade deals across Africa, Asia, and the Americas, as well as to impose regulatory norms worldwide. True, too, as EU leaders tirelessly repeat, taken collectively, Europeans are the second highest defence spenders worldwide, and first by a long way when it comes to develop-ment and diplomacy (Mogherini 2019). But all this, alone, does not add up to much: it neither protects Europeans against their vulnerabilities, nor projects European power on the world stage.

Today, friends and foes alike are intent on exploiting the European vulnerabilities generated by interdependence and openness to extract national gains. As a consequence, significant damage is being inflicted upon the European project as well as the rules-based international order.

President Trump even went so far as to question the collective defence clause of the North Atlantic Treaty Organization (NATO) to leverage European defence spending.[1] American leaders have long complained about dwindling European defence budgets. One needs only recall then US secretary of defense Robert Gates's stark words on the eve of his resignation in 2011, when he scolded Europeans for freeriding on US defence. But for an American president implicitly to question Article 5 of NATO is unprecedented. Perhaps it took French president Emmanuel Macron's remarks about the alliance's brain-death (Macron 2019) to rekindle President Trump's interest in NATO. Nevertheless, the damage done to transatlantic trust is likely to outlive Trump's incumbency of the White House. In fact, while President Biden has made reinvestment in Europe and the transatlantic alliance a lynchpin of his foreign policy, Europeans are both immensely relieved but not entirely reassured. After Trump, the question still lingers: 'could it happen again?'

When it comes to defence, Washington has stopped at veiled threats. The same cannot be said in the economic realm, however, where the picture is decidedly gloomier. Here, the US made full use of the global centrality of its currency and financial system to enforce secondary sanctions on Europeans in relation to the 2015 Joint Comprehensive Plan of Action (JCPOA) with Iran (Geranmayeh and Lafont Rapnouil 2019). It did so to prevent Europeans from respecting an international agreement which was negotiated and signed by the USA, too, and which is enshrined in international law through a UN Security Council (UNSC) resolution. Washington thus coerced Europeans into breaking the law and acting against their interests in non-proliferation, Middle East security, and more broadly rules-based multilateralism and international diplomacy. In response, while Europeans have been very vocal in defence of the JCPOA, in practice they have largely yielded to Washington. Faced with the threat of being cut off from trading with and investing in the USA, and more broadly from the US financial system and the dollar, European firms have either disinvested from Iran, as Total and Airbus did, or avoided even approaching the Islamic Republic for fear of American retribution. With almost no European trade and investment in Iran, and with the Belgian-registered SWIFT cutting Iran off from the global banking system, Europeans have been unable to deliver on their commitment under the

---

[1] As Montenegro entered NATO, President Trump, in an interview with Fox News, implicitly questioned whether NATO would come to Montenegro's rescue if it were attacked. See Sullivan (2018).

NATHALIE TOCCI   215

JCPOA to provide sanctions relief, pushing Iranians into fudging their own compliance with the deal, as a result. The JCPOA affair has been bad in and of itself. But it is also and perhaps above all a dramatic reminder of European economic vulnerabilities. Trump's USA imposed secondary sanctions on Iran, but Biden has threatened to do the same over the construction of Nord Stream, the Russian gas pipeline bypassing Ukraine and reaching Germany. With the exacerbation of the conflict between the US and China and the US drive towards the decoupling of the two economies, what if tomorrow the US were to threaten Europeans with extra-territorial sanctions towards China, disrupting €1 billion worth of European trade per day with China (Leonard and Shapiro 2019)? Given the state of great power rivalry, this is anything but a fanciful proposition; and given the precedents, everything points towards Europeans succumbing to such pressure.

European vulnerabilities as regards the USA are so striking because they are exploited by an actor who has been so instrumental in the establishment and development of the Union. However, such vulnerabilities are just as acute vis-à-vis other global players, whose intentions are even less benign than those of the USA. Europeans now appreciate that China behaves as a 'strategic competitor' in pursuit of technological leadership and as a 'systemic rival' in the promotion of its model of governance, which contrasts sharply with Western liberal democracy (European Commission 2019). It is doing so by acquiring influence over EU member states through trade and investment. It then uses this influence to hamper European consensus (for instance, vis-à-vis human rights in Xinjiang and Hong Kong, Taiwan or the South China Sea), as well as to divide and rule the Union. Its success in so doing was clear in the establishment of the 17+1 forum or the Italy–China Memorandum of Understanding over the Belt and Road Initiative (Casarini 2019). More broadly, China unashamedly exploits its structural advantages in its relationship with Europe. In the digital realm, for instance, significant parts of the Chinese digital infrastructure are controlled by large multinational corporations which are under heavy pressure to collaborate with the government, or are already controlled by it. Moreover, while placing heavy restrictions on European foreign investments in China, Beijing subsidizes its own national champions and favours their access to credit, thus creating a heavily tilted playing field. The resulting asymmetry means that China can gain considerable influence over the digital realm in Europe, while this does not work the other way around.

Last but not least there is Russia. Gone are the days in which Europeans projected their soft power eastwards, enlarging into central and eastern Europe (Grabbe 2005) and promoting Europeanization in the neighbourhood (Coppieters, Huysseune, Tocci, et al. 2004), while reaching out in a more diffuse manner to Russia, too (Haukkala 2010). Today, Russia projects its hard and soft power westwards, not limiting itself to the Eastern Partnership countries, but targeting EU member states too, through election meddling, support for anti-systemic nationalist parties, cyberattacks, and widespread disinformation campaigns (Gressel 2019). Moscow works by exploiting European vulnerabilities, be these systemic due to the openness of European political systems or political, by singling out and magnifying European fears. Russian support for Catalan separatists, Brexit, the migration crisis narrative, and the French *gilets jaunes* protest are only a few examples. In response, Europeans have issued communiqués, drawn up strategies, developed action plans, and established funds and governance units. However, the Russian 'hybrid' threat remains real and continues to hover over the Union.

A *Cri de Coeur* for European Sovereignty

Appreciating this European predicament, several European leaders have sparked a debate over European power, geopolitics, and sovereignty. In different but related terms, all these appeals are premised on the understanding that in the current (and future) circumstances, the Union will either sit at the great power table or end up on the proverbial menu.

High representative of the Union for foreign and security policy and vice-president of the Commission, Josep Borrell (2019), has stressed the need for the European Union to 'learn to use the language of power'. Commission president Ursula von der Leyen has defined hers as a 'geopolitical Commission', a concept heavily centred on the notion of power and its relationship with geographic space (von der Leyen 2019). Far more dramatically, French president Emmanuel Macron has declared that the Union will disappear altogether unless it understands itself as a global power (Macron 2019).

In this context, the notion of European sovereignty has been heavily stressed. In his speech in the Bundestag, Macron (2018) argued that:

> To cope with upheavals worldwide, we need a sovereignty that is greater than our own, but which complements it: a European sovereignty . . . That is why Europe must be stronger. That is why it must have more sovereignty, because Europe will not be able to play its part if it becomes itself the plaything of powers, if it does not take more responsibility for its defence and security and makes do with playing secondary roles on the global stage.

In the same vein, in his State of the Union speech in Strasbourg, then president of the Commission Jean-Claude Juncker (2018) stated: 'The geopolitical situation makes this Europe's hour: the time for European sovereignty has come.'

In several ways, this discussion is misplaced. Geopolitics, with its distinctly retro feel, is an unfortunate term to use. Yes, geopolitics is certainly back and evident in the intent and action of global powers such as the USA, Russia, and China, as well as regional ones like Turkey, Iran, and Saudi Arabia. But in a world whose major challenges are in the transnational domains of technology, climate, demography, and public health, geopolitics does not fully capture what is at stake.

Sovereignty, for its part, is a misnomer. If Weberian political sovereignty means the monopoly on the legitimate use of force within a given territory, then sovereignty is neither what the EU is likely to achieve nor what it needs to address vis-à-vis European vulnerabilities in the current international environment. True, former president Juncker often repeated his appeal for a European army. But he was repeatedly rebuffed by most member states and other EU leaders, who, while strongly supportive of systemic cooperation and even integration in security and defence matters, rejected the ambition of creating a twenty-eighth army alongside the existing 27 (Mogherini 2019). The point, in fact, is not that of making Europe sovereign in a classic federalist sense of the term. As Juncker (2018) himself put it, it is about 'sharing sovereignty' in a manner that makes European nations stronger.

That said, the current debate about geopolitics and European sovereignty does capture something important. The political intuition behind these statements and slogans is absolutely correct. This is because the twenty-first-century rationale for the European project is a profoundly global one (Tocci 2019). The EU does not exist only to secure peace on the continent and to enhance European prosperity through the benefits of the single market. It needs to act globally if Europeans are to rise to the major global challenges of our age. In the twenty-first century, size and weight matter. And Europeans, all of whom live in what are, on a global scale, small to medium-sized states, can achieve that critical mass only by standing together.

In security and defence, Europeans are threatened internally by criminal and terrorist networks. Externally, they are surrounded by fragile and collapsed states in which areas of limited statehood have opened the space up to regional conflict, and risk being torn apart by a global confrontation between the USA and China, in which an escalating trade, technological, and ideological war conceals the spectre of a possible military confrontation in years to come. Faced with all this, what can little Luxembourg, little Spain, or even little France and Germany do? Precious little. In security, including defence, scale matters. And all member states, including the largest ones, are simply too small to protect their own citizens from the turmoil brought about by the messy transition from one global order to what will become the next over time (Tocci 2018).

When it comes to well-being and prosperity, Europeans care about the quality of their work, as much as their leisure, education, and healthcare; they care about the food they eat, the water they drink, and the air they breathe. In the complex and connected world which we inhabit, none of these goods can be secured by small to medium-sized states like our own. Just imagine having to negotiate a free trade agreement which ensures the well-being of Dutch or Portuguese citizens, if the Netherlands or Portugal had to negotiate alone with the likes of the USA,

China or India? Imagine what it would be like if tech giants like Microsoft, Amazon or Google were to negotiate how much tax to pay or competition to allow if they faced not the Commission, bringing the weight of almost 500 million consumers to bear, but Bucharest, Nicosia or Vilnius? And could 27 small and separate European countries succeed in saving our planet from pandemics, climate change, and environmental degradation? Clearly not.

European unity is thus crucial. Only by standing together can Europeans address geopolitical crises as well as broader global challenges. To negotiate effectively with China, stand up to Russia, build a more balanced partnership across the Atlantic, govern migration, eradicate pandemics, counteract climate change, and jump on to the train of artificial intelligence and biotechnology, while ensuring digital safety, unity is the necessary condition. Separately, Europeans will simply be small, fat chickens in a jungle: as small, rich states standing apart, they will not fare well in an increasingly transactional and leaderless world. Fostering unity will take hard work. It means winning over central and eastern European member states to the Commission's Green New Deal for Europe (Leonard 2019). It means working towards a common (not a single) strategic culture, providing real financial incentives for defence cooperation, and concomitantly working on an ever stronger relationship between the EU and NATO. It means persuading member states to block their ears to the bilateral siren calls from China, because it is only by establishing and implementing common investment screening procedures, and common rules governing cooperation on aviation, infrastructure, data protection, environment, and energy, that all member states can fully maximize the benefits of their national cooperation with China.

The Quest for European Autonomy

As terms, 'power' and 'autonomy' are more appropriate than 'geopolitics' and 'sovereignty'. Through their Union, Europeans must strive to exert power—the ability to make others do what they would not have otherwise done (Dahl 1957)—in order to protect and promote their security, prosperity, and liberal democracies. Such power must be aimed at ensuring European freedom of action in the world, as President Macron put it at the 2020 Munich Security Conference;[2] it is aimed at achieving European autonomy, as first posited by the 2013 European Council and elaborated by the EU Global Strategy in 2016 (High Representative of the EU 2016).

The goal of such autonomy, as the etymology of the word itself suggests—*auto/*self + *nomos/*law—is the ability to live by one's laws without undue interference,

---

[2] Author's participation in President Emmanuel Macron's panel at the Munich Security Conference, 16 February 2020.

attacks or destabilization. The laws in question—national, European, and international—do not seek autarky, closure, or aggression. In this respect, the EU is simply not attuned to playing the geopolitical game in the same way great power states do. In the context of the EU, which is not a state but rather the most consolidated form of multilateralism in history, those laws cannot but be open and cooperative in nature. In fact, by becoming better able to act, Europeans will be, by definition, better able to work effectively with partners. The goal of autonomy is therefore not to act against, but rather to act with, our partners. Only as a second-best option will the EU opt to act alone when its vital interests are at stake and its partners are unwilling to cooperate with it. It is a cooperative autonomy the EU is after.

The ambition to be cooperatively autonomous pertains to every sphere of external action: from security and defence to trade and finance, through to new fields such as cyber, space, and artificial intelligence. It therefore encompasses the sphere of security and defence—commonly known as strategic autonomy—which in turn implies both decision-making capacity and civilian and military capabilities, as well as the willingness to use them through joint operations, beginning in key theatres such as Libya (Tocci 2020). All this will not come for free. Systematic European defence cooperation does entail real savings through the reduction of fragmentation and duplication and increased inter-operability and economies of scale. However, it must also mean devoting fresh resources to defence: Europeans must unequivocally put their money where their mouths are. In this respect, in the context of the current Multiannual Financial Framework, downgrading commitments relating to the European Defence Fund, Military Mobility, and the European Peace Facility from the proposals originally proposed by the European Commission was a terrible message for Europeans to send out. Further down the line, strategic autonomy in security and defence will also require that Europeans tackle the taboo subject of a nuclear deterrence. Interestingly, in his address to the French War College, President Macron (2020) raised the possibility of a European strategic dialogue on France's nuclear deterrent. So far, the rather vague French proposition has fallen on deaf (German) ears. But it must be a question of when, not whether, the nuclear deterrent question is addressed if European strategic autonomy is to become a realistic prospect.

The march towards autonomy does not stop at defence, however. It is crucial in the economic, energy, climate and digital realms, too (Leonard, Pisani-Ferry, Ribakova et al. 2019). The last five years have demonstrated that the EU continues to wield significant economic and standard-setting power, having the economic size to shape its own economic destiny, set its own rules for economic life, negotiate on an equal footing with partner economies, tame would-be monopolies, and contribute to global standard setting. In the last five years, the Union has reached free trade agreements with Canada, Japan, Mercosur, Vietnam, and Singapore, and has done so in a global environment in which nationalism, closure, and protectionism are on the rise. It has also succeeded in making the General Data Protection Regulation a dominant global standard, notwithstanding the growing conflictuality within the digital sphere, notably between the USA and China.

However, the recent past has also shown that Europeans are far from being fully economically autonomous. The vulnerability vis-à-vis US secondary sanctions as well as Chinese strategic investments or Russia's hybrid threats highlights this all too well. European cyber vulnerabilities were estimated at €400 billion in 2018 and are expected to grow in the light of 5G and the Internet of Things (Franke 2019). Addressing these vulnerabilities, and thus acquiring full economic and digital autonomy, requires the revision of *inter alia* European investment, competition, financial, and monetary policies.

Innovation and investment are essential. So far, the EU has punched above its weight in the digital sphere. It has been a rule shaper, even if the major tech companies are not European. The EU has proved to be an effective regulator, both because rule making is part of its DNA and because the Union still boasts a market of 446 million consumers. However, the EU's demographic weight in the world is fast declining, and consumers alone are unlikely to enable the Union to continue being a global regulatory power. If Europeans are to play a role in shaping the rules that will govern artificial intelligence, biotechnology or quantum computing, they need to invest in a strong research, scientific, and technological base. Currently, Europe lags behind every global player in this respect.

Reversing this trend will require access to capital for small and medium-sized enterprises. It will also depend on support for European champions that may indeed acquire dominant positions within the EU market, but which are the only way to prevent unfair practices within Europe while enabling the Union to play a role in the global governance of the digital sphere in the decades to come. In the heated 5G debate, for instance, supporting European champions such as Nokia and Eriksson would allow Europeans to access this key technology without exposing themselves to the security risks inherent in allowing Chinese Huawei to enter the EU market. In parallel, Europeans must also protect assets critical to national security from foreign interference through *inter alia* greater coordination in the monitoring of foreign investments. Existing dependencies, for instance, on chip companies risk spilling over into new dependencies, expanding the scope for abuse by companies with questionable data security standards.

The EU can become economically autonomous if it enforces a level playing field in domestic and international competition, changing the lens through which EU competition policy is viewed: from being exclusively aimed at the internal market to becoming more internationally oriented and promoting European fair play in the global market. This requires revisiting state aid rules also beyond the current Covid-19 crisis, enabling the channelling of funds towards strategic industries to be considered in key areas such as artificial intelligence, biotechnology, quantum computing, energy and space, as well as extending the application of state aid rules beyond European companies to all enterprises investing in Europe.

Finally, the EU must promote its financial autonomy by creating credible alternative payment systems to circumvent secondary sanctions, establishing credible blocking regulations, considering asymmetric countermeasures, and protecting SWIFT, the international payment network which allows international wire transfers to be made. Alongside this, financial autonomy would require the promotion of the international role of the euro through deep and integrated capital markets, a euro-area safe asset, and swap lines to partner banks allowing them to act as lenders of last resort to local banks that trade in euros.

Completing the picture in the financial domain, Europeans would also need to establish a coherent and effective European international financial architecture. In this field, the USA has set up its Development Finance Corporation, while China has championed the Asian Infrastructure and Investment Bank to finance its mammoth Belt and Road Initiative. The EU cannot simply stay put and lose its proud primacy in the development field: moving fast on the High Level Group of Wise Persons' recommendation to establish a European Climate and Sustainable Development Bank, ideally by merging the European Investment Bank's external component with the European Bank for Reconstruction and Development, is essential (Council of the EU 2019).

Clearly, autonomy is a long-term goal. The focus of ongoing efforts must be on achieving a higher degree of autonomy compared to the dependencies that exist today. This will take time, money, and above all courage. But it can be achieved in the long term, only if action begins now.

Conclusion

The exercise of European power aimed at hedging against weaponized interdependence and achieving European autonomy will continue to revolve around the EU's enduring ability to be a global rule maker and rule shaper. The nature of those rules will continue to be open and multilateral; closure, autarky, and unilateralism are simply not viable long-term strategies for a quintessentially liberal project like the European Union. In fact, the exercise of European power cannot be geopolitical in the way Putin's Russia or Xi's China is. The EU is not a sovereign state, and sovereignty is arguably not what it is after. Likewise, geopolitics is simply not the stuff the Union is made of. The EU being an entity held together by common liberal rules and norms, these rules and norms will continue to remain front and centre stage in the exercise of European power in the world. The Union will be less likely to set or shape rules through direct policies of conditionality than it did in the heydays of international liberalism. It will also have a harder time in diffusing its liberal norms and socializing others to them in an increasingly non-liberal world. But the EU can still exercise power and achieve autonomy on the world stage.

To do so, unity is a necessary condition. In a world in which size, weight, and scale are poised to matter ever more in world affairs, European unity is a precondition for the exercise of power and the achievement of autonomy. But unity alone is insufficient. Alongside unity, Europeans must also demonstrate responsibility, and moving forward this will require money and above all courage.

Exerting European power in the twenty-first century means assuming greater responsibility on the global scene, above all when such responsibility comes at a price. This means spending more on defence, not because the US demands it, but because Europeans cannot simply assume that the USA will take care of their security indefinitely. Responsibility also requires risk taking. It means for instance acting in Libya, because we have seen that unless Europeans do so, others—Russia, Turkey, the United Arab Emirates—will instead, in a manner that will certainly not be conducive to European interests, notwithstanding the many differences and divisions between member states (Tocci 2020). Responsibility does not stop with defence, however, and also relates to economics. This entails assuming the costs of European economic and digital autonomy, even if it means paying the short-term price of transatlantic friction or Chinese retribution.

The EU today is faced with unique challenges, but also with unprecedented opportunities. The mode of exercising power which the Union has employed over the last two decades is no longer available, at least not without modification, as the world around us changes systemically. This ought to shake Europeans out of their comfort zone and make them realize that a global EU is not simply nice to have; it is essential if Europeans are to stand proudly by their way of life in the years to come. This bestows upon the EU a new and exquisitely global *raison d'être*, one that encompasses a unique danger if the Union fails to rise to the challenge, but also holds the promise of a re-energized European project if the opportunity is seized. The new EU political leadership appears to understand this in theory. Its task now is to deliver on its words in practice.

References

Allison, Graham (2017). *Destined for War*. New York: Mariner Books.

Barber, Lionel, Henry Foy, and Alex Barber (2019). 'Vladimir Putin Says Liberalism Has Become Obsolete.' *Financial Times*, 28 June. https://www.ft.com/content/670039ec-98f3-11e9-9573-ee5cbb98ed36.

Borrell, Josep (2019). 'Hearing at the European Parliament.' September, European Parliament, Strasbourg. https://www.europarl.europa.eu/news/en/press-room/20190926IPR62260/hearing-with-high-representative-vice-president-designate-josep-borrell.

Casarini, Nicola (2019). 'Rome-Beijing: Changing the Game—Italy's Embrace of China's Connectivity Project, Implications for the EU and the US.' Commentary, Istituto Affari Internazionali, Rome. https://www.iai.it/sites/default/files/iaip1905.pdf.

Coppieters, B., M. Emerson, M. Huysseune, N. Tocci, et al. (2004). *Europeanization and Conflict Resolution*. Gent: Academia Press.

Council of the EU (2019). *Europe in the World: The Future of the International Financial Architecture*. An independent report by the High-Level Group of Wise Persons on the European financial architecture for development. https://www.consilium.europa.eu/media/40967/efad-report_final.pdf.

Dahl, R. (1957). 'The Concept of Power.' *Behavioral Science* 2: 201–15.

Damro, C. (2015). 'Market Power Europe.' *Journal of European Integration* 22(9): 1336–54.

Dûchene, F. (1973). 'The European Community and the Uncertainties of Interdependence.' In M. Kohnstamm and W. Hager (eds.), *A Nation Writ Large? Foreign Policy Problems before the European Community*. London: Macmillan.

Dworkin, Anthony and Gowan, Richard (2019). 'Rescuing Multilateralism.' In *Report on European Sovereignty*. London and Berlin: European Council on Foreign Relations.

Ehteshami, A. and Mohammadi, A. (2017). 'The EU and Geopolitics in the Mediterranean.' Medrest Policy Briefs, Istituto Affari Internazionali. http://www.iai.it/it/pubblicazioni/eu-and-geopolitics-mediterranean.

European Commission and European External Action Service (2019). 'Joint Communication: EU–China: A Strategic Outlook.' https://ec.europa.eu/commission/news/eu-china-strategic-outlook-2019-mar-12_en.

Farrell, Henry and Abraham Newman (2019). 'Weaponized Interdependence.' *International Security* 44(1): 42–79.

Franke, Ulrike (2019). 'Harnessing Artificial Intelligence', Report on European Sovereignty, London and Berlin: European Council on Foreign Relations.

Geranmayeh, Ellie and Manuel Lafont Rapnouil (2019). 'Meeting the Challenge of Secondary Sanctions.' In *Report on European Sovereignty*. London and Berlin, European Council on Foreign Relations.

Grabbe, Heather (2005). *The EU's Transformative Power: Europeanization through Conditionality in Central and Eastern Europe*. Basingstoke: Palgrave Macmillan.

Gray, John (2018). 'The Problem of Hyper-Liberalism.' *The Times Literary Supplement*, 27 March. https://www.the-tls.co.uk/articles/public/john-gray-hyper-liberalism-liberty/.

Gressel, Gustav (2019). 'Protecting Europe against Hybrid Threats.' In *Report on European Sovereignty*. London and Berlin: European Council on Foreign Relations.

Haas, Richard (2018). 'Liberal World Order R.I.P.' *Project Syndicate*, 21 March. https://www.project-syndicate.org/commentary/end-of-liberal-world-order-by-richard-n—haass-2018-03?barrier=accesspaylog.

Haukkala, Hiski (2010). *The EU–Russia Strategic Partnership: The Limits of Post-Sovereignty in International Relations*. New York: Routledge.

High Representative of the EU for Foreign Affairs and Security Policy and Vice-President of the European Commission (2016). *Shared Vision, Common Action: A Stronger Europe—A Global Strategy for the EU's Foreign and Security Policy*. https://europa.eu/globalstrategy/sites/globalstrategy/files/eugs_review_web.pdf.

Juncker, Jean-Claude (2018). 'State of the Union: The Hour of European Sovereignty.' 12 September, Strasbourg.

Krastev, Ivan and Mark Leonard (2014). 'The New European Disorder.' European Council on Foreign Relations, Essays, November. https://www.ecfr.eu/page/-/ECFR117_TheNewEuropeanDisorder_ESSAY.pdf.

Leonard, Mark (2019). 'Ursula von der Leyen's Geopolitical Commission.' *Project Syndicate*, November. https://www.project-syndicate.org/commentary/von-der-leyen-geopolitical-european-commission-by-mark-leonard-2019-11.

Leonard, Mark and Shapiro, Jeremy (2019). 'Empowering EU Member States with Strategic Sovereignty.' In *Report on European Sovereignty*. London and Berlin: European Council on Foreign Relations.

Leonard, Mark, Jean Pisani-Ferry, Elina Ribakova, Jeremy Shapiro, and Guntram Wolff (2019). 'Redefining Europe's Economic Sovereignty.' In *Report on European Sovereignty*. London and Berlin: European Council on Foreign Relations.

Macron, Emmanuel (2018). 'Commemorative Ceremony in the Bundestag: Speech by M. Emmanuel Macron, President of the Republic (Excerpts).' Berlin, 18 November. https://uk.ambafrance.org/France-and-Germany-must-build-EU-sovereignty-Macron.

Macron, Emmanuel (2019). 'Emmanuel Macron in His Own Words.' *The Economist*, November. https://www.economist.com/europe/2019/11/07/emmanuel-macron-in-his-own-words-english.

Macron, Emmanuel (2020). 'Discours du Président Emmanuel Macron sur la stratégie de défense et de dissuasion devant les stagiaires de la 27ème promotion de l'école de guerre.' Elysée, 7 February. https://www.elysee.fr/emmanuel-macron/2020/02/07/discours-du-president-emmanuel-macron-sur-la-strategie-de-defense-et-de-dissuasion-devant-les-stagiaires-de-la-27eme-promotion-de-lecole-de-guerre.

Manners, Ian (2002). 'Normative Power Europe: A Contradiction in Terms?' *Journal of Common Market Studies* 20(2): 235–58.

Mogherini, Federica (2019). 'Address at the Munich Security Conference'. 17 February.

Sullivan, Eileen (2018). 'Trump Questions the Core of NATO: Mutual Defence, Including Montenegro.' *New York Times*, 18 July.

Tocci, Nathalie (2007). *EU and Conflict Resolution*. London: Routledge.

Tocci, Nathalie (2018). 'The International Liberal Order and the Future of the European Project.' IAI Commentaries. https://www.iai.it/en/pubblicazioni/demise-international-liberal-order-and-future-european-project.

Tocci, Nathalie (2019). 'Navigating Complexity: The EU's Rationale in the 21st Century.' IAI Commentaries. https://www.iai.it/it/pubblicazioni/navigating-complexity-eus-rationale-21st-century.

Tocci, Nathalie (2020). 'Why the EU Needs Boots on the Ground in Libya.' Worldview Column, *Politico*, February. https://www.politico.eu/article/europe-libya-strategy-boots-on-the-ground/.

Tsoukalis, Loukas (2016). *In Defence of Europe*. Oxford: Oxford University Press.

Von der Leyen, Ursula (2019). 'Political Guidelines to the Next European Commission.' September. https://ec.europa.eu/commission/sites/beta-political/files/political-guidelines-next-commission_en.pdf.

Youngs, Richard (2017). *Europe's Eastern Crisis: The Return of Geopolitics*. Washington, DC: Carnegie.

15

The European Union as a Global Power?

Enrico Letta

The EU through Momentous Change

In recent history, very few moments have the evocative thrust of a rebirth after a traumatic event, the exemplary charge of rebuilding upon the ruins. Always and at all latitudes, a community rises and returns to prosperity if it leverages three main elements: the reference to its identity, the acceptance of fatigue, and the circulation of the best intellectual and creative energies able to redesign a shared vision of the future. The history of European integration is no exception. On the contrary, great steps forward have been taken in response to crises. This time, we, as Europeans, are called on to rebuild upon the economic and emotional ruins of a terrible disease. This will once again require creativity, fatigue, and an identity. It is this third element in particular that the Union's global ambitions can help shape and strengthen. Three world challenges of the twenty-first century—migration, technology, and climate change—may represent the foundation upon which we build our global identity and, in doing so, help transform the EU into a global and humane power.

European integration started after the Second World War. It was a peace project whose goal was putting an end to the continent's divisions and promoting harmony between its peoples through a categorical rejection of nationalism. The well-known method used by the founding fathers was to create sufficient economic interdependences among member states to bind their national interests inextricably together, defusing any temptation to wage war. Alongside this peace project, one can also identify a power project, which fostered a union of European countries capable of increasing their prosperity, well-being, and influence in the world. The two projects have reinforced one another and can be considered two sides of the same coin. The first step towards understanding the Union's global ambitions is thus to sketch out the most crucial moments of transition in its integrative project and then relate them to global geopolitical dynamics.

The first key shift was the creation of the seminal European Community. It was built to heal the wounds inflicted on the continent during a long hegemonic power struggle between its leading nations. The Franco-German border is a symbol of this conflict. The European Community was born from the ashes of a war whose primary battlefield was the Old Continent.

Enrico Letta, *The European Union as a Global Power?* In: *Europe's Transformations: Essays in Honour of Loukas Tsoukalis.* Edited by: Helen Wallace, Nikos Koutsiaras, and George Pagoulatos, Oxford University Press. © OUP 2021. DOI: 10.1093/oso/9780192895820.003.0015

The second crucial moment in the Union's history was the end of the Cold War. This was certainly fought in ways that set it apart from previous conflicts, but it had still retained a global character and, more importantly, Europe as its most relevant battleground. For the European project, the fall of the Berlin Wall in 1989 initiated a decade-long reboot. A swift German reunification, which allowed the birth of the single currency; the Maastricht Treaty, which turned a predominantly economic community into a Union with elements of strong political integration; and eastwards enlargement were among the most significant geopolitical achievements of the decade.

The common thread running through these events was the central position Europe occupied on the geopolitical chessboard. One could argue that this perception of centrality worked as an incentive for European countries to maintain a predominantly intra-European horizon, mostly focusing on dynamics between European countries. After the Iron Curtain collapsed, however, Europe's loss of centrality became more and more evident. Today, three decades later, Europe is now in its third phase, exhausted by more than a decade of deep and overlapping crises, which have called its very existence into question. Let us briefly review some of the salient traits of these crises.

The economic crisis has severely tested our development model with serious repercussions for the economic fabric, social protection mechanisms, political systems, and the very functioning of our democracies. Some steps forward have undoubtedly been taken in the integration of the Eurozone, thanks above all to its enlightened management via Mario Draghi's monetary policy, but the architecture of the single currency remains incomplete and lacking adequate political and democratic legitimacy. Again, just as we saw the erosion of trust between north and south during the sovereign debt crisis, so we saw the rise of divisions and suspicions between east and west during the tragic migration crisis. Too many lives were lost in the Mediterranean or on the barbed wire of the newly erected borders, without anyone being able to find solutions which reconciled security-based and humanitarian perspectives.

The images of desperate people trying to reach Europe in their thousands have had a powerful impact on European public opinions, exacerbating the polarization of our societies. Nationalist forces have taken advantage of the European stalemate to fan the flames of fear and uncertainty, turning them into a growing and widespread rejection of European integration *tout court*. Thus, a large member country like the United Kingdom has chosen to withdraw from the Union. This is a significant loss, especially for the Union's global actions, if we consider the UK's diplomatic, security, and defence capabilities.

Last but not least, we have been hit by the most acute crisis of all, and one of a fundamentally different nature: the Covid-19 pandemic. The magnitude of its consequences will be immense and we have only begun to glimpse them at the time of writing. In this crisis, the Union's very existence is once again at stake, and the way in which it defies it will determine European dynamics for many years to come.

It is all the more relevant if we add that, in this third stage, the world is no longer *Eurocentric*. Asia increasingly carries the lion's share of the global economy and is already a protagonist on the international stage. The game changer has been easier access to technologies, which have proven to be less and less prone to monopolistic capture. Hence, this easier access to technologies has reinforced and deepened the tie between economic and demographic power. The rise of giants like India and China has for this reason been sudden and impetuous, and has significantly altered the geopolitical balance.

Change has not come from Asia alone. If we look west, to our closest ally since the Second World War, we realize that things are not as they used to be there, either. Donald Trump has shown a very different attitude towards Europeans than his predecessors, effectively questioning the solidity of the bridge connecting the two sides of the Atlantic Ocean. In 2021 a new world is opening up. Trump is gone and with him a model of all that is negative for us in politics. President Joe Biden has arrived, working for the revival of multilateralism, for human rights and to fight the return of dictatorships.

The list of radical changes is long, but for the purpose of our analysis, we should mention three more: Africa, our great neighbour, is experiencing an unprecedented demographic boom that makes well-balanced development throughout the continent even more urgent. Furthermore, the latest revolution in technology—a field in which Europe risks being left behind—is changing every aspect of our lives. The pandemic-provoked lockdown has only accelerated some of these trends. Finally, climate change is questioning every paradigm of our economic and societal models, and is even putting our species at risk. Can the EU live up to its global ambitions in such a transformed world?

In order to do so, it must complement the intra-European perspective— sufficient in yesterday's world—with one that looks beyond our borders and towards the most important global dynamics. The internal perspective, although still necessary, is no longer adequate to sustain European integration. In retrospect, it is as if the fall of the Berlin Wall marked the need for integration to accelerate and move beyond the past. One could see it as a metaphor for what Europe needs to do now, 30 years later: the European Union has brought us peace; the Wall has fallen; now the future awaits.

One of the 'positive' aspects of the aforementioned crises has been the EU awakening from a dangerous, deterministic, and almost dogmatic inertia as regards the reasons *why* it should go further. Why do we need the EU? We can no longer answer the question by merely saying 'because we do'. By rejecting the hegemonic model, which saw it plunge the world into darkness until the twentieth century, Europe shall become a beacon of hope, a value-based global power devoted to emancipation and respect for human dignity. This is the essence of the new role that Europe can play in the world.

To complement the intra-European regional focus with an extra-European global outlook, we must foster an alignment between values and interests. In other words, we should urgently show that European values overlap with European strategic interests. This shift is crucial, lest intra-European issues continue to prevail, condemning our continent to an inexorable marginalization when it comes to shaping the world's future. Where should we begin? A logical starting point would be in the three areas identified above: migration, climate change, and what I call technological humanism. They are not only the most urgent challenges we face; I would argue they are also three domains in which there is an explicit overlap between our values and our interests, making them the perfect basis upon which to build the Union's new global role.

Migration Policy

The lack of an effective European migration policy has left an indelible mark. When we leave human beings to die in the Mediterranean, Europe betrays the promise of humanity that it made to its citizens and to the world. It is clear that Europe can never be a credible principled global actor unless it finds a new and supranational way to address this epochal phenomenon. To achieve this effectively, we must remedy one of the most dishonourable pages in our recent history.

It is not just a matter of values; it is also about political wisdom. If we are unable to find a balance between respect for human rights and the orderly management of flows and borders, Europe risks getting stuck in an unhelpful dichotomy between closed ports and abolished borders. In the prolonged absence of credible and adequate solutions, populist and xenophobic rhetoric playing on fears and simplifying reality will inevitably triumph.

History has taught us that the national responses adopted in times of urgency may be better than nothing, but also that they do not represent a sustainable way to manage large-scale, long-lasting phenomena. Only a collective European response can achieve the critical mass required to do that. Yet, it is not just a matter of European versus national solutions; it is also a question of having the right toolbox. Until now, Europe has tackled the issue with obsolete tools that are unsuited to the new context of migrations. A striking example is represented by the fact that the headquarters of Frontex—the European agency responsible for coordinating actions along the EU's external borders—is located in Warsaw, Poland. This choice of location suggests that when the architecture of European competence in this field was designed, it was done just with eastern—not southern—borders in mind.

A similar logic of inadequacy applies to what is arguably the most critical European tool in migration policy, the Dublin Regulation. As is well known, the Dublin Regulation states that the responsibility for arrivals lies with the country of their first port of entry. The geography of the phenomenon means that southern European countries—especially Italy, Greece, and Spain—are doomed to be burdened with a disproportionate and often unmanageable weight, unless the regulation evolves to deal with a completely different scenario.

There have been various efforts by the European Commission to reform the Dublin Regulation, but the situation has reached a stalemate, which the new Pact on Migration and Asylum hopes to resolve. Even though migration is a competence shared between the Union and the member states, which therefore requires qualified majority voting, it is so politically delicate and controversial that de facto reform will require political unanimity.

In essence, in an issue as sensitive as this in terms of public opinion, every government has instinctually sought not to be overwhelmed by populist messages. In other words, there has been a temptation to leave the most exposed countries to their own devices, bypassing solidarity mechanisms and leaving the responsibility with them, which are then branded as negligent states.

Despite repeated efforts by Mediterranean countries, the most intransigent states, which include Hungary, have never been willing to move forward on this. The price of stalling has become unsustainable, in terms of human lives first of all, but also in terms of accountability: the institutions in Brussels are blamed instead of the countries imposing vetoes.

We need to walk along other paths, even if it means summoning the courage to make radical choices. A possible way forward could be similar to one that was already used for the European Stability Mechanism: temporarily leaving the framework of the EU treaties to enter into a binding agreement between a coalition of the willing. In other words, this would entail establishing a new treaty defining clear and fairer rules of burden sharing, starting with the elimination of the first-port-of-entry rule. Needless to say, it would be essential for this treaty to provide for operation based both on qualified majority voting and automatic mechanisms, to prevent us finding ourselves in the same bottlenecks as we do today.

Other critical provisions would include the creation of a central European authority endowed with the necessary powers to relocate asylum seekers automatically or quasi-automatically on the basis of criteria drawn up jointly by the signatory countries. It would also be critical to distinguish the management of flows of asylum seekers from flows of so-called economic migrants, and to deal with integration principles and responsibilities, starting with the requirement to learn the language of the country of destination. The other major chapters would concern control of the EU's external borders, the coordination of rescue rules at sea, and the EU's relationships with the countries of origin. In a nutshell, the new treaty should reflect a systemic perspective that considers each phase of the migration process, from the country of origin to the destination country.

The Commission would still play a key role, since it has the expertise and the tools. From an institutional point of view, it would be a temporary solution which relied on a multi-speed Europe. The concept should, however, be pursued, given that the European Union is not a supermarket for solidarity. Those who oppose the European distribution of migrants must also accept, as a consequence of failing to demonstrate European solidarity, the loss of some advantages that come with it.

The proposed solution should be complemented by a strategic and comprehensive European Mediterranean policy. There have already been two major attempts to push forward a Mediterranean agenda for the European Union, but both failed: the first was with the 1995 *Barcelona Strategy*, while the second was 2007's *Union for the Mediterranean*. The third attempt cannot fail, because the history of our continent shows that the fates of Europe and the Mediterranean region are bound intimately together.

Relaunching a Mediterranean policy requires a real diplomatic effort in the sphere of migration which can ensure the harmonization between the internal mechanisms described above and European external actions. The reader will notice that the internal–external alignment described in the first part of this chapter is the logical thread running through these proposals. Only a systemic approach ensuring consistency can be effective. That the envisaged relocation systems would benefit greatly from well-informed diplomacies, which would in turn leverage their knowledge of migration patterns for more logical relocations provides a good and tangible example of the advantages deriving from a coherent approach.

Lastly, a coherent diplomacy concerning migration could not ignore the necessity of Europe being a co-protagonist in African development, promoting mobility both within Africa and between the two continents. In addition, the fact that not all migrants who arrive in Europe for economic reasons want to stay here forever should not be underestimated. Hence, a policy focused on mobility rather than permanent settlement would represent a game changer in the management of this phenomenon, resulting in a more adequate solution for a complex situation.

To sum up, the first pillar of a truly global Union is represented by an ambitious European migration policy that knows how to combine values with security considerations and highlight a forward-looking strategy. The same logic applies to the second pillar: a European way forward in the technological revolution.

Technological Humanism

Technology and data management present another epochal challenge facing the European Union. We live in a world in which we are inextricably interconnected by a continuous flow of information, most of it exchanged online. Many have said that data is the new oil, underlining the strategic role that access to, and ownership of, information has achieved. Continuing with the metaphor, data can be compared to oil for another reason, too: once spilled, it is impossible to put back in the 'barrel'. That is why, for the first time in its history, humanity is tasked with the ethical, philosophical, and legal problem of managing the multiplication and diffusion of an individual's digital identities. As a matter of fact, digital identities are those created by the data flows we generate every time we perform a digital action on a smartphone, computer or digital television, and by the multiple applications of artificial intelligence.

As with any transition, this historical moment requires us not only to identify and seize opportunities, but also to set standards and design policies that can mitigate potential risks without endangering non-negotiable values. How will this massive technological revolution be addressed? Simplifying somewhat, it is possible to identify three different philosophies: The first is the American approach, which could be summed up by the motto *Market first*. It emphasizes the centrality of market logics in which the idea of buying and selling data for commercial purposes prevails. The second—Chinese—philosophy is at the other end of the spectrum and could be defined as *State first*, because it is the state that defines what and who is a 'good citizen' through a system of social credit scoring. A third—European—way focuses instead on the protection of the individual and their related data; one could define this strategy as *Person first*.

Neither of the first two models—Market first and State first—offers enough safeguards for citizens and the appropriate level of respect for fundamental human rights. We cannot risk degenerating into the kind of surveillance state that daily deprives people of their privacy rights and assesses them based on their online behaviours, as the Social Credit System does in China. Neither can we entrust everything to the hands of the private sector through deregulation policies. The European Union should therefore seek to serve as a model for the protection of digital freedom.

The General Data Protection Regulation[1]—the GDPR—is a step in the right direction. It protects citizens both when they are within Europe's borders and when they are in any other country in the world, guaranteeing them a nascent form of 'right of ownership' of their computerized identities. In this way, the architects of this complicated system of regulation have prioritized the security of the individual, inspiring a model of protection and efficiency that has brought the discussion on the defence of privacy back on the right ethical and democratic track. The GDPR is far from perfect, but its inspiring philosophy is the correct one and should open the way to legislation in other spheres.

---

[1] https://gdpr.eu/what-is-gdpr/.

The coronavirus pandemic offers a concrete example. It shows that we should not place the right to privacy in contradistinction to other fundamental rights, such as the protection of human life. In this time of crisis, several states have implemented high-tech measures aimed at limiting or slowing down the spread of the virus. At the same time, though, some of these measures openly violate individuals' right to privacy by means of traceability systems and personal identification. This has sparked a debate suggesting a dilemma between privacy and health; however, I believe this dilemma to be false. First of all, any measure taken during an emergency should be strictly limited in time and scope. Secondly, solutions should provide for safeguard mechanisms that ensure independence and, most of all, anonymity when data are accessed and managed.

Another example which reveals the ambition of the European vision is the pan-European consortium created by the joint efforts of researchers, scientists, and technology experts from eight countries. The project[2] seeks to develop digital solutions to curb the rapid spread of Covid-19, while safeguarding the rights of European citizens. It stands out precisely for its high ethical and democratic standards in relation to data access and management, with appropriate protocols for the encryption and anonymization of personal information to protect the identity of the people who use the devices. This initiative shows us how it is possible to find solutions that are compatible with both the core European values and the protection of our communities.

Nonetheless, if the European Union is to become a global actor in the digital field and foster technological humanism at the global level, it should do more. So far, both member states and the Union have invested too little in the development of new infrastructures relating to the management of anonymized data. Organization, data collection and analysis are absolutely vital operations as they pave the way for public action that is capable of addressing economic, social, and environmental issues. It is also a strategic necessity to develop European value chains in the field of critical digital infrastructures. Similarly, an effort is needed to invest in decentralized technologies (blockchain, for example, which enables the anonymity of personal data), where Europe remains a world leader. It is important to note that the common efforts to develop a European approach to Artificial Intelligence have found, after years of discussions and consultations, a concrete outcome in the 2021 Coordinated Plan on Artificial Intelligence, which strengthens EU's role in the global leadership in trustworthy AI. It is crucial for Europe to continue to pursue a campaign capable of engineering a new cultural paradigm in which citizens are aware of the importance of protecting the integrity of their digital identities.

This is not some form of blind techno-optimism; it is a strategic consideration. The landmarks that new technologies have allowed us to achieve are profoundly

---

[2] https://www.pepp-pt.org/.

transforming many aspects of our lives; they cannot be left to second guessing. The pandemic and the lockdown have also shown the growing importance of the digital world in most of our activities. Even though the digital will not, and should never, replace human interaction, it is not an exaggeration to say that many fields of public policy will be—and already have been—shaped by data collection. All this can and should be done with complete respect for individuals' rights, without surrendering either to the market logic or to a dystopian logic of state control. Europe has accepted the challenge, and should continue to foster its model of technological humanism, and leverage it to catch up with other global players.

Climate Change

The fight against climate change is by far the most important challenge humanity has ever faced. Never in the history of our species have we found ourselves having to safeguard the sustainability of the planet. The global pandemic recalled a fundamental principle of integral ecology: everything is connected. It is still early to draw conclusions on the specific link between coronavirus and climate change, and it is not for me to do so. However, many experts argue that there is a link between the latter and infectious diseases.

This is a further confirmation of how environmental protection policies can no longer be a niche issue, separate from other policy areas. Climate change is an epochal challenge, not only because it affects every area of our lives, but also because it is influenced by them: each of our individual and collective behaviours has repercussions on the ecosystems in which we live. Hence, it is of fundamental importance that we adopt a transversal perspective and promote actions aimed at reorienting every policy area towards sustainability. To use an effective formula, it is not about creating policies of sustainability, but sustainable policies. This is the philosophy that underpins the European Green Deal, which represents legislation that is both crucial for our future and a focal point around which we can strengthen the European identity.

A European identity is an urgent and necessary element in a paradigm shift that must take place in every area of our lives, but also globally; it must involve everyone. No one can bring it about alone; we are all experiencing this with the pandemic, but it is a principle that applies to climate change too. The issue, then, is an economic, political, diplomatic, and cultural one. It requires that the world's elites in those policy realms leave their silos and work towards achieving tangible results. Europe has done much more than many others in this field, but if it is the only one acting, it will not be enough. We need to be clear: if we cannot convince the Chinese, the Indians, and the Americans of the urgent need to act unequivocally, it will be difficult to get adequate outcomes. Nobody can make it on their own, because we all depend on everyone.

This principle—we all depend on everyone—is something that unites climate change with the migration and Covid-19 crises. In all three, the EU could not defend itself simply by closing borders. Refugees, pollution, and disease are significant examples of interdependencies that transcend borders. Interdependence requires cooperation and multilateralism.

That is why our role as Europeans is even more important. We must become the protagonists of a new *climate diplomacy* based on scientific evidence. And the more concrete and effective the results of our policies are, the more powerfully such a diplomacy will influence global trends. Thus, it becomes essential that the European Green Deal, which the other actors can use as a model to adapt to their own specific contexts, is rigorously implemented so as to unlock its full potential. In doing so, the EU will be able to give a real demonstration of the advantages of the transition to a cleaner and more sustainable ecosystem, and in turn reinforce its role as a global player.

Once again, the need for economic recovery caused by the global spread of coronavirus can leverage on a rigorous and far-reaching implementation of the Green Deal.

There are some priorities if the implementation of the Green Deal is to be successful. First of all, it is necessary to maintain the political momentum around this topic. Sustainability and climate change have become the most discussed subject in the world. Conferences, seminars, debates, and events have proliferated everywhere. It is a subject that has rightfully entered the public discourse of many countries and influenced their political and diplomatic agendas. We cannot afford it to be just a passing phase. The ecological transition will keep us busy for several years, and it is essential that it remains a political priority.

In this sense, it is positive that the centrality of the fight against climate change has been front and centre on the agenda since European Commission president Ursula Von der Leyen's first day in office. She has made its entire mandate about it and entrusted the climate portfolio to her first vice-president, Frans Timmermans. The decision to make part of the resources of Next Generation EU conditional on transversal objectives consistent with the green and digital transitions is another move in the same direction. Additionally, the extraordinary energy of millions of young people and their mobilization on a planetary level has certainly played a role—and I hope it will continue to do so—in crafting this political thrust. Young people have sent a message that is difficult for politics to ignore: its primary responsibility will be keep climate change the focus of attention and of actions.

There are two other decisive principles that must guide the European institutions as well as national governments in their implementation of the Green Deal. Firstly, it is crucial to uphold the principle that growth and prosperity are not incompatible with the protection of the planet. In other words, it is necessary to demonstrate in every possible way that green is not only good for the planet, it also benefits businesses and creates jobs. In order to do so, we must plan for the careful and intelligent management of the reconversions and disruptions every transition brings, to ensure that nobody is left behind. Hence, measures that uphold the consistency of this principle in our external actions are also to be considered. Trade policy is a clear example: it would not be fair to ask European entrepreneurs to shoulder the effort and investment of the energy transition without protecting them from unfair competition from outside our common borders. This would also be a way to use the economic power of the single market as an incentive for other global players to make progress, too: that much-desired upward convergence.

In other words, to be affordable, and therefore effective, ecological transition has to be fair. Here, we come to the second principle that must inspire the implementation of the legislative package: equity. This concept, also known as climate justice, refers to the fact that we cannot avoid taking existing conditions into consideration. In practical terms, the implementation of the Green Deal must take into account that the weight of the necessary actions and investments should not be disproportionate to everyone's abilities. If that is not the case, it could be, for example, that smaller economic actors end up penalized. This should be avoided.

Referring once again to the pandemic, the same principle remerges: a phenomenon may affect everyone and yet be far from an equalizer. The less well-off are particularly exposed to the adverse effects of climate change, mainly due to their lack of access to resources that would allow them to protect themselves from the consequences. Equity, however, also has an intergenerational dimension. The mass mobilization of young people reminds us that the main consequences of today's choices will be experienced by those who come after us. To underline the future weight of our responsibility, the following comparison could be helpful. Over the lifespan of those born in the 1960s, the planet will see its inhabitants increase threefold in what is effectively the biggest demographic boom in human history. However, my generation has been able to rely on a similar level of resources to those enjoyed by our parents and grandparents; will this still apply to our children and, above all, to our grandchildren? The essence of the global role that the EU will be called upon to play in the twenty-first century may well lie in this collective urgency and awareness.

To conclude, one should stress that a strong European action to fight climate change cannot be distracted by the global pandemic. The latter has caught everyone unprepared and is showing us every day that nothing will go back to how it used to be. Here, it will be vital not to create competition among policy objectives, since they are in fact very closely connected. Prosperity, social justice, health, and safeguarding the planet: the ability to keep them together requires remarkable political leadership and vision.

Conclusions: A Matter of Method

We have seen so far that the EU is in a crucial phase of its existence, which is different from those that characterized its path before. Its loss of centrality in the world confronts the Old Continent with an urgent need to live up to the new global dynamics, if the Union is to continue to play an influential role in shaping them. The realignment between values and interests, and the reinforcement of a global European perspective, are indispensable elements in achieving this.

We have therefore identified three important and necessary policy areas on which the Union can build its external action and strengthen its identity in the world. To complete the picture, however, it is essential to add a methodological principle that must pervade the action of the Union: placing the citizen at its heart.

The increase in voter participation at the last European elections is an encouraging sign. Yet, it also illustrates citizens demanding to be placed at the core of the processes and decisions that impact on their lives. The Union cannot disappoint these expectations and should devise ways to regain their citizens' trust. A good opportunity to do that is to accelerate the fight against tax havens within the Union, those powerful symbol of unfairness. This is one of the very few positive aspects of Brexit, and it should be seized without hesitation. The departure of the British takes with it the veto they have always wielded against pan-European tax harmonization schemes, which is an essential element of the fight against tax evasion and avoidance. It would be a way to show that, on the Old Continent, the balance between rights and duties applies to everyone, without exception. It would demonstrate that the rules which ordinary citizens—craftspeople, small entrepreneurs, and everyone else—must abide by also apply to multinationals, tech giants, and industrial conglomerates. It will not be simple at all, but it would be the best way to claw back some of the citizens' trust.

Finally, the global pandemic has urged us to rethink the paradigm of space. Placing citizens at the centre also implies a re-evaluation of the concept of proximity, therefore stressing the value of the local level. This is the dimension that is closest to citizens, their first safety net. Hence, a good way to combine environmental and economic needs with the rediscovered importance of the local would be to revive the *Europe of the Regions* agenda. This could be done by emphasizing the need to find cohesion between economic activities, value chains, people, and the specificities of those cultural systems and ecosystems. To be clear, it would not mean rejecting the benefits of global markets or free trade, which remain essential for our prosperity. Rather, it would stress our commitment to ensure balance between openness and safeguards.

The current era requires openness to be intelligent and clearly defined. It has to find the right balance between *global projection* and *local protection*, without the two dimensions being—or even being perceived as—contradictory or conflicting.

Here, the capacity to discern and judge matters; because it influences civil understanding and the fears that inevitably condition it, it takes ability and empathy to understand, courage to grasp a different horizon, and will to overcome the temptation simply to close up. The Union's ruling classes, at all levels of government, have a responsibility to guide and listen to the communities in this process of discernment, and to promote the tools necessary to prevent them being overwhelmed by the wind of change. If this method is adopted, the EU will unlock its full potential as a global, humane power.

16

The Partnership between the USA and the European Union

The Key to Ensuring that the Western Model is Not Eclipsed by China

Anthony Gardner

It is an honour to contribute to this volume commemorating the enormous impact that Professor Loukas Tsoukalis has had over many years in many fields, including European Union studies. It is to him that I owe my own interest in and professional dedication to EU affairs.[1]

One of the reasons why I have been drawn to EU studies and, in particular, the USA–EU partnership is my growing conviction that the 'West' cannot maintain its relevance without a strong and self-confident European Union and USA working together to defend and promote 'Western values'. While the term 'West' is hard to define with precision, it obviously has a conceptual, rather than geographic, meaning. Often the 'West' is used as shorthand for the values of the rule of law, individual liberties, democracy, the separation of spiritual and temporal authority, and economic liberalism (particularly free trade and free competition).

Many countries, including many outside Europe and North America, with some in Asia and Latin America, have for the past 70 years ascribed to these values, although some have not respected all these values consistently. The foundation of this Western alliance has always been the *European–US partnership*. The North Atlantic Treaty Organization is often considered to be the essence of the partnership. But with the dramatic increase in transatlantic trade and the end of the Cold War, commercial ties between the USA and an increasingly integrated

---

[1] Tony Gardner had the pleasure of studying under Loukas Tsoukalis when he was a graduate student at Oxford University. According to Tony, Loukas inspired him to continue studying the EU at Columbia Law School, before he went on to work at the European Commission and then practise EU antitrust law at an international law firm in Brussels. These experiences, in turn, led him to serve as Director for EU affairs at the National Security Council and, ultimately, to be appointed Ambassador to the European Union. One of the books Tony read in preparation for his diplomatic mission was Loukas' *Unhappy Union* about the challenges facing the EU.

Anthony Gardner, *The Partnership between the USA and the European Union: The Key to Ensuring that the Western Model is Not Eclipsed by China* In: *Europe's Transformations: Essays in Honour of Loukas Tsoukalis*. Edited by: Helen Wallace, Nikos Koutsiaras, and George Pagoulatos, Oxford University Press. © OUP 2021. DOI: 10.1093/oso/9780192895820.003.0016

Europe have become as important as security ties. With the EU's rapid enlargement and adoption of a robust set of Western values in its Charter of Fundamental Rights, there is a strong case for arguing that the US–EU partnership is key to the continued relevance of Western values.

Prophecies of Western Doom Are Not New

Prophecies of Western demise have been popular before and proved far too gloomy. It has been roughly one century since Oswald Spengler's famous book *The Decline of the West*, whose first volume was published in 1918 during the calamity of the First World War. And yet the West has proved resilient and has subsequently exercised unparalleled global influence despite a major financial crash, a second world war, and many other great crises.

'Declinism' remains a thriving cottage industry. Articles and books such as *Suicide of the West, Is Democracy Dying?* and *Why Liberalism Failed* continue to flood our bookstores and newspaper stands. One of the great problems with 'declinism' is that it often looks at the past with rose-tinted spectacles, conveniently forgetting that not all was well in the past and too often exaggerating the problems of the present. Anyone who believes that the USA and its Western allies had an easy time bending the world community to their will in the aftermath of the Second World War is conveniently forgetting the many instances when this was not the case, including the creation of the Soviet bloc, the rise of communist China, the building of the Berlin Wall, and the defeat of France and the USA in Vietnam. Anyone who is currently despairing of the bitter polarization of US politics would do well to look at Ken Burns' magisterial television series on Robert F. Kennedy. The series reminds us that the country was poised on the precipice of civil war after the assassination of two Kennedys and Martin Luther King, race riots, and massive anti-war demonstrations. Even the dysfunction of Trump's America, including the exacerbation of racial conflict and income inequality, looks relatively mild by comparison.

It is true, however, that there are a few important ways in which the current crisis facing the West is more profound than previous crises. Freedom House, the non-governmental organization that has tracked the degree of freedom around the world since its founding in 1941, recently warned that democracy is facing its most serious threat in decades: 'the right to choose leaders in free and fair elections, freedom of the press and the rule of law are under assault and in retreat globally' (Freedom House 2018). Its 2019 *Freedom in the World* report recorded the thirteenth consecutive year of decline in global freedom. Of the 41 countries that were consistently ranked free from 1985 to 2005, 22 registered net score declines over the last five years (Freedom House 2019). There are many possible explanations for this. Freedom House itself concludes that more and more people are doubting the ability of democracies to solve the urgent challenges of the twenty-first century, including climate change, the impact on society of the accelerating pace of technological change, demographic shifts, and increasing inequality in the distribution of wealth. As a result, many voters no longer trust established political parties, institutions, and media.

Many autocrats who openly scorn Western values are, rather ironically, now coming to power through the ballot box rather than by *coup d'état*, as has so often been the case in the past. As Elizabeth Andersen, the executive director of the World Justice Project, a Washington-based civil society initiative, has noted: 'One of the most striking things about the degradation of the rule of law is that it is being effected through laws and legal institutions. The law itself is being hijacked and used to erode checks on power.'[2] There are many examples of this, including Recep Tayyip Erdoğan, president of Turkey, and Vladimir Putin, president of Russia. Following the failed 2016 coup, Erdoğan has carried out a campaign involving the passing of censorship laws, attacks on independent media, pressure on independent book publishers and academics, and the culling of libraries to remove critical books. Not satisfied with choking democracy at home, Putin appears to be bent on making the world 'safe for autocracy' and on spreading doubt about the moral superiority of Western values in order to destabilize Europe and the USA.

In a widely cited interview with the *Financial Times* in 2019, Putin claimed that 'the liberal idea' has outlived its purpose as people around the world turn against immigration, open borders and multiculturalism. Donald Tusk (2019), president of the European Council, retorted that: 'Whoever claims that liberal democracy is obsolete also claims that freedoms are obsolete, that the rule of law is obsolete and human rights are obsolete.'

Rodrigo Dutertre, president of the Philippines, and Jair Bolsonaro, president of Brazil, are two more elected populists who openly stoke anti-democratic, nationalist, and xenophobic sentiments. One of the ironies of their electoral success is that their policies may well aggravate, rather than address, many of their supporters' legitimate complaints (such as income inequality).

Are Prophecies of Western Doom More Believable Now?

The challenge to Western values is also of greater concern now than in the past because the phenomenon affects Europe and the USA, the world's bastions of democracy, and not just developing countries. Poland and Hungary have regularly flouted EU law and undermined democratic principles, including the independence of the judiciary and the media. Hungarian prime minister Victor Orbán has

---

[2] As cited in Barber (2019).

promoted his vision of an 'illiberal state' on the ground that authoritarianism works better than Western liberal democracies.

Right-wing populists remain strong in Italy, France, Austria, and elsewhere in the EU, and are gaining ground in Spain. Even in the United Kingdom, parliamentary democracy has come under unprecedented strain during a highly divisive Brexit debate in which prime minister Boris Johnson exploited nationalist emotions. Brexit has also underscored the problem that the Franco-British tandem, instrumental in propelling the European project forward, is not working as effectively as it should.

The USA is exhibiting a remarkable erosion of its democracy while political partisanship rises to unprecedented levels. In 2019, Freedom House issued a sober warning about the USA: 'President Trump ... is straining our core values and testing the stability of our constitutional system ... Trump has assailed essential institutions and traditions including the separation of powers, a free press, an independent judiciary ... '.[3] In their recent book *How Democracies Die*, political scientists Steven Levitsky and Daniel Zitblatt offer a stark warning of how easy it is for elected leaders to undermine democracy by 'capturing' independent referees such as the judiciary and law enforcement, side-lining political opponents and the media, and subverting electoral rules.

Another reason why the current challenge to Western values is more serious now than in the past is the belief that there are other political models that can generate economic growth and social progress. China, above all, has shown the world that prosperity is possible within an authoritarian system. That has challenged one of the tenets of the liberal world order: that a stable, participative democracy is a prerequisite for steady and inclusive social progress.

But are we really on the brink of a post-Western age in which non-Western actors are destined to shape international affairs? If so, are they likely to create a value system that competes with, and eventually supplants, the Western framework that has formed the bedrock of the liberal international order since the Second World War? More and more pundits, including Kishore Mahbubani in his provocative book *Has the West Lost it?*, seem to think that we are navigating a fundamental period of realignment rather than a moment of temporary disruption. The realignment purportedly consists of an end to Western global dominance and a shift in the global balance of power towards Asia.

The Chinese Model Is Unlikely to Supplant the Western Model

While it is obvious that the West is declining in economic power relative to Asia, I doubt that the West has 'lost it'. Commentators repeatedly fall into the trap of

---

[3] Freedom House, Freedom in the World, 2019. https://freedomhouse.org/report/freedom-world/freedom-world-2019/democracy-in-retreat.

linear thinking. In 1989, Francis Fukuyama famously predicted that with the collapse of communism 'we may be witnessing...the end point of mankind's ideological evolution and the universalization of Western liberal democracy as the final form of human government' (Fukuyama 1989). Many people forget that Fukuyama made that confident prediction a few years after the OPEC oil embargo and the Iranian revolution, both events that triggered yet another bout of hand-wringing about the decline of the West and the apparent helplessness of the USA. In the few short years since Fukuyama penned his prediction, his linear extrapolation has clearly proved to be wrong. Now, observers are increasingly subscribing to another linear extrapolation, this time in the opposite direction.

One hundred years after Spengler's vision of Western decline, the West stubbornly refuses to die. There may be many explanations for this, but one important one in my view is that the West—specifically, the Western system of values—has proven to be far more adaptable to external and internal pressures than other regions and value systems did in the past.

Another core reason for the West's resilience is that one system of values can only die if another one gains widespread popular appeal. There are many countries in the world that are interested in undermining liberal democracy. There is no shortage of 'strong-man' autocracies peddling populism. But they are characterized by significant differences and will therefore struggle to form a common front.

The only system of values that could possibly claim to rival the Western model is an Asian system based on Chinese values. (I specify 'Chinese', because it is highly unlikely that India will have either the resources or the ability to inspire admiration for a rival system, especially given the divisive policies currently being promoted by prime minister Narendra Modi.) None of the other non-Asian models is sufficiently attractive or organized to challenge the Western one.

A rival Asian system based on Chinese values will not happen soon. Samuel Huntington (1997) rightly pointed out that in the post-Cold War world, the most important distinctions are cultural rather than ideological, political or economic: 'We know who we are only when we know who we are not and often only when we know whom we are against.' Increasingly, in my view, millions of people around the world know that they do not want to be like the Chinese, even if they don't necessarily see themselves as enemies of China.

The Chinese model of development has certainly created economic miracles, above all by lifting hundreds of millions of Chinese from poverty into a middle-class lifestyle. These miracles are justifiably celebrated and suggest that autocratic systems can, even over the medium term, generate prosperity. Nonetheless, China faces an enormous and imminent demographic challenge, due to its rapidly ageing population and declining workforce. It will likely grow old before it gets rich.

The main reason the Chinese model may fail to exert global influence is unrelated to the economy, however. The more the world learns about the repressive nature of

Beijing's rule, the more unlikely it will be that China can hope to provide an attractive model. The mass internment of Uighurs in Xinjiang and the Orwellian system of social scoring are just several examples of how Beijing maintains autocratic control. As much of the world appears concerned (albeit in varying degrees) with an individual's right to control how their information is collected and used, especially by governments, China appears determined to resist any such personal data rights. The Great Firewall continues to limit severely what Chinese citizens can see online, just as severe censorship prevents what they can see offline. Under Xi Jinping, China is increasingly turning from a one-party state into a system of one-man rule that resembles a cult of personality: term limits for his presidency have been abolished; 'Xi Jinping thought' has been written into the Chinese constitution; businesses of all sizes in China are increasingly under the control of the Chinese Communist Party apparatus; party members, but also ever larger swaths of the general public are being forced to study and regurgitate their leader's utterances; billboards on city streets quote his wisdom. We have seen this movie many times before worldwide and we know that it doesn't end well, especially in China. Gideon Rachman (2020) of the *Financial Times* hit this nail on the head when he described why he has gone from being a believer in China to a sceptic:'A personality cult makes the adoption of bad policies more likely, as frightened and sycophantic advisers tell the great leader what he wants to hear, rather than what is actually happening.'

The dangerous consequences of centralized power, as well as a one-party autocracy's obsession with control and secrecy, were made manifest during the outbreak of the coronavirus in China. The Chinese Communist Party refused to act quickly on reliable information about the threat. Worse still, it persecuted outspoken doctors who bravely raised the alarm, forcing them to sign confessions and pledges to stop spreading 'rumours'. The Party resorted to its old playbook of blaming local officials while exonerating the Party's top leadership. The Party's performance in bringing the outbreak under control subsequently turned out to be far swifter and more effective than the performance of most Western nations, yet this was at the cost of brutal measures that only a highly centralized government can achieve.

At a recent conference in Singapore, I argued that China would not emerge any time soon as the world's dominant power, because it is not capable of attracting widespread support for its values. To put it bluntly, it can't make the world dream in the way that the USA has been able to do, not only because of Hollywood and its ubiquitous products and services, but also because of its leadership (now rather tarnished) of a global community of democracies. The audience laughed, but the point is serious: the USA will continue to exercise significant global influence for as long as it remains the preferred place for the talented and the hard-working to study, work, get ahead, and get rich. The Trump administration's immigration restrictions, xenophobia, and aggressive unilateralism pushed some of this group towards other destinations in the West, such as Canada, Europe, and Australia. But the Biden administration is likely to open US doors to global talent once again. The continued attractiveness of the American model will depend, however, on whether recent negative trends in social mobility, income inequality, and race relations are addressed, as I believe they will be.

China can compel countries to bend to its will through force, threats, or the power of investment. But it cannot inspire. How many refugees in the world today dream of going to China rather than the USA or Europe? I will never forget the images of the Ukrainians from all walks of life who braved the cold and risked their lives in the Maidan Square to demand that Ukraine join the European family of nations. Many of them died gripping the EU flag, because they wanted their country to embrace Western values.

Another reason why Chinese-dominated Asian values may not replace Western values is that authoritarian governments have a tougher time than democracies coping with shifting pressures, whether it be the melt-down of a nuclear reactor or a highly infectious virus, such as the coronavirus. Despite all the shortcomings of representative democracy, it is the most capable of reform. In China, domestic discontents can be bought off for a long time when economic growth is robust—6 per cent and above in China's case for decades. But what happens when that growth rate inevitably slows down?

China is now facing serious pushback, not only in the USA but also in Europe. Both will continue to get much tougher on China regarding its unfair trading practices. While too many of the West's economic ills are laid at China's door (rather than blamed on automation and the inevitable process of globalization), there is no doubt that Chinese unfair competition has contributed significantly to the weakening of Western economies and the fracturing of their societies. President Trump preferred an aggressively unilateral, bilateral, and transactional approach that eschewed multilateral rules and institutions. Under the Biden administration the USA and the EU are once again taking similar approaches to the Chinese challenge. Both prefer to work within the rules, by reforming them and making them tougher.

Europe and the USA Are More Resilient than Commonly Believed

Under the von der Leyen Commission, for example, the EU has pledged to toughen its trade defence instruments, including resorting more frequently to anti-dumping cases and blocking access to the EU's public procurement market to those countries (especially China) that do not offer equivalent access to EU companies. Moreover, the EU is finally getting serious about the need to scrutinize acquisitions of European companies in strategic sectors, especially when they are carried out by foreign state-owned competitors that have benefited from subsidies. The EU's state aid rules will almost certainly become tougher with regard to third countries. Why should the EU apply state aid rules to subsidies provided within the EU, only to allow third countries to engage in massive state aid in support of their companies operating in the EU?

I am confident that under the Biden administration the USA will work closely with the EU on a wide range of trade challenges they face from China: together they can leverage the power of their internal markets to force China to make overdue reforms with regard to its abusive trade and investment rules. The USA and the EU can further tighten their export controls, improve their supply chain diversification and resilience, bring more cases to the WTO, and align their policies regarding Chinese acquisitions of companies in strategic sectors.

During my diplomatic mission and thereafter, I have been struck by how often experts on Europe focus on the laundry list of problems besetting Europe, including the European Union. There are, indeed, many problems: fraying solidarity among EU member states, the rapid ageing of the continent, an inability to make bold reforms quickly, and the difficulty of stimulating growth and innovation are certainly among them. But the ritual of invoking all that has gone wrong usually ignores what has gone right. During much of 2015, when Europe was coping with a migration crisis, repeated terrorist attacks, a potential Greek exit from the euro, and the overhang of the financial crisis, I was regularly fielding calls from the White House and the State Department asking me when Europe was going to 'fall apart'. I replied that it would not. Some of my interlocutors thought that I had gone native.

But I was right. The Schengen area of free movement did not fall apart, as many had feared. (And despite an initial free-for-all in which EU member states closed off borders during the coronavirus outbreak, the EU managed to re-establish common rules of the road relatively quickly.) The migration crisis was addressed, as numbers of refugees from the eastern Mediterranean and northern Africa dropped and control of the EU's external borders was strengthened. Grexit did not occur. And the populist wave turned out to be much less severe than widely anticipated. Although centre-right and centre-left parties were weakened, they retained control in the European Parliament; Emmanuel Macron came to power in France and launched a pan-European liberal and pro-European movement that is still ongoing (albeit in a weakened state); the Five Star populist party in Italy gained and then lost influence; President Zuzana Čaputová in Slovakia won on a platform that emphasized anti-corruption and civil rights. Pro-European sentiment has increased across Europe, partly because of the example of how Brexit is likely to make the UK poorer and less influential. And although Poland and Hungary continue to infringe EU norms, they have regularly backed down when the European Commission, supported by EU courts, confronts them.

While Western values were under attack in the USA during the Trump presidency, the system of checks and balances proved to be robust. Partisan voting patterns continue in Congress, but the courts have frequently ruled to curb executive over-reach. Subscriptions to quality media are increasing as the public seeks reliable news. The *New York Times* and the *Washington Post*, for example, experienced a significant 'Trump Bump'. In the USA, as in most other parts of the West, the judiciary and law enforcement held up under assault.

Civic engagement, especially among the young, has never been higher. If the Biden administration succeeds in its battle for "the soul of the nation", the assault on democratic norms under the Trump era may eventually be considered an aberration. Despite all the external and internal challenges that the USA is facing, it remains an unparalleled machine of wealth creation. Microsoft, Apple, and Amazon have breached trillion-dollar stock market valuations. Many new multi-billion-dollar companies seem to sprout in the USA every year. While the USA and Europe no longer dominate the key industries of the future, they certainly continue to play an important role in many areas.

The cause of Western values is not necessarily lost, at least not if we refuse to be fatalistic. Prophecies of decline run the risk of being self-fulfilling.

> The lessons of declinism are manifold, but the central one is that obsessively fretting about your possible decline can be a good way to produce it. None of the things that let the West run the show in the past were the result of worrying about China: when Watt perfected his steam engine, he was not worrying that someone was making one in Cathay.   (Gopnik 2011)

It is one thing to worry, even obsess, about China's unfair competition and to focus on remediating a world trading system that allows this to happen. It is another thing entirely to think that the answer to Western economic decline is to copy China. That is a hopeless strategy. As European Commission vice-president Margrethe Velero (2020) aptly put it: 'We should let the Chinese be Chinese, we are definitely not good at it. So, it is much better for us to stand by what we believe in.'

The European Union and the USA Must Collaborate to Protect Their Shared Values

One way to ensure that these values remain relevant is for those countries that still subscribe to them to work more effectively together. I agree with the conclusion of Freedom House that: 'Only a united front among the world's democratic nations...can roll back the world's current authoritarian and anti-liberal tendencies.' During my diplomatic career, I frequently thought of Benjamin

Franklin's own admonition: 'We must, indeed, all hang together or, more assuredly, we shall all hang separately'. He was thinking of the young colonies facing the British Empire, of course, but the sentiment applies just as powerfully to the need for the USA and the EU to work together more effectively to protect and promote the values that allowed them and the world to thrive.

Decline, as the late conservative commentator Charles Krauthammer observed, is a choice; it is not an inevitable fate. It is not too late for a revived USA–EU partnership to breathe new life into the Western model of values that now appears to be in retreat. During my diplomatic mission, I witnessed the power of this cooperation in many areas, including trade, sanctions, law enforcement, climate change and environmental protection, foreign aid and humanitarian assistance.

Trade and investment flows are at the core of the relationship. The $5.5 trillion transatlantic economy is the largest and wealthiest in the world, accounting for over one-third of the world's gross domestic product (GDP) in terms of purchasing power. The USA and the EU are each other's largest trading partners: the USA–EU merchandise trade amounted to roughly $807 billion in 2018, double what it was at the start of the century. In all, 45 out of 50 US states export more to Europe than to China, in many cases by a wide margin. In addition, 55 per cent of total US global investment outflows go to Europe, and Europe accounts for 54 per cent of global investment inflows into the USA. Affiliates of US companies in Europe generate sales of over $3.1 trillion and employ 4.8 million workers, while affiliates of European companies in the USA generate sales of $2.3 trillion and employ 4.6 million workers (Hamilton and Quinlan 2019).

Together, the USA and the EU spearheaded multilateral trade liberalization, at least until the Trump administration. During the Obama administration, they significantly expanded, for example, the product coverage of the Information Technology Agreement. That expansion covered roughly 9–13 per cent of world trade and is expected to increase global GDP by $190 billion per year. During the Obama administration, the USA and the EU were the key proponents of the Trade in Services Agreement, covering 70 per cent of the world's services economy, and the Environmental Goods Agreement to eliminate tariffs on many 'green' goods crucial for environmental protection and climate change mitigation. The Trump administration put negotiations on both agreements on hold. The USA and the EU also cooperated intensively to combat a wide range of unfair Chinese trade practices, together bringing cases before the World Trade Organization (WTO).

A significant ambition of both the Transatlantic Trade and Investment Partnership (TTIP) agreement and the Transpacific Partnership (TPP) agreement was to set the rules of global trade based on the model that the USA and EU largely share. While the EU has struggled to get some of its free trade agreements ratified by some of its member states, it has been extremely successful in striking and implementing significant new deals in recent years. If the USA and the EU do not set these rules together in the coming decade, then other countries whose weight in the global trading system is rising fast will set their own of a lower standard. Unfortunately, the Trump administration pulled out of TPP and made little progress on the TTIP agenda. While the Democratic Party is divided on the issue of trade and while President Biden has made clear that signing free trade agreements is not a priority, it is likely that his administration will seek to engage with Europe in reforming the WTO, liberalizing transatlantic trade in some areas and pushing for multilateral trade liberalization with high-specification standards, especially with regard to labour, the environment, and intellectual property protection.

During my diplomatic mission, I also witnessed the power of the USA–EU partnership when they cooperated intensively in implementing restrictive sanctions on Russia and Iran. Without the sanctions on Russia, Putin would likely have been tempted to exploit Russia's military advantage even further. Similarly, USA–EU cooperation on Iranian sanctions was instrumental in bringing Teheran to the negotiating table to limit its nuclear ambitions. Acting alone, neither the USA nor the EU could have crafted sanctions that were equally effective in either case. The USA can inflict serious short-term pain on its own through unilateral sanctions, but only at the cost of transatlantic disunity and the long-term ineffectiveness of these sanctions.

The USA and the EU have been essential partners in addressing the critical challenges of climate change and environmental degradation (until the Trump administration). During President Obama's two terms in office, the USA and the EU worked together to achieve a very significant commitment to address climate change at the 2016 Paris climate accords, and they will no doubt do so once again under Biden's Democratic administration. They have also been critical players in the drive to protect the world's oceans and endangered species.

Law enforcement is one of the lesser known aspects of the USA–EU partnership, but it is vitally important. The USA has gradually built up its cooperation with Europol, the EU's police agency, in the light of Europol's growing contributions in the joint struggle against serious crime and terrorism. USA–EU agreements, such as those dealing with the exchange of passenger name records, data privacy protections for the transfer of law enforcement data, and US access to records of financial transactions held by the Society for Worldwide Interbank Financial Telecommunication (SWIFT), which is based in Brussels, have made a substantial contribution to enhancing transatlantic and even global security. The USA and the EU now need to negotiate an agreement on their reciprocal access to electronic evidence to help law enforcement authorities respond quickly to serious crime and terrorist attacks.

Together, the USA and EU provide two-thirds of the global humanitarian assistance for the alleviation of emergencies arising from natural and man-made disasters, and 80 per cent of global foreign aid for longer-term development assistance programmes. The USA and the EU have forged a close partnership over many decades in ensuring that their dollars and euros are spent as effectively as possible. I witnessed how they successfully, albeit belatedly, addressed a major health crisis that could have turned into a global pandemic. (These lessons could have proven useful in dealing with the outbreak of coronavirus as well, had the Trump administration shown interest in cooperating with the EU.) In many areas in Africa, moreover, the USA and the EU have collaborated closely on founding shared principles on food security, resilience, and electrification among other things. They are among the largest donors to the Global Fund to Fight HIV/AIDS, Tuberculosis and Malaria, and to the Global Alliance for Vaccines and Immunization. Their work may not get as much press as China's infrastructure projects in Africa, such as those that form part of the One Belt One Road (OBOR) initiative, but they are important nonetheless. And unlike OBOR, whose legacy includes saddling some African beneficiary countries with heavy indebtedness, and financing projects with poor environmental and labour standards as well as projects with poor commercial justifications, the projects which the USA and EU support are more often sustainable and respect international standards.

In summary, the decline of the West may not be imminent. The West has come through crises in the past, only to emerge stronger and healthier while its competitors have faltered. It may be more than simply wishful thinking to believe that the USA and the European Union can once again revitalize their essential partnership and, together with their vital allies in the Western alliance, exercise global leadership. According to Samuel Huntington (1997)

> The West should not attempt to reshape other civilisations in its own image but preserve and renew the unique qualities of Western civilisation. That responsibility falls overwhelmingly on the most powerful Western country, the US. Neither globalism nor isolationism, neither multilateralism nor unilateralism will best serve US interests. Its interests will be advanced if it instead adopts an Atlanticist policy of close co-operation with Europe, one that will protect the interests and values of the previous and unique civilisation they share.

If the USA sticks to its longstanding bipartisan foreign policy—regrettably abandoned by President Trump—of working closely with its key allies, especially in Europe, it is possible that the Washington-designed post-war order will continue to shape the world. The 500-year-long era of Western global supremacy will eventually fade, but not quite yet.

References

Anderlini, Jamil (2020). 'Xi Faces China's Chernobyl Moment.' *Financial Times*, 11 February. https://www.ft.com/content/6f7fdbae-4b3b-11ea-95a0-43d18ec715f5.

Barber, Tony (2019). 'Rise of Autocracies Spells End to the West's Global Supremacy.' *Financial Times*, 6 November 2019. https://www.ft.com/content/cc420908-e910–11e9-aefb-a946d2463e4b.

Freedom House (2018). *Freedom in the World 2018: Democracy in Crisis.* https://freedomhouse.org/report/freedom-world/freedom-world-2018.

Freedom House (2019). *Freedom in the World 2019: Democracy in Retreat.* https://freedomhouse.org/report/freedom-world/democracy-retreat-2019.

Fukuyama, Francis (1989). 'The End of History?' *The National Interest*, No. 16 (Summer 1989).

Gopnik, Adam (2011). 'Decline, Fall, Rinse, Repeat.' *New Yorker*, 12 September 2011. https://www.newyorker.com/magazine/2011/09/12/decline-fall-rinse-repeat.

Hamilton, Daniel and Joseph Quinlan (2019). *The Transatlantic Economy 2019: Annual Survey of Jobs, Trade and Investment between the United States and Europe.* Foreign Policy Institute, Johns Hopkins University SAIS. https://transatlanticrelations.org/wp-content/uploads/2019/03/TE2019_FullStudy.pdf.

Huntington, Samuel (1997). 'The West and the Rest.' *Prospect*, 20 February. https://www.prospectmagazine.co.uk/magazine/thewestandtherest.

Rachman, Gideon (2020). 'How I Became a China Sceptic.' *Financial Times*, 20 January. https://www.ft.com/content/cecbc5c8–3ab5–11ea-b232-000f4477fbca.

Tusk, Donald (2019). 'Remarks before the G20 summit in Osaka.' Japan, 28 June. https://www.consilium.europa.eu/en/press/press-releases/2019/06/28/remarks-by-president-donald-tusk-before-the-g20-summit-in-osaka-japan/.

Velero, Jorge (2020). 'Vestager: Facial Recognition Tech Breaches EU Data Protection Rules.' *Euractiv*, 17 February. https://www.euractiv.com/section/digital/news/vestager-facial-recognition-tech-breaches-eu-data-protection-rules/.

17

Are We Still Allowed to Dream?

Herman Van Rompuy

Historically, the concept of Europe is young. It only really solidified in the seventeenth century. The reference to the Greek goddess Europa is misleading. For several centuries, it was a dream of writers and thinkers. Sometimes it was also the ambition of rulers like Napoleon, who wanted to impose the new realm of the Enlightenment upon the whole of Europe—under French leadership, of course. The next attempt was under Nazi Germany, which set out to impose its non-values on the rest of our continent. These were not dreams, but nightmares and horror stories.

It was only after the tragedy of two world wars that some European countries made the dream of a united Europe a reality, politically, at least in western Europe. On 9 May 1950, Robert Schuman made his famous statement in the Salle de l'Horloge in the French Ministry of Foreign Affairs on the Quai d'Orsay. This was followed by a success story in which the Union expanded first into southern and then into central and eastern Europe, until it encompassed 28 countries and 500 million inhabitants. The British have recently left us, but this is not the final stage in the difficult relationship between the continent and the United Kingdom. The common market has been extended into a single monetary zone. National currencies, once symbols of national sovereignty, have disappeared. The 27 states are working together in many other areas, and in others still, like defence, cooperation is set to increase in the future.

Of course, after 70 years, the dream is now being experienced differently. That is normal and very human, for there is no point referring always to the beginning of a 'love story'. Most of the time, we refer to what still has to be done and to the speed of our progress. In the light of history, the EU is a success story: a dream come true. In the light of what is needed still, a sobering frustration reigns supreme. However, this is no reason to surrender to the 'pessimism of the mood' and engage no more with the 'optimism of the will'.

Over the last decade, we have experienced multiple crises, a series of setbacks which began with the banking crisis and was followed by the Eurozone crisis. When these were over, it was time for the refugee crisis and the pressure on the Schengen zone, Brexit, and most recently, the Covid-19 virus crisis. Against all the odds, we overcame two existential crises, the Eurozone and Schengen crises, in 2012 and 2016. Then, to the surprise of many, the EU27 have remained united

Herman Van Rompuy, *Are We Still Allowed to Dream?* In: *Europe's Transformations: Essays in Honour of Loukas Tsoukalis*. Edited by: Helen Wallace, Nikos Koutsiaras, and George Pagoulatos, Oxford University Press. © OUP 2021. DOI: 10.1093/oso/9780192895820.003.0017

over four years of negotiations with the UK. And Brexit will be more of an existential threat to the survival of the UK than it will be to the survival of the EU. Over these ten years and more, the EU has been more concerned with its survival than with its future and its place in its neighbourhood, let alone in the world.

During these ten years, new problems have arisen: the democratic deficit in two countries (Hungary and Poland), the political weakening of many member states as a result of rising populism and political fragmentation, the loss of European technological/digital sovereignty, the pressure on our external borders, the grow- ing inequalities among our member states and within our societies, and a decline in solidarity among the member states. But big changes are also taking place in the rest of the world, such as, Russia's anti-Western course and military aggressive- ness towards its surrounding countries, Chinese economic expansionism, terror- ism, the now omni-evident climate change. I would add that, like the EU and its member states, each of the other global actors has its own internal problems; indeed, some are facing still more profound societal crises, although undemocratic systems have a trained capacity to conceal it longer.

A rational analysis of trends inside and outside the Union leads to one conclusion: there is a need for more European integration and cooperation. The challenges are so wide ranging that they transcend the powers of a nation-state. Rationality is not life's only dimension—far from it. We have to acknowledged the power of emotions. But negative emotionality also makes us forget people's long- term interests.

Is popular support slowing down for an 'ever closer Union', or is there a lack of political leadership? Two-thirds of Europeans think that membership is a good thing for their country.[1] Many do not like or love the Union very much—it is no longer a dream—but they do not want to miss out on it. Many citizens are suspicious of any institution of any kind. Citizens feel that they have too little control over decision making, sometimes because they are deeply divided them- selves, and sometimes because leaders have long misjudged the priorities of many voters. People today are anxious about many real or perceived threats, such as unemployment, job insecurity, terrorism, climate change, pandemics, irregular migration, military threats, corruption, and rising inequalities. They demand more 'protection' from every level of government. If this protection is insufficient or provided too slowly, they even question democracy itself. At the same time, there is a lot of resistance to 'change', especially in our 'way of life': think what is needed to combat climate change or a pandemic. These uncertainties and fears are also—but not only—projected onto the EU, which has the disadvantage of being further away from the citizens and therefore even less under their control.

---

[1] Spring Eurobarometer 2019 (https://www.europarl.europa.eu/at-your-service/files/be-heard/ eurobarometer/2019/closer-to-the-citizens-closer-to-the-ballot/report/en-eurobarometer-2019.pdf).

Modern citizens navigate between 'space' and 'place'. They are part of globalization every day in their preference for travelling, music, and sport, for example, just as much as when they are confronted by a pandemic. But at the same time, they are also people who live somewhere, and live territorially, historically, socially and familially in a small space. Each one of us tends to live both 'somewhere' and 'anywhere', though to varying degrees. But we need to build and perform in such a way that our fellow citizens do not see 'home' as the ultimate and only solution to the big problems of our time. We are not at that stage yet, but we must be careful not to feed into the idea that we are only safe behind our borders. The current pandemic has led to a number of remarkable changes in attitudes in the Union. For example, many citizens were surprised to find that the Union was almost absent at the beginning of the crisis in the spring. Health is a national competence, but few people knew this. Citizens noticed that each country reacted differently and that borders were gradually closing de facto as in the pre-Schengen period. It became clear that Europe was not a superstate. Many asked for 'more Europe'!

The Union has surprised itself by finding an agreement on a recovery fund, the bulk of which is made up of non-repayable grants or transfers, mainly for the benefit of the regions most affected by the crisis. Germany, in particular, has abandoned various taboos in this regard. The response to the pandemic is an example of concrete solidarity that was chosen over selfishness and austerity. The continuation of the European dream runs ahead along concrete paths.

It is in these confusing times that the Union must find its way. There are three major challenges: climate change, European sovereignty, and social cohesion.

The Commission's Green Deal is a project which, if implemented, will be more important than the single market of the great Jacques Delors' Economic and Monetary Union. It would be a tectonic energy shift. It is also a gigantic opportunity. The European Council endorsed the objective of carbon neutrality by 2050 in December 2019. The prize at stake is not self-evident, because the climate theme is also highly controversial in its implementation. The question here, too, as with a budget cut is: who pays what? Behind the debate on burden sharing, there is also a hidden resistance to changing our habitual ways of life or giving up business as usual. We all change under pressure; only then. But showing leadership in times of weakened governments run by weakened traditional parties is even more difficult, however necessary it may be. And, by the way, do not expect courage from populists. By definition, they only want to be popular.

A great deal is already happening on the ground in terms of climate policy. The EU is on track to meet its climate targets for 2020. But more is needed, even more than what was asked for at the Paris conference of December 2015, because the situation is far more dramatic than previously thought. However, it should not be forgotten that the implementation of climate objectives is to a large extent a competence of the national and regional authorities. The Union is also the sum of the member states. The success of this transition also requires the full commitment of industry players. All sectors will have an important role to play not only in reducing their own emissions, but also in providing solutions to achieve climate neutrality. The competitiveness of our industrial fabric for the next 30 years relies on including the green dimension. We can and must become a world leader in green technology. We are not starting from scratch; Europe is already the world leader, holding 28 per cent of the world's green patents today.

Overall, the Commission estimates that the funding part of the Green Deal is supposed to secure at least €1 trillion for sustainable investment over the next decade, and it will be a mix of different sources. That is not an Apollo programme—it is one Apollo programme per year. To achieve the climate change target in a fairer way, the European Commission proposed a Just Transition Mechanism (JTM) and a Just Transition Fund (JTF). The fund envisages €100 billion of investments for 2021–7; the intention is that it should support the territories most affected by the transition towards a climate-neutral economy. Once again, it is also about solidarity.

This project is also a test of the Union's credibility and relevance. We must get results. A 'delivery gap' is not an option. The Green Deal is a dream to save humanity from a nightmare.

There is a direct link between the pandemic and climate change. It appears more and more that deforestation is driving animals—carriers of viruses—to areas where people live. This is why it is important that climate investments represent 37 per cent of the recovery fund to deal with the economic consequences of the pandemic. This is a good example of integrating long-term measures into short-term crisis management. Generally speaking, in the future, the world will have to deal even more with exogenous developments such as climate change and pandemics. The devastating fires in Australia and the coronavirus teach us that the exception is almost becoming the rule. Crises are not just endogenous—they aren't specific to our individual economic, political or societal systems. Disruptions are not just technological, like the digital revolution—disruption exists at all levels.

A second theme is European sovereignty. This does not concern defence alone, but also and especially the digital economy, energy, migration, and the euro. We are making progress in all these areas, but too slowly.

Technological sovereignty implies Europe's ability to become a leader in digital technologies and to shape the rules and standards around these technologies. We have the largest single market in the world, but this must continue to operate according to our rules and to respect reciprocity fully in our relations with other global players. Europeans must also own their data. The underlying risk is that if Europe cannot compete among the leading technological nations, it will go from being a rule maker to being a rule taker, and across the board. If you are not in the game, your chances of shaping the rules are extremely limited. And there is recognition that, in many areas of digital innovation, Europe is no longer a leader. Of the world's 15 largest digital firms, not one is European.

We are lagging a long way behind, especially on artificial intelligence (AI), but also on battery cells, which are so essential to the future e-car industry. We are too dependent on other continents. We have European technology—5G, for example, where we own 55 per cent of the related patents—but our companies often lack the requisite scale. Sometimes we have inventions, but lack the economic and financial infrastructure to translate them into innovations.

Although Europe might have lost the 'battle' for personal or consumer data to companies such as Google, Facebook, and Amazon, it is still well placed to become a leader in industrial data.

Europe's added value lies in its large industrial base and the many traditional manufacturing companies it houses. By better leveraging and sharing the data possessed by European industry, Europe could develop new technologies, services, and products.

Moreover, in developing its own digital industry, Europe must not simply replicate the USA or China by creating a European Google, Facebook or Huawei. That would probably be neither desirable nor possible. These companies are the result of market and framework conditions that we do not have in Europe. The US model focuses on venture capital, an open digital market and little regulation. On the other hand, Chinese firms often have access to state subsidies and public data that most European firms do not—a mass of data with insufficient safeguards for the individual. We can confidently say that Europe's future does not lie in becoming more like the USA or China, but rather in making Europe more like herself.

Therefore, instead of replicating, Europe will have to carve out a third way: its own European approach to digital industry. Competitiveness matters, but so do values. Given the important implications of emerging technologies for people's lives and the economy, it is obvious that AI in particular is a resource that needs to be used in sustainable, safe, and transparent ways, and that we must ensure it is.

Protecting and promoting our interests and values without falling into protectionism is a difficult balancing act.

We are not autonomous enough! France and Germany have finally understood that scale and size matter and are now starting to work together on this. Although they may disagree on macroeconomics (for example, on Eurozone reform), they are still working together on microeconomics. After all, there can be no European sovereignty without competitiveness. The EU cannot be a geopolitical actor if it continues to lack sufficient autonomy.

We are also making progress on energy sources that will reduce our dependence on Russian gas and oil. Micro interests must give way to the macro public interest. Achieving the ambitious climate targets for 2030 (a reduction of at least 55% in greenhouse gas emissions) and 2050 (net zero emissions) along with the projected increase in renewables will contribute greatly to our achieving energy autonomy.

On migration, we are better now at protecting our external borders, but it is still not enough. The estimated quadrupling of the African population by the end of this century is also a time bomb for the EU. Only when we have irregular migration under control—and we have made significant progress in that area since 2016—will we be able to convince our citizens of the inevitability of legal migration, for both the skilled and unskilled. After all, our working population is declining dramatically in many countries. Just to give you an indication: without any influx from abroad for the rest of the century, Italy's population would end the century at half its current size.

The tension between humanitarianism and migration control is gradually increasing. The impression is that we have gone from one extreme to the other. Fears of further political instability linked to irregular migration further exacerbate the imbalance that already exists between the two. There is little consensus within the Union on migration, other than through the control of external borders. The Commission recently proposed a Pact on Asylum and Migration, including different types of solidarity with those countries that are most likely to receive irregular migrants because of their location. It will be a difficult exercise.

The euro makes us more autonomous. It is the second largest currency in the world, accounting for one-third of all payments, but the US dollar is used as a political extraterritorial political lever against which we have no recourse. Here, too, we need to strengthen ourselves by launching a euro safe asset.

In the light of the Covid-19 crisis, Western countries will rethink their production chains and will no longer want to be dependent on a single supplier in strategic sectors such as medical equipment. They will want to keep more strategic activities in Europe in their own hands. The world will not de-globalize economically, but there will now be a greater tendency to emphasize strategic autonomy or sovereignty. Private companies in the West that usually look for the cheapest solution and do not care much about geopolitics have learned their lesson.

All this does not detract from our choice of a multilateral, rules-based order with institutions that function (see Chapter 12 in this volume). The World Trade Organization is toothless at the moment. That is a real threat. Unfortunately, there is no consensus on remedies in the Western world. In practice, the European Union is the only global player that still genuinely believes in multilateralism. The rest are against or pay only lip service to it. With its new free trade agreements (with Canada and Japan), the EU proves that it is resolutely anti-protectionist.

Social cohesion is a real challenge. Our societies are individualized, fragmented, and increasingly unequal. There is a growing contrast between the highly educated and the rest, between cities and the countryside, between young and old, between natives and migrants. These dichotomies are translating into electoral outcomes.

It makes governing increasingly difficult in times when much is at stake. To govern better, we must govern together.

This is certainly the case in the Covid-19 crisis, where new inequalities are emerging. Not everyone can protect themselves in the same way against illness and death. Not everyone can work at a distance. Not everyone will soon have access to the vaccine in the same way. Older people face many more health risks than young people, but young people lose their jobs more quickly.

The elimination of major inequalities is primarily a task for national governments. The EU countries are better at this than most other countries in the world, and much better than the Anglo-Saxon world, but the disparities are increasing in a number of countries. The EU has deployed new instruments against international tax fraud and evasion. There is a growing consensus in the OECD on the need to tax global digital companies that have paid hardly any taxes thus far.

The American and Chinese challenge is great. Naturally, both countries also have their own internal problems. But with greater autonomy, the EU can seek to preserve our 'way of life' and carry the necessary geopolitical weight to defend and promote our values and interests. We play a geopolitical role in several sectors in which we are united—climate, trade, currency. Geopolitics in today's a-polar world is an entirely different beast from the geopolitics of 30 years ago (see Chapter 13 in this volume). It also means something different, now that the USA is turning back on itself and Russia has been reduced to a regional player.

Once upon a time, geopolitics was equivalent to military intervention. The successive failures of the USA and Russia (considering Syria, too, now) show the bankruptcy of geopolitics of this kind.

Trade wars have also hit their limits. We do not know whether the Chinese Belt and Road initiative will create a lasting economic sphere of influence.

The EU needs to invent its own geopolitical role. Let us start in our neighbourhood, around the Mediterranean, especially in the western Balkans and in the Eastern Partnership countries. Geopolitics starts at home. Enlargement should not be a dirty word. The association agreements with Ukraine, Georgia, and Moldova were not political mistakes. The Union can still be attractive. The Union cannot be a geopolitical actor if it does not play a major role in its neighbourhood.

A 'divided empire falls apart' (Mark, 3:24)[2] as the Bible has it. Populism thrives *inter alia* on inequalities. It is the enemy of the European idea and of democracy, although the populists realize that, after Brexit, two-thirds of Europeans cherish EU membership. Populism weakens national governments and creates enormous political volatility and instability. How can the Union be strong when the member states are weak? Despite this, leadership is needed more than ever. The leaders of the EU institutions—Ursula von der Leyen and Charles Michel—must come up

---

[2] 'And if a kingdom be divided against itself, that kingdom cannot stand' (Mark 3:24, King James Version).

with ideas. We desperately need mobilizing ideas. The Green Deal is a good example. France and Germany continue to bear a major responsibility. Their agreement on a recovery fund was essential in order to reach a final agreement with 27.

I hope that the planned Conference on the Future of Europe will be about policies and not about institutions and treaty changes; that it will be about creative ideas and not only passive listening. Climate change, sovereignty, and social cohesion are the great themes of our time.

The pandemic crisis makes our populations even more anxious and insecure. Vulnerable to reason or susceptible to emotions? In the long term or the short term? Stability or adventure? Solidarity or tribalism? How can we prepare for new crises without more social solidarity and political courage among our leaders at the national and European levels? Much is at stake again. The EU institutions have their role to play as engines, but they can do nothing if the 27 member states do not engage.

Athena's owl flies at dusk. I remain a man of hope. The European caravan will continue its journey towards 'an ever closer Union', because it is a necessity in the new world in which we live.

APPENDIX

Chronology, 1970–2019

Nikos Koutsiaras

	Global events	Developments in European integration	Select publications of Loukas Tsoukalis
		Werner Report on the realization by stages of economic and monetary union (EMU) in the EC.	
1971	End of the gold convertibility of the dollar; Smithsonian agreement.		
1972	Nixon goes to China.	Introduction of the 'Snake in the tunnel' system of exchange-rate management in the EC.	
1973	End of the Bretton Woods 'pegged rate' currency regime: floating exchange rates; first oil shock.	Denmark, Ireland, and the UK join the EC.	
1975	Global recession and steel crisis.	United Kingdom EC membership referendum: 67% vote in favour of EC membership.	
1977		Adoption of the 'Davignon Plan' for the restructuring of the European steel industry.	*The Politics and Economics of European Monetary Integration.* London: George Allen & Unwin.

Continued

	Global events	Developments in European integration	Select publications of Loukas Tsoukalis
1979	Second oil shock; conclusion of the Tokyo Round of GATT trade negotiations; Margaret Thatcher becomes prime minister of the UK.	Launch of the European Monetary System (EMS)/ Exchange Rate Mechanism (ERM); first direct elections to the European Parliament.	*Greece and the European Community.* Westmead: Saxon House (editor).
1980			'Management of Industrial Surplus Capacity in the European Community.' *International Organization* 34(3): 355–76 (co-authored with António da Silva Ferreira).
1981	Ronald Reagan is sworn in as the 40th president of the United States.	Greece becomes the 10th member state of the EC.	*The European Community and Its Mediterranean Enlargement.* London: George Allen & Unwin.
1982	Latin America's debt crisis; global recession.		'Looking into the Crystal Ball.' *Journal of Common Market Studies* 21(2): 229–44.
1983			(a) 'Money and the Process of Integration.' In H. Wallace, W. Wallace, and C. Webb (eds.), *Policy-Making in the European Community.* Chichester: John Wiley & Sons Ltd: 115–41; (b) *The European Community: Past, Present and Future.* Oxford: Blackwell (editor).
1984		Fontainebleau European Council— negotiation of the UK rebate.	
1985	Plaza Accord: agreement between France, West Germany, the USA, the UK, and Japan to intervene in currency markets.	Commission EC's White Paper on the completion of the internal market.	'The New International Monetary "System" and Prospects for Reform.' In L. Tsoukalis (ed.), *The Political Economy of International Money: In Search of a New Order.* London: Sage Publications for The Royal Institute of International Affairs: 283–304.

1986	Launch of the Uruguay Round of GATT trade negotiations; Big Bang reform of the London Stock Exchange.	Portugal and Spain join the EC; signing of the Single European Act (SEA).
1987	Louvre Accord: agreement between France, West Germany, Canada, the USA, the UK, and Japan aiming at stabilizing currency markets.	'Community Policies on Steel 1974–1982: A Case of Collective Management.' In Yves Mény and Vincent Wright (eds.), *The Politics of Steel: Western Europe and the Steel Industry in the Crisis Years (1974-1984)*. Berlin: Walter de Gruyter: 186–221 (co-authored with Robert Strauss).
1989	Fall of the Berlin Wall and end of Soviet rule over central and eastern Europe.	Delors Report on economic and monetary union in the EC.
		'The Political Economy of the European Monetary System.' In P. Guerrieri and P. C. Padoan (eds.), *The Political Economy of European Integration: States, Markets and Institutions*. London: Harvester Wheatsheaf: 58–84.
1990	German reunification; (–1991) the Gulf War.	Launch of intergovernmental conferences on EMU and political union; the UK joins the ERM.
1991	Dissolution of the Soviet Union; end of Cold War; Yugoslav wars begin; global recession.	
1992		Signing of the Treaty on European Union (TEU); (–1993) ERM crisis; TEU is rejected in the Danish referendum; 51% of the voters approve TEU in the French referendum.
		1991/1993:* *The New European Economy: The Politics and Economics of Integration*. Oxford: Oxford University Press.

Continued

	Global events	Developments in European integration	Select publications of Loukas Tsoukalis
1993		EU membership criteria laid down by the European Council in Copenhagen; a second referendum in Denmark approves TEU.	
1994	Conclusion of the Uruguay Round of GATT trade negotiations.		
1995	Creation of the World Trade Organization (WTO).	Austria, Finland, and Sweden accede to the EU.	
1997	Asian financial crisis.	Signing of the Treaty of Amsterdam; agreement on the Stability and Growth Pact.	*The New European Economy Revisited.* Oxford: Oxford University Press.
1999	NATO military operation, during the Kosovo War, against the then Federal Republic of Yugoslavia (Serbia and Montenegro).	The euro is launched as the official currency in 11 member states.	'Greece: Like Any Other European Country?' *The National Interest* 55 (Spring): 65–74.
2000		The European Council adopts the Lisbon strategy; the far-right Freedom Party joins a governing coalition in Austria—sanctions introduced by the other 14 member states.	
2001	9/11 terrorist attacks against the USA; China accedes to the WTO; launch of the Doha Round of trade negotiations.	Signing of the Treaty of Nice.	*Competitiveness and Cohesion in EU Policies.* Oxford: Oxford University Press (co-editor with R. Hall and A. Smith).
2002		Euro notes and coins are introduced in 12 member states.	
2003	The Iraq War.		2003/2005:* *What Kind of Europe?* Oxford and New York: Oxford University Press.
2004		The European Council adopts the Treaty establishing a Constitution for Europe; EU enlargement with ten new member states (the Visegrád Four, the Baltics, Cyprus, and Malta).	

2005	'Constitutional Treaty' is rejected in French and Dutch referenda.	'The Long-Term View.' In Loukas Tsoukalis (ed.), *Governance and Legitimacy in EMU*. Florence: European University Institute—Robert Schuman Centre for Advanced Studies: 111–17.
2006	Establishment of the European Globalization Adjustment Fund.	(a) 'The JCMS Lecture: Managing Diversity and Change in the European Union.' *Journal of Common Market Studies* 44(1): 1–15; (b) 'Why We Need a Globalization Adjustment Fund.' In *The Hampton Court Agenda: A Social Model for Europe*. London: Policy Network: 81–7.
2007	Bulgaria and Romania join the EU; signing of the Lisbon Treaty.	
2008	Ireland holds a referendum on the Lisbon Treaty: 53.4% vote no to the treaty. Onset of the global financial crisis. Lehman Brothers file for bankruptcy; coordinated action by the world's major central banks; G7 Finance Ministers and Central Bank Governors meet in Washington: agreement on a Plan of Action; G20 Washington Summit on Financial Markets and the World Economy.	
2009	Onset of the euro area economic crisis with Greece in the role of catalyst; a second referendum on the Lisbon Treaty is held in Ireland: 67% vote yes to the treaty. Great Recession; G20 Leaders' Summit in London; first formal summit of BRIC (Brazil, Russia, India, China).	(a) 'In a Changing World Where Size Matters.' In L. Tsoukalis (ed.), *The EU in a World in Transition: Fit for What Purpose?* London: Policy Network; (b) 'A New European Contract.' In A. Hemerijck, B. Knappen, and E. van Doorne (eds.), *Aftershocks: Economic Crisis and Institutional Choice*. Amsterdam: Amsterdam University Press.

Continued

	Global events	Developments in European integration	Select publications of Loukas Tsoukalis
2010	Arab Spring begins; South Africa joins BRIC (S).	Creation of the European Financial Stability Facility (EFSF) and the European Financial Stabilization Mechanism (EFSM); Economic Adjustment Programmes for Greece and Ireland; introduction of the European Semester/ annual cycle of EU economic and fiscal policy coordination.	
2011		Economic Adjustment Programme for Portugal.	(a) 'The Delphic Oracle on Europe.' In L. Tsoukalis and J. Emmanouilidis (eds.), *The Delphic Oracle on Europe*. Oxford: Oxford University Press; (b) 'The JCMS Annual Review Lecture: The Shattering of Illusions— And What Next?' In N. Copsey and T. Haughton (eds.), The JCMS Annual Review of the European Union in 2010. *Journal of Common Market Studies* 49: 19–44.
2012		Restructuring of Greek sovereign-debt held by private investors; second Economic Adjustment Programme for Greece; establishment of the European Stability Mechanism (ESM); decision of the Council of the EU to create a euro area banking union; signing of the Treaty on Stability, Coordination and Governance in the Economic and Monetary Union; European Central Bank (ECB) President Mario Draghi delivers his 'whatever-it-takes' speech in London; ECB announces its Outright Monetary Transactions (OMT) programme.	(a) 'Markets, Institutions and Legitimacy.' *Journal of Democracy* 23(4): 47–53; (b) 'The Political Economy of the Crisis: The End of an Era?' In H. K. Anheir and D. Chalmers (eds.), Changing the Debate on Europe—The Inaugural Dahrendorf Symposium. *Global Policy* 31(s1): 42–50.

2013	The Fed announces the future tapering of its policy of quantitative easing (QE): 'taper tantrum', panic.	Croatia becomes the 28th member state of the EU; Economic Adjustment Programme for Cyprus; establishment of the Single Supervisory Mechanism (SSM).	'We Need a New Grand Bargain in Europe.' *Zetischrift für Internationale Beziehungen* 1(3): 125–35.
2014		The Single Resolution Mechanism (SRM) enters into force; the National Front and the Danish People's Party win the European Parliament elections in France and Denmark respectively.	*The Unhappy State of the Union: Europe Needs a New Grand Bargain.* London: Policy Network.
2015		The ECB starts implementing QE; third Economic Adjustment Programme for Greece; Justice and Home Affairs Council of the EU approves by majority voting a relocation plan for asylum seekers.	(a) 'Alcuin Lecture 2103: Is There a Future for the European Union—and with Britain in It?' *Cambridge Review of International Affairs* 28(4): 589–98; (b) 'Rebalancing and Completing the European Monetary Union.' In M. Dawson, H. Enderlein, and C. Joerges (eds.), *Beyond the Crisis: The Governance of Europe's Economic, Political and Legal Transformation.* Oxford: Oxford University Press: 44–61.
2016	UN Leaders' Summit on the Global Refugee Crisis; Donald Trump wins the 58th US presidential election.	Agreement between the EU and Turkey on migration; the European Commission issues Communication to the European Parliament and the Council: 'Towards a Reform of the Common European Asylum System and Enhancing Legal Avenues to Europe'; UK European membership referendum: 51.9% vote in favour of leaving the EU.	*In Defence of Europe: Can the European Project Be Saved?* Oxford: Oxford University Press.
2017		UK invocation of Article 50 of TEU.	

Continued

	Global events	Developments in European integration	Select publications of Loukas Tsoukalis
2018	US–China trade war begins; the USA leaves the Iran nuclear deal.	Signing of the EU–Japan Economic Partnership Agreement.	
2019	'Year of protests'		'Brexit and Globalization: Collateral Damage or an Accident Waiting to Happen?' In P. Diamond (ed.), *The Crisis of Globalization: Democracy, Capitalism and Inequality in the Twenty-First Century*. London: I.B. Tauris: 109–25.

* Year a/Year b indicates first and second edition respectively.

Index